JOHN MAURICE CLARK

CONTEMPORARY ECONOMISTS

General Editor: John Pheby, Professor of Political Economy,
De Montfort University, Leicester, England

The *Contemporary Economists* series is designed to present the key ideas of the most important economists of this century. After an opening biographical chapter, the books in this series focus on the most interesting aspects of their subject's contribution to economics, thus providing original insights into their work. Students and academics alike will be fascinated by the wealth of these economists' contributions and will be able to look with fresh eyes on their discipline.

Published titles

John F. Henry   JOHN BATES CLARK
Steven G. Medema   RONALD H. COASE
Michael Schneider   J. A. HOBSON
James Ronald Stanfield   JOHN KENNETH GALBRAITH

John Maurice Clark

A Social Economics for the Twenty-First Century

Laurence Shute
Professor of Economics
California State Polytechnic University, Pomona
Pomona, California

First published in Great Britain 1997 by
MACMILLAN PRESS LTD
Houndmills, Basingstoke, Hampshire RG21 6XS and London
Companies and representatives throughout the world

A catalogue record for this book is available from the British Library.

ISBN 0–333–53645–2

First published in the United States of America 1997 by
ST. MARTIN'S PRESS, INC.,
Scholarly and Reference Division,
175 Fifth Avenue, New York, N.Y. 10010

ISBN 0–312–16525–0

Library of Congress Cataloging-in-Publication Data
Shute, Laurence.
John Maurice Clark : a social economics for the twenty-first
century / Laurence Shute.
      p.   cm. — (Contemporary economists)
Includes bibliographical references and index.
ISBN 0–312–16525–0 (cloth)
1. Clark, John Maurice, 1884–1963.   2. Economists—United States–
–Biography.   3. Statics and dynamics (Social sciences)   I. Clark,
John Maurice, 1884–1963.   II. Title.   III. Series.
HB119.C53S55   1997
330'.092—dc20
                                                      96–34662
                                                          CIP

This book is printed on paper suitable for recycling and made from fully managed and
sustained forest sources.

10   9   8   7   6   5   4   3   2   1
06   05   04   03   02   01   00   99   98   97

Printed in Great Britain by
The Ipswich Book Company Ltd
Ipswich, Suffolk

Contents

To J.D. and D.J.D.

"There *is* no beginning; we know nothing about beginnings; there is always continuity with the past, and not with any one element only of the past, but with the whole interacting organism of man."

Charles Horton Cooley
Social Process (1918)

Preface

John Maurice Clark was one of the seminal social thinkers of the twentieth century and his work provides the foundation for a dynamic economics of the twenty-first century: for a *Social* economics. The extent and depth of Clark's contributions were often obscured by his quest to build bridges to orthodox, received, schools of economics; to convince them; to win them over. Moreover, Clark also sought to build bridges to the heterodox schools in economics, including the Institutionalist and Marxian – he considered Marx an Institutionalist. In this process, however, Clark often used language so temperate as to obscure the prodigious reconstruction in economic theory that he was formulating. He argued persuasively that prices were not the aim, end or final measure of things economic, nor were costs definite, absolute measures: they were functions of the institutional structures of society. It was necessary, in Clark's view, to create an economics of responsibility – of social responsibility. His work remains astonishingly modern in content and scope today, at the dawn of the twenty-first century.

Manuscript sources which have been consulted are listed in the bibliography. Wherever the J.M. Clark Papers are mentioned, the reference is to the primary collection in the Columbia University Libraries unless otherwise stated. Copies of all of J.M. Clark's unpublished works are in the author's possession.

This work has had a long gestation period and I am grateful to more people for assistance and encouragement than I can possibly mention. Above all, however, I would like to thank Joseph Dorfman, Donald Dewey, and Abraham Hirsch – each of whom at crucial periods contributed in memorable ways. Sharon Sterling contributed a great deal by formatting this on computer disk.

Although this work is written for the professional economist and social theorist, it is hoped – in keeping with Clark's lifelong approach – that much of this will be intelligible to thoughtful men and women everywhere; the themes are universal and most definitely not simply "economic" in today's narrow and constricted sense of the word.

1 Background and Origins

John Maurice Clark, who became a leading American Economist in the mid-twentieth century, was born on 30 November 1884 in Northampton, Massachusetts. He was the third son of John Bates Clark, himself the leader of the mainstream in American economics towards the close of the nineteenth century, and Myra Almeda (Smith) Clark, a graduate of Vassar College. As a member of this family, the young Clark had a number of unusual opportunities to make a decisive impact on the American intellectual and social tradition.

That he did so in fact is still remarkable. As the historian of American economics has noted: "There have been few cases of successive generations of a family substantially contributing to the advancement of knowledge. Certainly in the field of economics it has been rare." However, "The United States can . . . boast of that rarest of cases: a father and son both of whom achieve[d] the rank of seminal thinkers. This was the fate of John Bates Clark and John Maurice Clark, both of Columbia University."[1]

THE CLARK FAMILY BACKGROUND

His place of birth is indicative, since the Clark family had deep roots in the soil of Puritan New England.[2] Throughout the writings and actions of both the younger Clark and his father, the themes of those Puritan pioneers who had struggled to build a "Zion in the wilderness" run intensely and steadily. On the eve of his eightieth birthday, John Bates Clark remarked to an audience of friends and colleagues assembled in his honor that he had once visited one of his great-grandfathers who fought in the Revolutionary War. "I saw him," Clark said, "conversed with him, . . . and I have his journal, kept during the war." The elder Clark then emphasized, "at second hand, I remember the American Revolution."[3] The father's theme of continuity with the past was characteristic of the son as well. John Maurice Clark was, to the end of his life, to frequently underscore the notion that the direction and significance of his labors were to be seen as a continuation of his father's work.[4] Indeed, "Throughout his career [J.M.] Clark proclaimed his debt to

1

his father. Even in his sharpest advances beyond the frontiers of tradition he insisted that the seeds were to be found in his father's works, particularly *The Philosophy of Wealth*."[5]

The Clark family heritage, issuing as it did from the Colonial New England culture, "represented a combination of qualities which is not always well understood," as the children of John Bates Clark observed at the time of his death in 1938.[6] With historical perspective somewhat clouded by lurid descriptions of witch trials and such, some fail to gain an impression of a hard-headed and hard-working people maintaining a deep religious conviction arising from the Hebraic concept of a chosen people, who were called upon to express God's work through His (Divine) Laws. If the light and the way revealed through Martin Luther and later John Calvin pointed to the need for attention to this world and matters of a practical bent, this was but part of a grander scheme:

> The sense of heroic mission, of the destiny of New England, brought to the faithful a witness of hope. "Do you realize," asked President Sterns [of Amherst College] . . ., "that in building the Earth, your Creator selected North Central America, for his best adaptations to the human race? . . . it was treasured up and hidden by the covering of the Almighty's hand, till, for our fathers and for us, the time of its showing should come." The "time" was, of course, the accomplishment of the Protestant Reformation. The mission of America was to convert the world.[7]

Historians have recorded the undertakings of other groups filled with a similar sense of mission. But certainly the Puritan experiment was no less compelling in import. On these shores, "New England was to be a New Israel – a covenanted community."[8]

Piety, temperance, industry, thrift – the list could be extended – were no meaningless abstractions plucked at random from Benjamin Franklin's *Poor Richard*. They were traits coexistent with the widespread use of money; the quickened pace of technological innovation; and later, the extensive utilization of inorganic converters which was so profoundly reshaping the institutional fabric.[9]

The variegated developments of the nineteenth century involved substantial qualifications of this early zealousness and direction. Extensive intra- and interregional development brought numerous problems to the growing business system. One of the decisive books in shaping the thought of the century was *The Origin of Species*.[10]

Contemporaneous bearers of the faith viewed these gathering clouds with foreboding: "the decay of spiritual intensity is the theme of almost all the founders as they survey the tribal community in their declining years."[11] But, in retrospect, descendants of the Puritans could be less concerned, as the children of John Bates Clark observed:

In the 19th century the sternness of the early Puritanism was in process of modification and a culture was developing which combined courtesy in human relations with keenness of intellectual life and an equal keenness in the pursuit of individualistic commercial enterprise. It was a union of religion with secular practicality – religion making demands for rigorous thinking in a sternly logical school, and secular practicality embodied in a character which put principle first.[12]

JOHN BATES CLARK

It was into the nineteenth century of Puritan New England that the father of John Maurice Clark was born in 1847 at Providence, Rhode Island. During his lifetime, John Bates Clark was to become "the first American economist to gain the respect of . . . [those] European and British writers who had felt that America could produce practical men, but certainly not competent and great theorists."[13] And in the United States, it was the view of a leading scholar that "no other among American economists has come so near to founding a 'school'" as did John Bates Clark.[14]

The impact of Calvinism was early and profound in the life of Clark's father.[15] Both grandfathers of the elder Clark were Protestant ministers. His mother grew up in a household which regularly and faithfully took part in daily prayers as well as the Sabbath . Both parents of John Bates Clark "were active in church circles and in childhood he acquired the habit of church attendance which was to remain with him throughout his life."[16]

John Bates Clark was educated in the public school system in Providence and upon graduation from high school in 1865 entered Brown University. It is not unlikely that he would have gone on to enter the ministry. However, two events contributed to his later decision not to follow this path.

Some years earlier, in 1857, his father became associated with the Corliss Engine Works where he prospered as an official. John Bates

Clark's aptitude for mechanical devices was stimulated while wandering about his father's place of business – an association which "almost surely determined his choice of a profession."[17] Out of this early stimulus and later tinkering developed two patents which he regarded with a certain amusement years afterward.[18]

After two years at Brown, Clark transferred to Amherst College in the fall of 1867 because some of the most outstanding teachers had left Brown. His college work was interrupted, however, by a tragic second event. Sometime earlier his father had contracted tuberculosis and the family had been forced to move to Minnesota in order to better cope with the disease by means of an improved climate. But the situation now became critical and the son was compelled to suspend his studies and join the family in Minneapolis. Once in the Midwest he entered his father's plow business as a partner in order to help sustain the family. He evidently adapted himself without much difficulty to the exigencies of business, since "the enterprise was a decided success."[19] This business experience, "the only time in which he worked in a commercial enterprise,"[20] was to stand him in good stead in the years to come. In 1871 his father died and the following year, after selling his share in the business at a profit, John Bates Clark returned to Amherst College. "He was [then] twenty-four years old and brought with him into the work of his senior year a maturity and an insight based on first-hand contact with mechanical, mercantile and farming problems."[21]

With his background, it was appropriate that J.M. Clark's father should have chosen Amherst. The school had been founded in 1821 specifically to combat the "tidewater heresy" of Unitarianism which had infected Harvard.[22] In the third quarter of the nineteenth century, under the administration of President William A. Stearns (1854–1876), "there was still a strong bent towards Puritanism, not to say ecclesiasticism, among the undergraduate body, and Amherst was consequently producing more preachers than any other American college." At this time, Julius H. Seelye, as Professor of Mental and Moral Philosophy was "the dominating personality on the faculty."[23] He was to prove instrumental in influencing Clark's choice of profession.

Himself an 1849 graduate of Amherst, Seelye began teaching at the college after postgraduate study in theology in Halle, Germany, under the theologian August Tholuck[24] and quickly won a reputation as a thorough, conscientious, but entirely orthodox teacher . . ." as he sought to deal with the difficulties and dangers to orthodoxy presented by Charles Darwin. Seelye seems not to have been a very original mind, but his exposition was effective and the famous "Senior Course" or lecture which he developed generally produced an indelible impression on the undergraduate minds – especially with those "of strong religious predilections."[25]

As the Professor of Mental and Moral Philosophy, it fell to Seelye to include a discussion of political economy in some of his lectures. That he was conversant with the subject is suggested by the fact that he was appointed, in 1874, to a three-person commission "to inquire into the expediency of revising and amending the laws relating to taxation and exemption therefrom," by the Governor of Massachusetts, and "wrote a considerable portion of the excellent report. . . ." In the fall of that year, he was elected as an independent to the U.S. House of Representatives. His election to the presidency of Amherst College in 1876 lends further support to the proposition that Seelye was as familiar with matters of this world as with those of the next.[26] Some of the tenor of Seelye's thinking can be grasped from this portion of his baccalaureate address in 1879:

> "Ask the machinery . . . whether the wealth . . . it brings to its inventor or its owner, is a compensation to society for the cramped intellect and enthralled will . . . thus ensured to the workmen. Ask the system of division of labor . . . whether the enervated bodies and enfeebled minds . . . are actually outweighed in the social scale by the abundance and the cheapness thus secured for the products of labor.[27]

For the purpose at hand, Seelye's principle importance stems from the counsel he gave John Bates Clark during his senior year at Amherst. Clark had already taken steps to enter ministerial training at the Yale Divinity School when Seelye, detecting a flair for political economy in his work, advised him to continue his studies in that direction.

Whether Seelye saw in his inquiring mind a talent more adapted to secular studies than to the religious calling, or whether he was moved by the specific promise of Clark's economic ideas and felt that his creative bent lay in this field, we can only surmise. The decision was made and Clark turned to economic studies, though he remained throughout his life an active leader in the church.[28]

Therefore, upon his graduation in 1872, Clark went to Europe where he studied for two years at Heidelberg under Karl Knies – one of the founders of the "older" German Historical School of economics. Later, he went to Zurich for six months and returned to the United States. He obtained a position at Carleton College in Minnesota where his most famous pupil was Thorstein Veblen – a source of much satisfaction to Clark in later years, though Veblen was to criticize much of Clark's writing.[29]

In 1875 he married Mary A. Smith, daughter of Jotham Smith, a prominent manufacturer in Minneapolis. However, shortly after the semester began, he was forced to take a leave of absence because of an illness which was to leave him with a "permanently reduced working strength" the rest of his life.[30] After some tutoring and teaching during his leave, at the University of Minnesota,[31] Clark returned to Carleton in 1877, and in 1881 he left for a position at Smith College. A few years later, Clark began teaching at Amherst College and Johns Hopkins University. In 1895 he was called to Columbia University, where he was to stay for the remainder of his academic days.

It was during the period at Smith that John Bates Clark joined the growing numbers influenced by the developing Social Christian movement in the United States. Christian Socialism had been partially inspired by the examples of men like the Reverend J. Frederick Denison Maurice, the Reverend Charles Kingsley, and Thomas Hughes.[32] Although the English Christian Socialist movement went into a period of decline as an organized force in England after 1854, it revived in the late 1870s to lend considerable support to various currents such as Fabianism in England and the Henry George movement in the United States and England.[33] However, the English example was but one of several factors leading to a pronounced Social Christian movement in the United States. If any single factor were to be selected, it would be "the pressure exerted by an expanding labor movement" following the Civil War.[34]

It is noteworthy that "the expansion of the social movement in religion follows a line of development parallel to that of the social sciences, especially sociology." Since John Bates Clark was in the initial stages of his push to the forefront of economic science – and economics then included sociology – it is understandable that he would have been animated by this general movement. Furthermore, the Social Gospel movement "showed its greatest strength in the countries where Calvinism was most deeply entrenched."[35] An early

article by the elder Clark illustrates his advocacy of this movement:
"The Nature and Progress of Christian True Socialism." Here he
wrote that "The cooperative principle in its different forms is the
Christian socialism of Maurice, Kingsley, [Thomas] Hughes, and
their worthy co-laborers. It meets an imperative human need, and
must grow surely, though not . . . rapidly."[36] Indeed, when his
youngest son was born, Clark named him John *Maurice* Clark after
the founder of Christian Socialism, the Reverend John Frederick
Denison Maurice.

J.M. CLARK – THE EARLY YEARS

The younger Clark's initial years, then, were spent in an atmosphere both pious and academic. Both these influences were strongly
tempered with a sense of social justice and the obligation of dealing
with the pressing problems of the day. The story of his life and
works is the remarkable one of a continuing and rich harvest of this
early seed.

Clark's childhood, with his brothers Frederick Huntington and
Alden Hyde, who later became an engineer and a minister respect-
ively, and his sister Helen Converse, seems to have been an
especially happy one.[37] He attended public school in Northampton
and the Horace Mann School in New York City. Throughout this
period, the father, "entered into the life of his three boys in their
childhood as few fathers do."[38]

A recollection is provided by John Maurice Clark regarding his
early training in economics by his father:

> [M]y regular education in economic theory began at the age of
> 9 or 10, in our first year at Amherst. . . . My father had in
> mind James Mill's training of his son, John Stuart Mill, and
> he copied the technique of explaining something during a
> walk, but he didn't follow James Mill's example by making me
> submit a written report for criticism and revision. All he did was
> to explain about diminishing utility and marginal utility – using
> the illustration of the oranges. And he was satisfied that I
> understood it, and concluded that the simple fundamentals of
> economics could be taught to secondary school or "grammar-
> school" students. . . . Twenty years later, it didn't look so
> simple.[39]

In this kind of family setting, the younger Clark was formed.

The "outside" world was not as idyllic. As Clark approached college age, the developing Republic outstripped an earlier individualistic day with a newly-formed pecuniary and industrial might while the Western frontiers were reached. As Alfred Marshall was inscribing *Natura non facit saltum* on the title page of his finely polished work and the elder Clark was developing his static analysis, George Bernard Shaw was wondering if "nature was not an incorrigible kangaroo." It was during this age of a qualitatively different drift of the business system that Clark entered Amherst College in 1901.[40]

Under the presidency of George Harris, Amherst retained the pious orientation of its founders. In fact, some claimed the college had retained too much of the older spirit and had failed to keep abreast of the times. Not hesitant to run counter to the popular moods of the day, President Harris had authored such volumes as *Moral Evolution* (1896) in which he defended the business system on the grounds that socialism would make no changes in the stratification of society: "Let a socialistic scheme be put in operation and warranted to run twenty years, and, provided there is no other change in society, the men who are rich now will be rich then." To Harris, "One of the most important considerations is the fact that the advance of civilization has gone along with the possession of private property." He continued:

> Progress has accompanied increase of ownership, and especially increase in the number of owners. . . . If history teaches anything, it teaches that common ownership and production would be a backward step in civilization.[41]

Perhaps even more striking was Harris's reply to the popular and widely influential utopian novel of Edward Bellamy, *Looking Backward*. His volume, *Inequality and Progress*, contrasted sharply with the view of progress in human institutions expressed by Bellamy. To Harris, "inequality always has been and always will be the condition of progress," and, "a state of equality would be a state of stagnation, a reversion to savagery and the tribe."[42] Coming as it did on the path of the trough year of 1897, Harris's volumes demonstrated a willingness to adhere to fundamental truths more than an ability to bend with the times. Indeed, it has been argued that there was a decline in the emphasis on social studies at

Amherst during the Harris administration:[43] it was during this period, in any event, that the college lost John Bates Clark to Columbia University.

Amherst also came close to losing the influential Charles Edward Garman, who, after coming to the college in 1880 as an Instructor in geometry, went on to become Professor of Moral Philosophy and Metaphysics, and "a career which must be regarded as one of the most stimulating and influential in the college annals."[44] Garman, who graduated from Amherst in the 1872 class with John Bates Clark and Herbert Baxter Adams, was probably the most challenging and influential undergraduate teacher for the younger Clark. Garman used pamphlets which he had printed at his own expense and distributed to the students to stress an approach which sought to have the student think for himself, "to weigh evidence, to accept nothing on authority, and to follow the truth no matter where it led." Using "a wealth of illustrations from science," he "drew his analogies, not from theology, but from sociology and economics, the live issues of the day, thus retaining the interest of his listeners, who found philosophy to be, not abstract, remote science, but a guide to conduct."[45] Garman noted, for instance, that "Service and furnishing employment are two different things." If a million pieces of paper were arranged on a desk and left to blow about before an open window, "Would that be employment or service?" He continued:

> Some employment may keep people from a state of suffering, and may keep idle hands busy. But why should not all employment be in the line of service, of public improvements instead of useless work for some rich man? Is there any excuse for this at all? Not an iota, and I want you to preach this belief when you get out of college.[46]

A friend of William James, Garman also pioneered in the teaching of modern experimental psychology, "and developed the field at Amherst to the point where it rested after him for thirty years." Judging by the students he produced, it is not difficult to understand that his courses and extracurricular associations with them provided "the most stimulating intellectual experience and probably the most lasting influence" for students at Amherst.[47]

Clark studied economics under the Canadian-born James Walter Crook. Crook had done his undergraduate work at Oberlin and gone on for graduate study at Wisconsin, Berlin, and Columbia University, where he received his doctorate in 1898.[48] During his first few years at Amherst, Crook used the standard texts for his introductory "Outlines of Economics": Francis A. Walker's *Political Economy* and Arthur Twining Hadley's *Economics*. The advanced theory course began with readings in the English Classical economists and concluded with readings in Alfred Marshall's *Principles of Economics* and J.B. Clark's *Distribution of Wealth*. Crook later used Charles Gide's *Principles of Political Economy* or Henry R. Seager's *Introduction to Economics* and John Stuart Mill's *Principles of Political Economy*. Although Clark was tolerably familiar with the principles of economics[49] by then, the advanced course in "Trusts and Transportation" must have been revealing, particularly in the light of his later work.[50]

After receiving his A.B. degree in 1905,[51] Clark enrolled in the Faculty of Political Science at Columbia University and earned his A.M. degree the following year with a thesis on railroad rate-making.[52] He continued with his studies at Columbia[53] until 1908 when he accepted a position as Instructor in Economics and Sociology at Colorado College. The sociology part of the young Clark's appointment might seem unusual today. However, at the time of his graduate study at Columbia, all candidates for the doctorate in economics were required to have a major and two minors, one of which had to be sociology. He was allowed to split his second minor between American history and Constitutional Law. As he recalled later:

> I took Burgess' course in "Privileges and Immunities of Individuals under the Constitution of the United States" – not his lecture course in principles – the one an economics minor would have been expected to take – but a case-course mainly taken by lawyers, which I thought would give me some brass-tack material relevant to public regulation of industry.[54]

The position at Colorado[55] Clark felt to be necessary. Having been so near his illustrious father for so long, the younger Clark now felt the need to remove himself from this influence as well as from the influence of his friends and associates while he devoted his energies to his dissertation on railway charges. Clark's undergraduate years had come during the heyday of the Muckrakers, with the works of writers like Henry Demarest Lloyd, Lincoln Steffens, Ida

M. Tarbell, Upton Sinclair, Frank Norris, and Ray Stannard Baker. Their articles in *McClure's, Cosmopolitan, Collier's,* the *American Magazine, La Follette's Weekly,* and William Dean Howell's *Atlantic Monthly* generated considerable public concern with the problem of trusts and the social and economic effects of monopoly, broadly defined.

Clark's interest in railway rate-setting is all the more understandable since "the elder Clark carried on an active campaign against what he considered predatory big businesses. Thus he strongly encouraged Ida M. Tarbell as she proceeded with her famous series of articles in *McClure's* (1902–1904) that in book form appeared as *The History of the Standard Oil Company* (1904)."[56] The younger Clark's dissertation, completed in 1910, followed the path of his Master's thesis and dealt squarely with the problems of twentieth-century enterprise.[57]

After receiving his doctorate, Clark returned to Amherst as Associate Professor of Economics, shortly before the famous administration of Alexander Meiklejohn.[58] He left Amherst in 1915 for the University of Chicago with an appointment as Associate Professor of Political Economy; he was promoted to full professor in 1922. From 1918–1919 he served as acting Managing Editor of *The Journal of Political Economy,* was Editor from 1919–1921, and was on the Board of Editors for several years. During his stay in the railroad and meat-packing center of the nation, the younger Clark was afforded an excellent opportunity to round out empirically his developing notions on trusts and the problems of railroad and business organization. Clark remained at the University of Chicago until 1926, at which time he was appointed Professor of Economics at Columbia University.[59]

John Maurice Clark's career was only beginning at this time, yet already substantive methodological questions appeared. He recalled in 1949 that at the age of nine, "I read enough to become a convinced free-silverite. And then I had the shock of discovering that my beloved and respected father was on the wrong side of the question. I decided there must be more to it. . . ." Clark continued:

> I suppose that was my first lesson in the need of preserving an open mind and holding economic ideas subject to possible reconsideration. [Herbert J.] Davenport and [Thorstein] Veblen gave me more extensive lessons, fifteen or twenty years later, only this second time it was my father's ideas I had to rethink,

after reluctantly admitting that these opposing ideas represented something real, that needed to be reckoned with. One had to do something about it, though the something didn't mean substituting Veblen for my father. It was a more difficult and discriminating adjustment that was called for.[60]

In order to more fully appreciate his contributions and efforts during his latter life, it will be helpful to examine the approach – methodology – which Clark developed at a relatively early age.

2 An "Examination of Premises"

During his teaching at Amherst, Clark began "an examination of *premises*" of the received economic thinking. Hardly indicative of a rebellious attitude on his part, Clark's search was largely brought on by the criticisms which thinkers like Thorstein Veblen and Herbert J. Davenport had directed against the theories of the elder Clark and the marginal utility school in general. As he much later recalled, "the development of his studies, relative to order of teaching positions held and relative to times when the studies were made":

> Overhead Costs came first, 1905–23. Next in time I'd put the working out of a position relative to Veblen's & Davenport's criticisms of J.B.C., centering on "*social productivity* vs. *private acquisition*." This pointed to examination of *premises*. . . . All this in the Amherst period. Criticisms of the psychological assumptions of utility theory remained a challenge, & led to the two 1918 articles on psychology, with Wm. James' *Psychology* the most obvious source; Cooley's *Human Nature and Social Organization* [*sic*] next, perhaps. Carleton Parker came later, I *think*, as did Cooley's *Social Process*. "Inappropriables" formed a natural key concept, and Ely's *Property and Contract* (1914) put content into it, followed by Roscoe Pound and Ernest Freund. Meanwhile Pigou's *Wealth and Welfare* (1912) and Hobson's *Work and Wealth* (1914) put "Welfare Economics" on the map relative to social productivity *vs.* private acquisition. Mitchell's *Business Cycles* (1913) led to the acceleration article, as you indicate.[1]

When Clark reviewed Davenport's *The Economics of Enterprise* in 1914, he noted that Davenport indicted the marginal productivity theory and argued "that there is no 'specific product' which an employer or any one else could trace through the technical processes of modern production and assign to particular instruments." To Clark, Davenport was "in some ways the most socially-minded of economists" since he was convinced that economics jumped to unwarranted ethical conclusions and was used as a cloak for injustice and inequality. The marginal productivity theory, which the elder Clark had pioneered, ignored predatory activities and taught "that income is the measure of social deserving," which made it an "apologist for the wrongs of the present order." Clark wrote:

> The greatest significance of the author's work lies in his vigorous resistance to the optimistic social conclusions that are often prematurely drawn from the static hypotheses, and in his sturdy insistence on more study of individualistic facts as the necessary basis of thought and action that shall be truly and sanely social. Great strides have been made since the torpor of *laissez faire* was dispelled, but vastly more remains to be done in building the economic theory of the future. "Static" economic theory has intentionally left out of account inconvenient disturbances and most of the forces of evil. The "dynamic" study of life as it is must put them in again.[2]

This searching the roots of economic analysis was to occupy a major portion of the young Clark's attention and notably shape his life work. He thus joined the "first" generation of twentieth-century American economists who were seeking to free economic analysis from a complete dependence on the marginal utility mold and enlarge the scope of economic inquiry. They were seeking, in the words of Wesley C. Mitchell, "to give economics once again the vitality it had in Ricardo's day."[3] Many of the trails first explored at this time were to become broadened in Clark's mature years into significant avenues of his economic thought.

THE NEED FOR REALISTIC PSYCHOLOGICAL ASSUMPTIONS

Already deeply interested in psychology, Clark came into further contact with leaders in the field during his teaching at the University of Chicago. The Chicago tradition of "functional" and experimental psychology had been developed by John Dewey, partly as a result of the impact on him of the thinking of William James and Charles S. Peirce. Although Dewey left Chicago in 1904 for Columbia University, psychological research in the Dewey tradition was carried on and expanded by James Rowland Angell.[4] Angell had also been stimulated by James, having received a Ph.D. under him at Harvard in 1892.

William James, who pioneered experimental psychology in the United States,[5] had helped to undermine the pleasure-pain theories on these shores largely with his *The Principles of Psychology* in 1890. James had written, for instance:

> So widespread and searching is this influence of pleasures and pains upon our movements that a premature philosophy has decided that these are our only spurs to action. . . .
>
> This is a great mistake, however. . . . [P]leasures and pains . . . are far from being our only stimuli. With the manifestations of instinct and emotional expression, for example, they have absolutely nothing to do. Who smiles for the pleasure of the smiling, or frowns for the pleasure of the frown? Who blushes to escape the discomfort of not blushing?[6]

Clark took an early opportunity to appraise the worth of the new psychology to economic theory. The results of his examination were largely contained in a World War I article. Around this same time, Clark also presented his views on what he considered a number of fundamental issues in economics.[7]

In "Economics and Modern Psychology," Clark began by sounding what was to become for him a characteristic note of urgency. "[I]f the world is to tolerate the leisurely luxury of speculative theorizing in this time of action," he declared, "and to have patience with the demands of logical analysis amid the pressure of expedients and expediencies, it may certainly demand in return of theory that it shall prove it knows the world is at war." To Clark this meant that modern economics must advance beyond the static equilibrium analysis and become at least "evolutionary and social" in scope.[8]

The first part of the essay was devoted to establishing the importance of psychology in the realm of economics, and to an examination of some aspects of contemporary psychological thought. Clark wrote that economics "is a science of human behavior." He urged emphatically that "it is a sheer impossibility" for the economist to avoid coming to grips with the subject matter of psychology. As he put the matter:

> *Any* conception of human nature that he [the economist] may adopt is a matter of psychology, and any conception of human

behavior that he may adopt involves psychological assumptions, whether these be explicit or not. If the economist borrows his conception of man from the psychologist, his constructive work may have some chance of remaining purely economic in character. *But if he does not he will not thereby avoid psychology. Rather he will force himself to make his own, and it will be bad psychology.*[9]

The hedonistic psychology – Bentham's felicific calculus – which served the received economics was tautological and "fruitlessly noncommittal." This was so, Clark wrote, because "the assumption that men seek their interests in purchases for consumption" is not capable of being tested. "A hypothesis capable of fitting any state of facts is one on which no predictions can be based. It is as true and means as much as the statement that white is white." This is particularly so "when told that the consumer's purchase is itself the evidence from which to infer what his interest is, and that man's interests are continually changing."[10] In effect this leaves the economist without a relevant theory of human behavior and vitiates much of their work.

Clark was objecting, in the strongest possible terms, to the prevalent notion that economists must take "wants" as given data and work from there. As he phrased this objection:

"We [orthodox economists] begin by taking wants as we find them, and our doctrines are drawn up on that basis: hence one want is as good as another in our eyes. Indeed it is only this impartial attitude that makes economics possible as distinct from ethics."

It was to remedy this state of affairs that Clark, as well as a number of other leading economists, was directing his efforts.[11]

As Clark saw it, the nineteenth century had been taken to be "an age of self-reliant foresight beyond other ages" by Alfred Marshall and his predecessors in economics. In such circumstances it is not difficult to see how an individualistic psychology could come to dominate their view of human behavior. But the demands of the twentieth century are far different. As he noted in another context, today, "we must view Smith's individualism in the light of such facts as railroads, holding-companies, centralized banking, business barametrics and giant power. The teleology of his 'unseen hand' must be appraised in terms of Darwinism; its optimism in the light of modern psychiatry."

Yet Clark did not believe the late-nineteenth-century individualistic psychology to be identical with the views of Adam Smith. He noted that a reading of Smith could provide economists with an important lesson in psychology "after too long an immersion in the utilitarianism of Jeremy Bentham." Clark asked, "should we not recognize man for the paradoxical blunderer that he is, and look for our standards of what is good for him in that deeper-than-rational nature with which his biological past has equipped him; viewing his 'rational' strivings as only one outgrowth of that many-sided nature and quite as likely to benefit him by their defeats as by their victories?" He continued with a second point: "On the whole, is not Smith closer to the modern view than is much of the over-rationalized utilitarianism of the nineteenth century?" That is, instead of building upon Adam Smith's broad view of human behavior as most economists commonly suppose, Clark asks if the post-Smithian Classical economists did not in fact *reject* Smith's outlook![12]

In order to contribute towards the construction of economics for the twenty-first century, Clark wrote that it was not necessary for the economist to consider every phase of the psychologist's realm. Since the economist is principally interested in "the general theory of individual desires," he need not concern himself with, for instance, "the detailed study of particular instincts and dispositions, nor the greater part of social psychology." The essential point was simply that the wants of the consumer could not be taken as given if a meaningful theory was to be developed, since the effect on individual economic actions generated by the economic system itself was thereby excluded.

> [T]he suggestions that mold men's wants and demand schedules may be a direct part of the business of earning a living, or they may be an incidental result of some economic process of production, or they may arise out of those spontaneous contacts of man with man which would go on just the same under any economic system. . . .

Only with this last possibility, "if at all; is the economist justified in ignoring the origin of wants to the same extent and for the same reason that he ignores 'free goods.'"[13]

To Clark:

> The twentieth century is an age which, beyond other ages, is aware how much man is molded by his environment, and is deliberately undertaking to control this moulding process. This fact must be a dominant note in constructive contributions to theory in the immediate future, if the proper balance of emphasis is to be restored.[14]

Psychologists had begun to speak "in terms of the reaction of the organism to stimuli which come, directly or indirectly, from the world outside. . . ." This meant that "[o]ur ultimate motives . . . are many and concrete, and not one abstract quality, whether pleasure or anything else." Clark added that these motives "are incommensurable."[15] The impact of the modern thinking in psychology was disturbing:

> We used to think that we sought things because they gave us pleasure; now we are told that things give us pleasure because we seek them. We built economics on the idea of rational choosing, only to be told that rational choosing is but a small and very imperfectly developed part of our mental life. We thought of the self as a sovereign will, in some sense independent of the universe. Men had their wants, and the universe granted or denied their gratification. Production consisted in turning out goods and services to suit these pre-existing wants. Now, however, we find . . . *[o]ur wants . . . are molded by our environment just as surely as are the means of satisfaction.*[16]

Drawing on the works of psychologists like James, Dewey, Angell, and Edward B. Titchener,[17] Clark pointed out that "the quest of welfare evidently involves far more difficulties than can ever be surmounted by the mere calculating faculty of the individual." This is not to deny the role of reckoning entirely: "Calculation is necessary, but not final." It was not a *sufficient* guide to the determination of economic welfare or the optimum allocation of resources. For example, since the existing environment – whatever it may be – is taken as given, the stimuli originating in the environment are excluded, thus making it impossible to determine whether or not economic welfare could be increased by alterations in the given system. "A marginal utility management of income may be a very efficient or a very inefficient one, according as the conditioning environment is favorable or unfavorable in a million and one particulars." Indeed, Clark referred to his article on psychology as an "inquiry into the wastes and maladjustments of free private enterprise." Without taking this effect of environment into consideration as a strategic variable, theory "can furnish no ultimate measure of social efficiency with which to judge different industrial systems." Clark asked:

> In trying to pass judgment, then, on the competitive system . . . , what profits it to demonstrate that our productive powers are organized into a system of efficiency, if price be taken as the measure of efficiency, and that prices are actually in proportion to the marginal importance of the various products to the consumer, this marginal importance being in turn determined for good or ill by the environment which the competitive system itself plays so large a part in molding? This appears strangely lacking in conclusiveness.[18]

This did not imply acceptance of the behaviorist psychology: in a letter, Clark remarked that he was "not a behaviorist at all."[19]

Furthermore, following the especially seminal sociologist Charles Horton Cooley, Clark pointed out that even under the static equilibrium conditions, the cost of making finer and finer distinctions among alternatives is not considered by the orthodox. "Decision involves effort of attention," Clark notes, and this fact occupies no space in the assumption of an independently-generated demand schedule. "A good hedonist," he continued, "would stop calculating when it seemed likely to involve more trouble than it was worth, and as he could not in the nature of the case tell just when this point had been reached, he would make no claim to exactness for his results."[20]

Because of the costs involved in decision-making on a consumer level, Clark observed that habit, "nature's machinery for handing over to the lower brain and nerve centers the carrying on of work done first by the higher apparatus of conscious deliberation," played a large part.[21] At the same time, habituation to a brand name throws a road-block in the calculating process and thus needs to be considered in a new light. Advertising seeks to substitute habit for conscious decision-making and the part this process plays in production needs therefore to be re-evaluated.

Further, it is in the nature of consciousness to be dynamic. Yet, "The principle of marginal utility and even the principle of diminishing utility in the strictest sense are inconsistent with this dynamic principle in human nature." This static principle of diminishing utility "is always legitimate as a temporary expedient, and it may be legitimate as a permanent attitude, but only if the things ignored are things that do not concern the economist."[22] This, Clark argued, was not the case.

Equilibrium analysis thus construed yields a unique price and quantity offered and demanded on the market. This notion is useful as a starting point, but a greater degree of sophistication can be realized. Clark asks, "why shrink from the idea of identical goods selling at different prices in the same market?" We need to develop a theory "which takes as its normal case the rivalry of slightly different commodities in a market where prices, even for the same commodity, may differ on account of distance, ignorance, or suggestion."[23]

Clark noted that most of the criticisms he makes are already to be found in the works of men like John Bates Clark, Frank A. Fetter, and especially Philip Wicksteed. He pointed out that Wicksteed "most admirably expressed" the notions which Clark was attempting to put forth. Among Wicksteed's points, according to Clark, were:

> The fact that a personal budget governed by relative marginal utilities is an unattained economic ideal, that there is a point at which it becomes poor economy to lavish attention on economies of this sort because the gains are not worth the outlay, that scales of choices are not even self-consistent, but rather so illogically constructed that it is quite possible to prefer A to B, B to C, and C to A, that the alternative sacrificed in making a purchase is but vaguely sensed – all these and others are included in his most positive treatment.[24]

However, the purpose of the first part of his article on psychology was "something more than mere criticism or the exhibiting of exceptions to orthodox doctrines." Clark was well aware that these kinds of points had been made before. His question was: "How can they be made positive use of?"

A PROVISIONAL "THEORY OF GUIDANCE"

The second part, therefore, was an attempt to develop, in admittedly incomplete form, a "theory of guidance" in contra-distinction to the theory of behavior of the standard theory. As Clark saw the problem: "The guidance, formation, and determination of economic choices is a process which, in large part at least, must needs be classed and treated as economic production." In modern terms, what Clark had in mind here, as he was to explain later, was the sum total of non-market and institutional forces operating in any given economy. This is subsumed under what is referred to now as the "index of total factor productivity."[25] This guidance of economic choices "is productive by all the recognized tests," yet "it is a form of production to which the traditional analysis of economic theory does not apply."[26]

Although the subject matter of his proposed reclassification of production was not new, Clark wrote, formal theory has shied away from it "partly because it could not be analyzed into laws of equilibrium and partly because it leads to an eternal circle of cause and effect between production and consumption, and many theorists have wanted to end their inquiry in some ultimate fact from which the chain of cause and effect could be assumed to start."[27] Furthermore, the "state of the arts" as a productive force has been neglected and treated "as if it were a form of all-pervasive free good." It is instead "an active organizing process" and needs to be considered as a part of production theory.

Finally, this "theory of guidance" which Clark felt it was necessary to develop could not be one in which a proportional relationship between prices and marginal utilities was obtained. This, he argued, was so because in actual life the guidance of economic activity by its very nature served "to upset the stability of the personal budgets which is essential" to this process of price-utility calculation. He continued:

Such a study of production must needs start with a declaration of independence from the old-time supremacy of the theory of value (which was a theory of equilibrium). It will, of course, lay as much emphasis as ever on price as an instrument of productive organization, but will tend to discredit it [price] as the aim, end and final measure of all things economic.[28]

As Clark saw the matter, there were at least three aspects or "co-ordinate fields" of the production process which worked together to yield value:[29]

> The first is the production of objective gratifications: "utilities" of form, time, and accessibility [or place]. The second is the shaping, informing, and guidance of human impulses which are responsible for their taking the form of definite desires and attaching themselves to definite concrete objects. The third is the maintenance of order to protect the enjoyment of these gratifications from destructive interference. Manufacturing may serve as an example of the first field of production, salesmanship of the second, and jurisprudence of the third.[30]

Cause and effect were so inseparably interwoven that it was impracticable to deal fully with production, as Clark viewed the problem, within the paradigm of static equilibrium analysis. That is to say, for example, that the molding of tastes or desires was as productive as the actual manufacturing of a product. Clark observed that a product might possess greater usefulness or "value" (in the sense used earlier) when advertised and made to be an object of desire, *even after it had been produced.* The notion of "consumer sovereignty" is inconsistent with Clark's analysis.

The third of his "co-ordinate fields of production" examined the productive process in an even broader light. Given products are not even the same goods when "consumed" in different surroundings or in different legal or institutional settings. An apartment, for instance, in a building where a neighbor practices the cornet is clearly not the same apartment without such noise. Or a good produced in the surroundings of war or immanent theft is not the same good as one produced under more 'stable' legal or institutional conditions. It would miss Clark's point to merely maintain that these are two different goods and let it go at that. He has his sights set on the *process* of production rather than the production of goods.[31] His point was that the very institutions under which goods and services were produced were as *productive* as capital goods: factory plant and equipment.

Economic theory, Clark held, "has been almost exclusively confined to the field of gratifying *existing* wants." The resulting generalizations were dependent upon the assumption of *ceteris paribus.* But this view often involved some ambiguity concerning which things were being held constant.

Some of the generalizations are true, that is, so long as there is no change in the social efficiency embodied in the fundamental laws and customs or in the methods of directing people's wants; other statements are true on condition that no such change is possible; while some are strictly true only on the assumption that the two outside fields of production are carried out in absolute perfection.[32]

Clark therefore made a distinction in order to amplify his third productive agency.

Observing that the fullest utilization of a product is only possible when others are prevented from using it instead, or altering its form in a manner unsatisfactory to the user, Clark distinguished two main categories of what he termed "preventive values." The first "preventive value" was the "power to withhold" or "exclusion value." This characteristic resulted from the institution of private property which "is created by the state," although administered jointly by private individuals in cooperation with the state. "The exclusion value which the courts and police have produced," he explained, "is one of the most highly valued of all utilities." Clark pointed out that the dealer who sells goods does not create ownership, he merely transfers title. As for the possibility of doing without this type of public control:

Private production of preventive values is quite possible without public aid or control, but it is little more than a clumsy name for a state of brigandage and anarchy. For in this particular matter private interests are in direct and inevitable conflict.[33]

The second main type of "preventive value," such as "careless storage of gasoline" or "practicing on the cornet," he labeled "protective utility or value." Here various laws and ordinances operated to protect one's property from undesirable outside effects which might lessen its value.[34]

Clark mentioned, parenthetically, a third preventive value: "invidious value," or "superiority over one's fellows." Although it is conceptually possible to reclassify all values as to whether or not they are invidious or non-invidious, "it would be an optimistic scientist who could expect to establish an absolute test and measure of the extent of invidious utility in a family budget." Clark added that the scientist "would need to be still more optimistic to hope to determine just what part of the invidious values is a social waste, and how this waste can be scientifically prevented." The best solution, he thought, seemed to be "pitiless publicity" such as Thorstein Veblen had used so effectively.

At this point Clark wrote that if this reclassification of production is carried through and "it results in discrediting price as the final measure of economic performance, economic values, costs, and efficiency become complex things to deal with. . . ." Clark proposed two broad "principles of efficiency" for dealing with the "measure of economic performance": the principle of alternatives and that of efficiency. Clark stressed that different courses of action could hardly be efficiently evaluated unless the alternatives were clearly understood. "The ambiguity of the idea of cost," he wrote, "is largely due to neglect of this principle of alternatives." However, Clark went far beyond Alfred Marshall's notion of Opportunity or Conjuncture Cost. Clark was concerned here with emphasizing the "cost" of various legal and institutional arrangements to society in a manner precluded by the marginal analysis.

To begin with, he explained "that the principle of marginal utility has not necessarily been shown to produce the best organization of personal consumption . . ." even if everyone functions according to the logic of the pecuniary analysis in a given system. People, from birth, are subjected to vastly differing sets of stimuli, all of which affect their ability to calculate effectively. Each person "is limited by the range of stimuli that have come within his experience."

> He is at the mercy of whatever system he happens to be born into for creating, transmitting, and directing stimuli. The slum tenement or the hill farm, the school, the church, the newspaper, the trade journal, the advertisement, the arrangement of the street one walks on, the laboratory, and the social contact of the saloon – everything, in fact, that discovers real or fancied truths, every act that may furnish an example, and every conceivable method of communication – all are parts of this system which determines men by determining the stimuli to which they are exposed.[35]

"It remains to be seen," Clark continued, "that we cannot prove that we cannot prove that our social organization of consumption is the best available, even if we could prove that it is the best possible *under a system of inherited inequality in purchasing power*, so long as that inequality may conceivably prove to be in itself fatal to the attainment of the really best distribution." For example, during wartime, the consumption expenditures of the rich were limited in the interests of producing other necessary goods for society. Here was an instance in which alternative courses of action were considered from the standpoint of society rather than from the individual viewpoint. Many policies of this type might be tried. Clark cited an example of a society without unemployment agencies: people might be working as efficiently as possible without them, "But it hardly follows that the million are working at the maximum efficiency possible to them collectively if they could collectively establish agencies which would substantially reduce the amount of unemployment." And Clark continued:

> Thus economics must be on its guard in reasoning from the sum of individual efficiencies to social efficiency that individual efficiencies of this limited and almost irrelevant sort are not added up uncritically into a false social sum. Rather than this the thing which economics needs to contribute to the search for social efficiency is a study of the effect on individual economic efficiency of the various outside influences which society is capable of exerting or modifying.[36]

This principle of efficiency, "the principle of alternatives," thus covered far wider ground than does modern welfare economics. Indeed, as Kenneth J. Arrow has pointed out, "If individual values can themselves be affected by the method of social choice, it becomes much more difficult to learn what is meant by one method's being preferable to another."[37]

The second principle of efficiency which must be utilized once the pricing mechanism is removed as the final arbiter of efficiency is the "principle of standardization." Clark distinguished two types of efficiency in this category: standardized and unstandardized. "Standardized efficiency" belongs to that class of norms which are capable of being achieved or defined so that attainment can be spoken of in terms of less than or equal to one hundred per cent. Though not always susceptible of quantitative measurement, these norms are of the kind which "can be definitely stated." With this class, "The amount of possible gain is finite; the standard itself is static."[38] Characteristically, the other group of efficiency norms comprised a broader category:

Where this standardization has not been accomplished or cannot be accomplished the idea of efficiency remains essentially dynamic. The possibilities are unknown and indefinite, and progress can be known only as exceeding what has gone before. Studies of this type of efficiency must needs lack absoluteness and finality. They are relative, not absolute, *and are limited in scope to the range of alternatives that are suggested for consideration.*[39]

Thus the norms of the unstandardized type obviously include most, if not all, the trenchant problems of efficiency in any economic system.

To illustrate these concepts, Clark used examples drawn from many areas. An engineer's report would lie more in the realm of standardized efficiency that would a newspaper article, for instance. "If newspaper writing is less standardized, calls for more of initiative, and depends more on the 'personal equation' than the composition of an engineer's report, that fact may be taken as evidence of its place in the realm of creative art rather than of mere information." A law delineating fabric quality might be enacted, but would be wholly inoperable in attempting to measure or standardize a Paris fashion gown.[40]

Clark cautioned however, that "economics must be on guard against applying to one type of efficiency the conceptions that belong to another." And he added:

The doctrine of natural rights and its surviving aftermath, the idea of property rights as a pre-existent something which courts discover and protect, but whose nature they do not mold – these are the conceptions of standardized efficiency applied in an unstandardized field.[41]

Another area in which the requirements of the standardized type of efficiency are commonly misapplied is that of the marginal utility criterion. He explained that "the work to which this idea [of marginal utility] is applied is largely unstandardized work, and the most definitely standardizable part of it (the work of finding out what one is really buying) is often beyond the consumer's power and possible only to a well-equipped laboratory. . . ."[42] And Clark makes a subtle point when he notes that generally, "the existence of standards of efficiency, especially if there is no danger of their being quickly attained, has the effect of lessening the need for individualism as a means of attaining efficiency."

Discounting "in advance any claim of conclusiveness for deductive theories or for judgments of efficiency as commonly drawn from them," Clark offers some tentative conclusions from the entire constructive attempt:

> In general, the study reveals many shortcomings in economic guidance under private initiative, and points toward the need of co-operative or public agencies to make good these defects. Where guidance is left too much to private business enterprises, large-scale production has an unnecessary advantage due to the fact that guidance is in a sense a "natural monopoly." On the other hand, co-operative guidance may bring producers so close together as to make far-reaching changes in the character of business competition.[43]

Clark concluded the study with a lengthy "Outline of Study of Guidance of 'Free' Economic Choices." The wide range of his thinking on economic process and guidance is immediately apparent here and foretells much of his later work. He closes with the observation that "[t]he task of self-guidance which modern industry imposes is largely beyond the powers of the unaided individual, and the social need of large-scale co-operative guidance is largely beyond the reach of individualistic commercial incentives."[44]

THE EMPIRE OF MACHINES

In a different vein, Clark a few years later penned a troubling account of the impact of the machine civilization upon mankind.[45] Clark's essay was primarily inspired by a reading of Samuel Butler's *Erewhon* (1872), in which Butler wrote of a society which outlawed machines before they could "supplant the race of men."[46] Adopting the device of referring to machines in "racial" terms, Clark wrote: "We have brought into existence a race of monstrous beings . . . whose powers are vastly beyond our own in many respects, and whose natures, needs, and behavior are utterly foreign to ours."[47]

Although in some ways reminiscent of the views of the followers of the mythical "General (or King) Ludd" over one hundred years earlier in England, Clark's principal aim was to emphasize the cumulative impact on the institutions of society of the machine. Humankind had come to the point of, willy-nilly, assuming that more machines spelled more "progress." But to one taking the larger view, this was an untenable, even teleological, assumption.

> The trouble with our ordinary way of looking at machines is that we see no more than the single machine, and this we see as nothing more than the sum of the mechanical details that make it up. We lack the imagination to suspect that we may be dealing with that order of being whose whole is more than the sum of its mechanical parts – in short, with something organic. Not a conscious being, perhaps. . . . Let us drop, as far as possible, our provincial habit of looking at everything on earth from the human point of view, and try to interpret things from the stand-point of machines as a race of beings, having their own life needs and vital forces. To them, men would be convenient instruments of production. It is surprising how well the facts fit into this hypothesis.[48]

Clark also argued that what he "called Euclidean Economics, in general, serves the interests of the machines."

> [Static theory] directs attention to the bribe they offer, and away from the conditions they exact. It has countenanced the machines in neglecting to assume the burden of human overhead costs, and in this, as in other matters, by insisting on putting man on a higher level than machines in respect to freedom, it has sometimes put him on a lower level in respect to care for his material needs. This has its fine side, but by teaching man that he is the end of all things, when he is not, his subjection is concealed and thus perhaps perpetuated.[49]

His device of writing of machines as a "race" underscored the degree to which the machine had stamped society. The machines, Clark wrote, "have domesticated man to their service in such shrewd fashion that only a few have been dimly aware of what was happening to us." The urban contours of nations are their product: "From Homestead to Hollywood the machines have reared cities after their own needs. . . ." And humans themselves have been pre-empted from the stage by these creatures. In industry, "[t]he working unit is no longer a man, or any group of men, but a 'plant'." The pattern of work is dictated by the machine with the result that man's labor "often lacks variety and still oftener lacks openings for initiative and discretion."[50]

Clark's solution to this state of affairs did not involve the abrogation of machines by civilization, but in learning, initially, to deal with them. At first, we must seek "a reasonable degree of racial equality." He continued:

> When this is achieved, we can deal with the machines in that spirit of confidence which characterizes the bargaining of equals. Then perhaps we can secure the real benefits they stand ready and willing to give us. But to do so we must have – save the mark – machinery! Economic machinery for bringing the collective human judgment and will to bear *at the point where things are being decided, in the process of industry itself*, rather than waiting till the decision is made by the engineers, and captains of finance, and then, through our 'political' machinery, taking belated and purely defensive action.

However, in order to turn "the collective human judgment and will" to the problem and construct the necessary "economic machinery," it was necessary, in Clark's view, to bring *a different type of economic thinking* to bear on the issue.

AFTER STATICS, DYNAMICS: THE STUDY OF CUMULATIVE EVOLUTIONARY PROCESS

The phrase "*a different type of economic thinking*" should be doubly underscored since it is not uncommon for theorists to tacitly assume that what passes for dynamic theory in the conventional thinking answers the need to which Clark was pointing. For instance, many would take the term "dynamic" to refer solely to the addition of a *time* variable. But Clark, in a number of articles, stressed that in addition to time, a new range of problems must be investigated and which are on the whole not amenable to treatment by means of price variables. At an early point in his writing, he made note of this type of misunderstanding when he spoke of

> the feeling of many a theorist that modern criticism is not completed by any constructive offerings, and that until something

positive is forthcoming to take the place of the theories which are under fire, he will not discard them. He is perhaps looking for something constructive *of the familiar general type*, and cast in the familiar mold. If so, he will never find it – for a reason.[51]

The "reason" clearly was that a theory qualitatively different from "the familiar general type" was precisely what Clark was seeking.

He made a distinction between "statics" and "dynamics" in the following manner:

> The contrast which we are considering is between realistic economics and economics simplified by the method of static abstraction, which studies levels of equilibrium under abstract conditions. These make equilibrium possible (1) by eliminating elements of disturbance and (2) by confining the adaptive forces and processes to those which are self-limiting and not cumulative in character. Static economics . . . is complete in its main outlines. . . . [and] controversies are largely matters of proper formulation rather than of the essential logic of the main structure . . . . The significant field for present work lies in the development of more realistic economics, which may be defined . . . as dynamics. Unlike statics, dynamics is in its infancy, and very possibly is destined always to remain in that stage, on account of the fact that conditions change so fast and so endlessly that analysis and interpretation cannot overtake them.[52]

This development of a dynamic economics would also serve to answer some criticisms of the elder Clark's statics which J.M. Clark recalled: "Veblen: JBC's conceptions limited by taking institutions for granted as a 'frozen framework' (and) therefore 'not an evolutionary science'[,]" and "Davenport: . . . [J.B.] Clark deals in 'Beneficent abstractions'."[53] To Clark the key problem of dynamics was "of processes which do not visibly tend to any complete and definable static equilibrium." He stressed: "The importance of this shift from the search for levels [of equilibrium] *to the study of processes can hardly be overemphasized. . . .*"[54]

In order to illustrate his view of dynamic economics, Clark took "the narrowest possible problem that can be called dynamic: That of discrepancies between actual values and their static levels. . . ." He asked: "Why do prices seldom reach their supposed static level and never remain there?" A first approach to this question would involve "the whole baffling problem of the business cycle." Here one must needs consider the "cumulative forces" at work as well as the "self-limiting" type. At once the problem ramifies into the areas of credit, human behavior, contracts, costs, and so on. "In short, the problem reaches out into the fields of technical production, of human nature and of social institutions."[55]

Clark notes that these are the very areas which Thorstein Veblen has explored, for instance, in *The Theory of Business Enterprise*. In his stress on the "dynamic" and the "study of processes," Clark is also deeply indebted to the work of the pioneering sociologist Charles Horton Cooley, whom Clark considered one of the founders of the Institutionalist movement in economics.[56]

Cooley, whose training had been as an economist, had argued the necessity of relating human behavior to the evolutionary "social process" of society.[57] His "organic view" of things emphasized the notion "that the life-process is an evolving whole of mutually interacting parts, any one of which is effect as well as cause." He urged that a distinction

> should be made between human-nature values and institutional values, the latter being those which have social antecedents of so complicated a character that we cannot understand them except as the outcome of a special institutional development. It is apparent that the values of the pecuniary market fall under the latter head.[58]

It was against this kind of background and stimulation that Clark saw that the construction of a dynamic economics would involve "going back to the premises and replacing static by dynamic assumptions and then building upon them."[59]

THE SELECTION OF THE PROBLEM

The task of constructing a new type of economics appeared to Clark to require the greater emphasis upon an inductive approach[60] as well as the examination of a substantially different range and type of problem. He explained in a letter to Wesley C. Mitchell:

> The nineteenth century deductive theorists stuck to problems susceptible of definite answers by their method; and ultimately

landed in partial sterility. The statistical method has brought fresh problems within reach of systematic treatment, but does not reach all problems. So the tendency to confine attention to the kind of problems that statistics can handle satisfactorily (or more narrowly the statistics we now have) means leaving out important problems, and perhaps ultimately landing in another kind of partial sterility.

I am wondering whether the yearning to be an exact science does not have its drawbacks, for the above reasons; and whether it does not tend to prevent us from choosing problems for the single reason that the world needs to have them answered somehow; and trying to produce whatever kinds of answers the problem and the available materials permit, whether exact or inexact.[61]

The fact that the economist selects a problem, or type of theory with which to approach a problem, destroys the assumed "scientific" dichotomy between "positive" and "normative" thought.[62] Clark argued that the act of simplifying economic life "lays upon the theorist a great burden of responsibility for the character and influence of the kind of selection he sees fit to make." He continued:

It robs him of his defense of scholarly detachment, when critics assail him, for instance, on the ground that his doctrines are out of touch with movements of reform and surgings of unrest. He may answer that he is not supposed to be in touch with them, in his capacity as a scientist; he is supposed merely to furnish a wholly objective description of things as they are. But he is open to the rejoinder that, *so far as his description is selective, it is not wholly objective. He selects things that are significant, and significance is at bottom a matter of some underlying purpose.*[63]

Furthermore, it was Clark's view that "a judgment of cause and effect . . . commonly requires insight as to *what might have been*, had conditions been different."[64]

Adopting John Stuart Mill's expression, he wrote that "the assumptions proper to dynamics" are different "from static premises in qualitative or 'chemical' ways; including the dynamic character of human nature and the evolution of institutions."[65] Even the idea of static equilibrium was taken to be an assumption:

It also appears that the conclusion of the more developed statics – the level of static equilibrium – is, in the earlier forms of the study, essentially an assumption based on observation; and the assumptions of the later form of the theory are, in a real sense, deduced from it, being the conditions necessary to bring it about. Thus the relations of premise to conclusion may with propriety be reversed, or the entire structure be regarded as an assumption, to be justified by its usefulness in interpreting facts of experience.[66]

Clearly, however, the main point as Clark saw it was that "the choice of the [economic] problem should be governed by the need for light rather than by the amenability of the materials to workmanlike manipulation."[67]

Thus the obstacles to be overcome in creating a new type of economic thinking involved much more than merely adding a time variable or using the drift of economic life as a source of inductive studies designed to illustrate "timeless" economic truths. A sort of professional vested interest or, as Clark put it, a "scientific 'instinct of workmanship'," tended in the direction of "choosing problems for whose solution there are available materials which will satisfy canons of accuracy and demonstrability." Clark's perceptive explanation of the problem of resistance to methodological change was that

In living economic theory the investigators find that their best possible efforts cannot exhaust the material that is of vital importance in its effect on the issues of their time and the needs of their age, and they tend to concentrate upon these aspects of things, not because other aspects do not exist, but because they appear less important. In an economic theory that is not living, this selection is governed by tradition, by professionally vested interest in an existing stock of doctrines and methods, and sometimes by the line of least resistance toward deductive studies, because they yield definite results more readily than inductive, and with less labor of gathering data. But the selection is never governed by sheer search for truth, for the search for truth is not a principle on which one may decide what parts of truth to include and what parts to leave out.[68a]

The equilibrium of the static economics was in the mind, not in life. Clark understood that the psychological effort involved in new undertakings was not inconsiderable: "It takes resolution to go forth from the ease and beautiful simplicity of a well-formed hypothesis and struggle with amorphous facts."[68b]

At this point the earlier strands of Clark's "examination of premises" begin to take shape as they become woven into the fabric from which a serviceable economic theory could be fashioned. At the outset, Clark urged: "Economics inevitably involves two things: a description of the way economic forces work, and a study of the economic efficiency – or inefficiency – which results." This meant to Clark that "economics as a theory of efficiency" is almost certain to encounter "problems requiring evidence not amenable to academic canons of accurate and absolute demonstration." The economic theorist must then be bold enough to act on the following proposition in his investigations:

> "It is unscientific to exclude any evidence relevant to the problem in hand." *This comprehensiveness is scientific*, even if it involves some sacrifice of other qualities for which science likes to strive.[69]

With this kind of generalization in mind, Clark then stated his principal theme:

> The task of economic theory . . . is clear. . . . There are principles underlying our multifarious social policies – principles as general and far-reaching as those underlying the "theory of value and distribution." In fact, they are all phases of one process, social housekeeping. And until "free exchange" and "social reform" are both interpreted as governed by one consistent set of laws, they are not interpreted correctly. The crucial task of such a theory is to reveal those causes and consequences of things men do which transcend the scope of free exchange. . . . In a broad sense the great task of the theorist of our tremendously dynamic age is to substitute an economics of responsibility for the economics of irresponsible conflict.[70]

The "economics of irresponsibility" which the twentieth century had inherited was, in Clark's view, ill-suited to fulfill the function of a modern, relevant, social thought. The "irresponsibility" resulted, of course, from the standard assumption that people effectively pursued their own best interests and that the summation of this set of actions yielded an optimal economic solution. The consequent relegation of problems of "social reform" to the obscurity of a "special case" or "applied economics" abrogated the social responsibility of the economist. When institutional change was assumed to be absent, this became true *a fortiori*. For, in Clark's view

> The balance of forces in social life is continually shifting – between the few and the many. . . . Existing institutions set the mold in which forces act, and govern their relative opportunities. And, with the familiar fact of institutional lag, they are likely to be adapted to the relative position of the forces as they were when the institutions took shape, a generation or a century or more in the past. They give weight to certain forces, usually not in proportion to their present strength or capacities.[71]

Hence, for instance, the relevance of Adam Smith's work: the *Wealth of Nations* emphasized the drag of contemporaneous institutions on the social forces and dealt explicitly with social reform.

A "non-Euclidean" economics dealing with the fact of cumulative change would contain "a more urgent and vital truth for the present generation" than the "Euclidean economics" of standard theory. Thus, Clark's early and extended "examination of premises" led him to conclude that a new type of economic thinking was needed in order to help formulate guidelines to the solution of the problems of a "world at war." A reformulation of the received thinking was out of the question: the existing paradigm had not been designed to manipulate the necessary variables. But Clark clearly sought the development of a theory broad enough to include the insights generated by the orthodox analysis. "Professor Mitchell's *Backward Art of Spending Money*," Clark wrote, "is a perfect example of the type of study that theory must make, if it is to be more closely relevant to real life than past theory has been."[72]

The term, an "economics of responsibility," – one of several Clark suggested for the newer viewpoint[73] – aptly connotes his orientation to the important questions of the day and his view that the resolution of these issues could most effectively come about through "the growth of willing co-operation" in the economy.

Against this background, the development of Clark's thought becomes more meaningful and his life-work can be most effectively examined. One of his most impressive theoretical efforts towards the construction of a "non-Euclidean" economics was *Studies in the Economics of Overhead Costs.*

3 The Emergence of Overhead Costs

In December 1923, Clark published his *Studies in the Economics of Overhead Costs*.[1] His interest in the nature of costs was first seen during graduate work at Columbia University, especially with his dissertation *Standards of Reasonableness in Local Freight Discriminations* (1910).[2] In order to better understand the genesis and framework of *Overhead Costs*, it is necessary to examine Clark's dissertation.

CLARK'S DISSERTATION – A FIRST APPROACH

In this early work, Clark set himself the task of investigating the economics of the phrase "reasonable charges and services" as this phrase pertained to the regulation of railway rates. Regulatory patterns in Europe, particularly in Germany and Austria, differed fundamentally from those in the United States. "The American system in its machinery of regulation," wrote Clark, "lacks rules and precepts which should constitute a formal definition of the term 'reasonable' as applied to freight charges: a lack which the foreigner does not experience to any such extent."[3] Although the United States judiciary and legislature provided a certain basis for regulation, the economics of the situation was cloudy.

In addition, the term "reasonable" was clearly relevant to a much wider area of the economy. Regulation – or even economic evaluation – of the pricing policies of *any* industry or firm implied notions of a "reasonable" excess of revenue over cost.

Clark appropriately began his dissertation with an examination of "Railways and the Law of Cost." He wrote that it had taken the educated public some time to realize that railways, with their relatively large "fixed" costs, were different in kind from a grocery store or soap factory. But now, he argued, it was time to recognize that the difference is in fact only one of degree. "Both have large fixed plants, and large 'general' or 'fixed' or 'joint' expenses to deal with, and the cost accounting of both is complicated – more so in the case of the railroad."[4]

37

The heart of the railroad problem, according to Clark, was not that railroads constituted a different type of industry: it was the economic impact of "unreasonable" price discrimination.

> The vital question with a railroad is the effect of its rates on the conditions of competition in those industries whose products it carries. It is as if a great manufacturing industry had to do with putting certain finishing touches on goods – finishing touches which could add value to any kind of article at all. If the charges for these services could be arbitrarily varied, it can easily be seen that those who carry on this final completing process would hold in the hollow of their hands the producers in all the processes which came earlier in the series. They would have an almost inconceivable power over the whole economic system.[5]

Central to the particularly intractable problems of rate-setting in the railway industry was the question of costs. For if one begins by looking at profits, or the excess of revenue over costs, the trail quickly leads back to the definition and meaning of costs themselves.

At this crucial point the classical economists offered little in the way of a solution with their general emphasis on constant costs. In Clark's view, this was because the classical world contained nothing quite like the twentieth-century large-scale enterprise of which the railways were so characteristic. With the increasing attention paid to variable proportions in production towards the end of the nineteenth century, the familiar distinctions between constant and variable costs began making greater inroads into accepted theory.[6] This was especially true, of course, with the publication in 1890 of Alfred Marshall's *Principles of Economics.*[7]

Clark pointed out that many costs in the railway industry are not easily assignable to either category of fixed or variable costs.

> The most oft-discussed peculiarity of railroads . . . is that resulting from the fact of production largely at "joint cost." For convenience this term "joint cost" will be used to express the general condition in which some items in the cost of production, such as the fixed charges and many of the operating expenses of railways, are not directly assignable to any single item or items of the product. . . . This is closely connected with the policy of "charging what the traffic will bear." . . . *These phenomena are*

not peculiar to railroads, but are general throughout the field of industry.[8]

The term "joint cost" had been employed by John Stuart Mill to refer to the necessary production of by-products in nearly fixed proportion, but to Clark this was a special case of the more general case where the by-products can be varied in production. He notes that Alfred Marshall had developed the joint cost idea along these lines in his *Principles of Economics* by arguing that even fixed proportions of by-products such as wheat and straw, or mutton and wool, could be varied in the long run with changes in technology or breeding techniques. Clark further pointed out that Marshall had recognized cases where particular charges could not be assigned to either fixed or variable costs on a strictly logical basis. Although Marshall did not use "joint cost" to cover this contingency,[9] Clark employs the term in this sense throughout his dissertation.[10]

Clark went on to write that the "final step" in merging the notions of variable and total cost with that of "joint cost" was taken by E.R.A. Seligman in a brief controversy with Frank Taussig in *The Quarterly Journal of Economics* (November 1906).[11] "The chief point at issue," wrote Clark, "seems to be whether it is proper to apply the law of joint cost to a plant producing a homogeneous output as well as to one whose output is of several kinds." Siding with Seligman, Clark concluded that it is proper to do so in the case of the railroads. Later in his dissertation, Clark took the position "that even in the general field of industry the related factors of joint cost and 'increasing returns' are enough in many cases and over long periods to divorce total income from total outgo even under perfect freedom and in the absence of monopoly."[12] This cautious early statement was to receive an emphatic reformulation in *Overhead Costs*.

To Clark, the principal point was that once the notion of "joint cost" is admitted, the possibility of price discrimination must also be admitted. In modern terminology, this is because marginal cost is a function of *variable* cost, not fixed cost, leaving the door open for producers to vary even a theoretically most profitable price and output depending on which inputs they regard as "fixed." With regard to the railways this means, in Clark's view, "that the 'special costs' traceable to particular services constitute a minority of the total outlays of railways, and that up to the point where traffic begins to tax the maximum capacity of a well-equipped road, the business is one of markedly 'increasing returns.' " Clark continued: "Each rate must cover special cost and make some contribution to the covering of joint outlays, the amount of which contribution is gauged by the value of the service or by what the traffic will bear under the circumstances, considering value of goods, competition of carriers and all other factors that may affect the problem."[13]

The ideas in this last sentence are restated by Clark in a subsequent chapter of his dissertation and provide an essential key to the understanding of his insight on costs. Clark was pointing out that the problem of allocating total cost into the categories of fixed and variable was relatively unimportant in an era of small-scale enterprise, since the proportion of fixed to total cost was small and therefore of little consequence. With the appearance of larger-scale production providing increasing returns to scale, this was no longer the case. At the same time the problem was complicated by the appearance of jointly-produced products. Now the variable costs upon which marginal costs are based became crucial and the allocation of total cost between fixed and variable become largely a legal-institutional-historical question – *up to the discretion of the producer!* "Hence," writes Clark, *"competition does not control the ascribing of reward to various productive agents within the competing unit."*[14]

With Clark's observation that "a business carried on largely at joint cost is a business of increasing returns, within certain limits," enough has been presented of his dissertation to furnish an introduction to his later work on costs.[15]

THE DISCOVERY OF OVERHEAD COSTS

Against the background of Clark's dissertation, his statement that "unused capacity" is the "central theme" of *Studies in the Economics of Overhead Costs* takes on new meaning. In the beginning of his study, Clark wrote that the term "Overhead Costs" "covers an entire family of ideas, but they have one essential thing in common." He continued:

They refer to costs that cannot be traced home and attributed to particular units of business in the same direct and obvious way in which, for example, leather can be traced to the shoes that are made from it. And most of the real problems involve one other fact; namely, that an increase or decrease in output does not involve a proportionate increase or decrease in cost.

Noting the difficulties involved in assigning these costs, he wrote that "at the bottom of most of these complexities lies a fact that is simple."

> That fact is unused productive capacity, or capacity of which full advantage is not taken. "Idle overhead," that great industrial sin, is simply the expense side of this unused capacity. Our study of overhead cost will be largely a study of unused powers of production.[16]

The concept of an economic (as opposed to physical) "optimum" or "capacity" output or plant size was of course a nebulous one, and Clark was aware of this. He noted that "no absolute figure can ever be set" and speaks of "a zone of some width rather than a point." The output level at which marginal cost was equal to average total cost "might furnish a theoretical measure of capacity, but one that would be hard to apply."[17]

To Clark overhead costs, unused industrial capacity, and non-linear production functions are *necessarily correlative*. Further, they are not simply an interesting aspect of economic theory, but describe essential features of a qualitatively different economic society than that to be found during the late eighteenth and early nineteenth centuries.

Clark's opening chapter, entitled "The Gradual Discovery of Overhead Costs," sketches out the essential changes which, in his view, have taken place in economic thought and institutions since the eighteenth century. "The entire idea of expenses of production" was, according to Clark, "a rather recent one." During the medieval period, merchants and craftsmen operated on a small scale and did not customarily think of their own time as an expense. Only their materials were so viewed, and these in a direct, traceable fashion. Later, as the volume of manufacturing output grew, the domestic or putting-out system developed. Under this scheme, "the employer paid the worker not merely for the latter's time but also for the use of his tools and of the premises where he worked."

At this early stage in modern economic history – the stage in which modern economic theory is grounded – "virtually every element which economists now think of as an expense of production was paid for in such fashion that each item could be directly charged to an item of product." Clark noted that "*in these very special circumstances*, expenses were virtually all traceable directly to units of product, and overhead costs were virtually non-existent."[18]

These early conditions clearly have changed, and the key to this change is the workers' progression from tool-user to machine-tender. Indeed the technological growth of machine industry had been so rapid that Clark thought it "small wonder that Henry [Carter] Adams sought the historical formula for the nineteenth century in a geometrical progression: man's application of power doubling every decade."[19] The change in these early "classical" conditions spurred on by technology has not, however, been matched by sufficient change in the standard theoretical formulations of economic life.[20] "From the slowness with which economic science has assimilated the facts of overhead expense," wrote Clark, "one is almost tempted to conclude that its prevalent ideas on expenses of production date back to the domestic system and are not really appropriate to any later stage of industrial development."[21]

Clark noted that, nevertheless, several earlier writers had given some attention to the existence of overhead costs: among them were John Stuart Mill, Robert Torrens, Nassau Senior, and Karl Marx. But it was the American economist Arthur Twining Hadley who expressed the modern situation "with remarkable compactness." Hadley observed that the rise of relatively large investment in fixed capital had resulted in profound changes in the economic system:

> Each producer can extend his output with a gain rather than a loss in economy. If he can increase his sales, there will only be a slight increase – perhaps none at all – in the expense for wages and materials, and a decided decrease in the share of the charges on fixed standard of cost which we can treat as the normal price; for the cost per unit of product depends on the quantity sold, falling as sales increase.
>
> The price which will induce new competitors to enter the field is also much higher than that which will lead old ones to withdraw. . . . Thus prices, instead of constantly tending to gravitate toward an equitable figure, oscillate between two extremes. The rate of production, at figures which give a fair profit, is usually either much larger than the rate of consumption, or much smaller. . . . The average price resulting from such fluctuations may perhaps be a fair one; but the wide changes of price are disastrous to all parties concerned.

Hadley also wrote that "in some cases the industrial units which are necessary for proper utilization of labor have become so large as to produce actual monopoly."[22]

Work like Hadley's stimulated Clark's questions concerning the efficacy of standard economic theory in this area. "If monopoly is natural and if competitive price tends to no definite level, much of one's old economics needs revising," Clark wrote. He continued:

> The "cost of production to the marginal producer" no longer governs value, for the most expensive production is practically always being carried on at a loss. And if the "marginal cost" of production means the additional cost of additional output in a plant working at part capacity, it does not cover return on investment and may not cover all of operating expenses. The idea that price is governed by marginal cost of production may be reduced to a tautology; the marginal producer is the producer whose cost of production is equal to the normal price.[23]

Clark believed that Alfred Marshall had "avoided a barren tautology" by the device of the "representative firm" which had taken advantage of the economies of large-scale operations. Of course, this approach obscured the issue which Clark was at pains to clarify: the widespread existence of unused capacity and overhead costs. In the United States, John Bates Clark had argued that competition "was continually driving prices toward the cost of production of the most efficient concern, at a speed governed by the rapidity with which its processes could be imitated or its own plant could expand, though he [the elder Clark] also noted the importance of the variable costs of inefficient producers."[24]

Against this background, Clark restated the range of problems covered by overhead costs. "The backbone of the science of economics," he wrote, "is the balancing of value against cost." This furnishes the standard by which all economic activity is judged. In the orthodox view, those activities which do not measure up to this benchmark "may be worthy, charitable, public-spirited, even vitally necessary to the public welfare or the public safety, but they are not paying business and are often thought of as a variety of poor relations." Moreover, the business system is characteristically found to be the most qualified set of institutions to achieve economic efficiency.

Economic efficiency consists of making things that are worth more than they cost, and it is the peculiar characteristic of private business, under a competitive system, to seize and exploit any opportunity to achieve this desirable end. Thereby – so runs the argument – it tends to produce as much of everything as can be produced without driving value below cost, and any more would not be economically worth producing.[25]

But what happens to this argument the moment a decline in demand is experienced, as in a depression? For the present, there are no alternative uses for the various productive factors. What are the costs of additional units of output under such circumstances? As soon as we try to provide an answer to this last question, in Clark's view, "we find ourselves perplexed by the existence of 'overhead costs'." Clark continued:

> To put it briefly, the costs we can trace are only a part of the costs of the business as a whole, which it must somehow manage to cover. What now has become of our rule of economic efficiency? Is the carload of lumber worth carrying if it covers all the cost that can be attributed to that single carload? Or is it only worth carrying if the railroad as a whole is covering all its costs, and what are they? Shall we count the costs that would keep on even if the railroad shut down entirely? *Evidently "cost" is an ambiguous term and the test by which we are accustomed to decide whether production is self-sustaining or not has lost its meaning and requires a thorough re-examination.*[26]

Clark's examination of that "ambiguous term," cost, began with a restatement of the principal conclusion in his doctorate. The "paradox of overhead costs" was that their existence led business *in the normal course of events* to engage either in price discrimination or in cutthroat competition or monopolistic agreements.

PRICE DISCRIMINATION AS A RESPONSE

First he explored the problem of discrimination, which arose in the following manner. Given some degree of unused capacity,[27] a firm will forgo revenue and thus incur a loss[28] if it refuses any business which only covers marginal cost and returns nothing on overhead (fixed) cost. Clearly *some* business must return an amount over and above marginal cost in order to recover overhead costs, however. Discrimination was the "only answer" to this problem, argued Clark. Thus Clark suggested the maxim, "Discrimination is the secret of efficiency," adding that the firm must know where to stop. That is, the "added business will cause no added overhead, and will be a gain at anything above differential [marginal] cost, *so long as it can be kept separate from existing business*, so that existing earnings are not impaired."[29]

In Clark's view, a multi-price market was not therefore a symptom of market imperfections. "In general, discrimination is not a sure symptom of monopoly, still less of extortionate prices. Nor is discrimination necessarily due either to monopoly or to 'joint cost.' *It is a natural result of overhead costs, and is found in practically every phase of business*." Indeed, to Clark, the *absence* of discrimination was what "needs explaining."[30]

The standard view of the matter was far different, however.

> Economists are accustomed to assume that under competition there can be but one price at one time in one market. This assumption is partly the result of observation . . . and partly an a priori premise, growing out of the fact that the economist's study of the laws of price has been cast in the mold of a search for the natural level of prices; thus assuming that there is some natural level toward which the different prices in a market gravitate.[31]

Furthermore, the standard view was ahistorical. Indeed the notion that only one price can prevail in a competitive market at a particular time, "and the further notion that the prices of individual commodities are governed and definitely determined by their individual expenses of production under a competitive system", approximates reality for only a limited historical period. That is, only for the period beginning with the end of guild restrictions and ending with the advent of industries with relatively large amounts of "fixed" capital. Even then price discrimination existed, largely because the commodities were not definitely standardized.

Discrimination itself characteristically comes about because of "the retarded action of the market which permits different prices to prevail at the same time." Thus after one firm lowers its prices, it takes a certain amount of time before customers realize that other firms have followed suit. In this time lag interval, the initiating firm reaps its economic rewards. Furthermore, it takes customers a certain amount of time to switch their trade as a result of real or imagined differences in quality or grade reinforced by advertising. Each firm therefore has a sort of "qualified monopoly" which "is a feature of the typical 'competitive' market."[32]

This question of the competitive functions of product diversity was to become an important point to Clark – especially after the publication of E.H. Chamberlin's *Monopolistic Competition* in 1933. In 1963, Clark took a strong position against the orthodox view that product differentiation, since it led to a demand curve facing the individual firm being less elastic "than this supposedly ideal condition of substantially infinite elasticity," was indicative of monopolistic competition. Clark wrote that

> such differentiation has been labeled as an element of monopoly and allegedly like monopoly, . . . in leading to smaller output and higher prices than would prevail under pure competition. *This is one of the most misleading theoretical generalizations that has ever gained wide currency in economics* . . . within the current generation.

He pointed to the automobile industry and noted that "the meaning-lessness of such a theoretical comparison becomes obvious if one asks what pure competition would mean" in this case. Sometimes product differentiation may afford an opportunity to insulate a firm from competitive pressures, "but by and large it is likely to loosen up more of such inflexibilities than it creates, bringing competitive forces to bear on them."[33]

With localized production and sales, the range of price differentials becomes smaller in size and duration. A similar result takes place as goods become more standardized. With large-scale production, the situation becomes more complex since markets are now national or international in scope. Assume, Clark writes, three different manufacturing concerns, each with different costs of production, selling in a national market. "Under such conditions, the natural price in any one part of the market will be hard to determine. Goods from each center of production can be laid down there, at cost of production plus transportation, and the price will generally be high enough to let in all three producers, giving the most favored one a profit. Add to this the fact that all of them have overhead costs, so that cost per unit falls as output increases, and

the price situation becomes thoroughly indeterminate." The resulting set of market prices "cannot be foretold by calculating what
each would do if he were an 'economic man'."[34]

Similarly, relatively heavy overhead costs might legitimately result
in "dumping" on the international market,[35] or discriminating between different regions in a single nation. The result might be to
lower prices in the domestic or regional market by covering some
of the overhead costs elsewhere. Thus, to Clark, the "Pittsburgh
Plus" system was not necessarily an indication of monopoly since
"the structure is not dictated by any such inevitable competitive
forces as those which shape the wheat market."[36]

Other techniques of discrimination were those of dividing buyers
into different groups, such as wholesalers, retailers, and consumers,
or rich and poor customers as in the case of doctors and lawyers
and the less highly paid. Discrimination might also take place
according to service, or time, with special rates for conventions and
student discounts, for instance. Further, it could manifest itself in
the form of credit services or changes in selling effort. Goods might
be sold at identical prices, but without identical delivery or repair
services, though it is often impossible "to say what is discrimination
and what is equal service."[37]

Finally, Clark pointed out that discrimination which merely
results in the transferring of business from one firm to another is
of little value. This was usually the case, he argued, with local
discrimination. Only discrimination which as "a clear tendency to
tap strata of demand which would otherwise remain untapped, and
to develop uses of our economic equipment which would otherwise
remain unexploited" has a clear economic value.[38]

Discrimination was not simply a narrow economic issue to Clark.
Moral and social issues were also involved which could make of
discrimination "the tool of favoritism and greed" or "the vehicle of
the highest social justice."

CUTTHROAT COMPETITION AND MONOPOLY

The existence of overhead costs could not only result in discrimination, but in cutthroat competition or monopolistic agreements.
Clark proceeded to analyze this second set of possibilities.

In Clark's view, the problem of cutthroat competition arose
in the following manner. Whenever industry output was less than

"normal capacity," it was in the general public interest to increase output so long as the increase in revenue covered marginal cost. But the marginal cost of an increase in output was, "socially speaking," practically zero since the existing capital stock had no alternative uses. Discrimination would, Clark had argued, enable some additional capacity to be utilized, although "no system of discrimination would completely overcome the difficulty." Any uniform increase in prices brought about by an attempt to cover at least some overhead costs would necessarily result in some limitation of demand and some sacrifice of output. "The only level of prices," Clark wrote, "which will surely call all available productive powers into use is a bankruptcy level." That is, since

> industry is in a chronic state of partly idle capacity, to insist that producers shall compete unchecked appears to amount to inviting competition, and private enterprise with it, to commit suicide.[39]

What remains? Clark asked is there anything deserving the name of competition remaining in the economy or "is monopoly essential to the life of private industry?"

He enumerated three tendencies which generate the surplus capacity necessary for the threat of cutthroat competition to exist. Clark noted that plant construction was governed less by "average" demand than peak demand since firms characteristically aimed at supplying anticipated peak demand during the up-swing in the business cycle. In the second place, new and typically small-scale producers were regularly building new plants in an attempt to satisfy new rather than existing demand. Some succeed, some fail; but a net addition to the capital stock is generated. Thirdly, technological innovations continually offer the existing firm hope for lowering their present cost structure. This tends to generate additional capacity. Clark noted that proposals for the regularization of industry would tend to reduce excess capacity, but not eliminate it. The main result would be to eliminate the inefficient producer, since plants would tend to be operated on an all or nothing basis.

Given the existence of surplus capacity in the economy and therefore the incentive for producers to cut prices in order to gain some already existing demand, there were general forces which militated against price cutting: group and business ethics in the community, the adoption of cost-accounting techniques, and a general sense of self-preservation.

Clark pointed to Alfred Marshall's phrase "spoiling the market" and proceeded to extend Marshall's analysis by pointing to five areas that the phrase covered. In the first place was the evident fact that price cutting would not cover total costs either from the standpoint of the individual firm or from that of the industry, for even the most efficient producers. Secondly, if the firm was a large one and its output constituted a relatively large fraction of industry output, the demand curve facing this producer was likely to be of finite elasticity; not the perfectly elastic one assumed in standard theory. Indeed, the elasticity of demand could even be less than unity. Thus price cuts would fail to bring in the increases in total revenue that traditional theory anticipated. Third, the market might be "spoiled" by increasing current sales without increasing current consumption. This would mean that when demand revived, the existing stocks would have to be used up before new goods could be sold. Fourth, "the purchaser's faith" or level of anticipations might be shaken when faced with a new set of prices. Thus any attempt to increase prices during a business revival would meet with resistance on the part of the consumer. Indeed this is related to the fifth form of "spoiling the market": the drop in prices characteristic of a producer's attempt to maintain demand, might result in the consumer's expectation that prices would drop even further. Thus price decreases would actually result in fewer goods being purchased.

Clark then turned his attention to the tendency of producers to form monopolistic combinations, rather than engage in cutthroat competition, as a response to the existence of large overhead costs. There were two facets to the monopoly problem in his view: one entailed the forces making for monopoly; the other, forces tending to check large combinations.

To Clark, the forces tending toward the formation of monopoly were composed of "at least three elements": economies of vertical and horizontal integration, and freedom from competition.

Not all vertical and horizontal integration could be viewed as a response to overhead costs, however. Nor could vertical integration be said to arise solely from the desire for increased profits, since "men of large property frequently . . . invest in wholly unrelated industries." Vertical integration – forward or backward – could be a response to overhead costs, as in the case where the businessperson's knowledge is utilized over a wider area of production. "In this sense," Clark wrote, vertical "integration is really a case of joint costs." The prospect of obtaining a more dependable supply of raw materials or of lowering the costs of buying and selling may also result in economies of integration. On the other hand, if producers have need of products or services which are relatively "minor or incidental" to the business, it will usually pay not to integrate and reap the advantages of specialization on the supplier's part. The extent of integration in an industry will of course depend upon the economic advantages, but integration tends to spread if one or more of the processes of production are "in the hands of large combinations or of a monopoly." "The greater the advantages of integration, the harder to keep competition alive."[40]

"A large part" of the gains from horizontal combinations are merely continuations of those which arise from the growth of single plants. Additional gains arise in the realm of "intellectual overhead costs"; the savings resulting from being able to specialize various plants; and the possibility of concentrating fluctuations in a single plant. This last economy might not outweigh the economies of specialization however. Horizontal combinations may result in a certain "unwieldiness" when spread over great distances. "It is fair to conclude that the chief forces making for horizontal combination are not the economies that result, but rather the natural urge to cease competing and combine."[41]

Finally, the tendency to form large combinations could be seen as simply an attempt to gain freedom from competition. Monopoly, wrote Clark, "must be defined, not merely as a state of being, but in terms of the tactics necessary to establish that state of being and maintain it." Thus as "a state of being" monopoly could not be unreservedly condemned. For example, efficiency in the selling field might be obtained:

> Under monopoly there could be a vast reduction of the competitive armies and armaments of billboards, circulars, traveling salesmen, and color-page advertisements, which, along with some real beauty, contributes so much to the ugliness of America, to the irrelevance of its landscapes, to limiting the ideals and ambitious of many clever artistic craftsmen, to the disappearance of our forests and the subsidizing of the more ephemeral levels of our literature – those which oftenest degenerate into the tawdry.

Other economies were "slight or of doubtful character." Clark argued that "research does not gain by eliminating all duplication." Large producers might absorb inefficient, small, ones merely to protect their position and in some cases have simply closed them down. Then there was the problem of firms "putting to sleep" various patents which were of marginal benefit to the large producer, though they may be of great use to the small one. On balance the getting of a monopoly "and the maintaining of it is likely to involve burdens that outweigh the benefits."[42]

Therefore, the tactics designed to promote monopoly become crucial, since "monopoly does not come ready-made." The businessperson must actively seek to create one, and it is in this process that the costs of monopoly are most clearly seen. The "doubtful character" of economies of scale enter, as mentioned: patents which are often purchased with a view toward "putting them to sleep." Weak or inefficient producers which are sometimes incorporated into an enterprise in order to eliminate real or "potential competition" were examples. Indeed "potential competition," in Clark's view, constituted the principal check to the creation of monopoly.

As with the phrase "spoiling the market," the term "potential competition" was held to cover a number of possibilities. The term might refer to the knowledge that an attempt to push monopoly power too far might result in the creation of many new firms and result in a degree of competition not previously in existence. This is what had plagued the earlier trusts until "they learned the virtue of moderation."[43] Or the term could refer to the reopening of semi-obsolete plants if market price rose to a sufficiently high level. Another type of potential competition came from existing producers in the particular field, but not in the particular market. Potential competition might also refer to mail-order houses, cooperatives, or cash- and-carry stores who stand ready to open additional branches of their firms. Lastly, it might come from producers already in the market, but with whom "agreements, understandings, or more informal truces" have been executed to restrict competition. These firms stand always ready to break existing agreements particularly if the dominant firm becomes too greedy. "On the whole," wrote Clark, "potential competition is a mild and tolerant governor of prices." He continued:

> It allows some profits beyond the absolute minimum necessary
> to sustain private enterprise, but as compared to public regulation

of prices it probably makes up for its laxness by the fact that it leaves industry freer from the cramping effect of the system of checks and balances involved in public control.

But potential competition "tends to lose its force unless it now and then emerges from the background and takes the form of actual competition. *Thus it is inherently impossible to have industry effectively governed by potential competition alone.*"[44]

In addition, the consumer unfortunately does not always receive the benefit of potential competition. The industry attempts to maintain prices at a "sufficiently moderate" level so that price wars do not bring the prospect of large profits. Prices and costs "were brought together, not by bringing prices down to costs, but by bringing costs up to prices, by dividing the existing business up among so many competitors that they all had unused capacity and correspondingly high costs."

A serious drawback to potential competition exists when entry into the industry is conditional upon a relatively large investment in tangible capital. Under this circumstance, the entry of another firm may require prices to fall appreciably in order that the increment of industry capacity be profitably utilized. Profits must therefore be relatively high before new firms will enter the industry and the impact of potential competition is correspondingly reduced. Potential competition functions better "where it depends on the relatively unobtrusive entrance of small and medium-sized producers, no one of whom is of sufficient importance to provoke a price war."[45]

Another important facet of overhead costs was the fundamental role they played "at every stage" in the business cycle. But this role was paradoxical in the extreme. On the one hand, the existence of relatively large overhead costs made the regular and uninterrupted operation of the firm especially desirable and profitable. Whenever output declined below a "normal" level, business experienced a loss. So much so, in fact, that the firm in every case was willing to incur some financial sacrifice in order to stabilize output and preclude the heavier loss of below- "normal" output. "The establishment is willing to take off-peak business at a reduced price, or to spend an increased amount in storing, carrying, or selling the product, or in testing out and building up a scheme for dovetailing different products together, taking trouble and spending money which they would not otherwise spend." Behind this added expense, wrote Clark, "must lie the realization that more regular work is worth a financial sacrifice." By this, Clark did not mean to argue that a perfectly unvarying rate of output was necessarily desirable, as will be seen. He observed that there was nearly always a certain amount of idleness of fixed capital such as the evening shut-down. But "where this is a very large item it amounts to an economic waste large enough to be worth considering quite seriously." There was always, in Clark's view, a conflict between the rhythm of the machine and that of humanity.[46]

On the other hand, "it is largely due to this very fact of large fixed capital that business breeds these calamities for itself, out of the laws of its own being." Using employment as an index, Clark noted that those firms which have the highest proportion of constant costs, relative to invested capital, are the ones which tend to fluctuate the greatest in output.

SOME RELATIONS TO BUSINESS CYCLES

The causes of this perverse behavior are many and varied, but among them "the underlying fact of large capital plays a central part, and the inelasticity of costs, sunk costs, and the shifting and conversion of overhead costs are all facts of major importance." Clark noted however, that it was clearly outside the scope of his present work to fully explore the numerous causes.[47] A few factors, having directly or indirectly to do with overhead costs were considered.

First there was the fact that costs and profits were a function of output and therefore demand as well as the efficiency of production. "One result of this is that the producer has a wider option in price policies than he would have if volume of sales had no effect on cost of production per unit." Given an increase in demand, the firm can increase profits without increasing prices; or the firm can raise prices in order to recover the loss on overhead from earlier periods of depression.

The next contributing cause of business cycles concerned the fact that the derived demand for new capital goods fluctuates more intensely than the primary demand for consumption goods in industries using these capital goods. Here Clark introduced and expanded a major theoretical tool which he had developed earlier: The Acceleration Principle.[48]

Clark wrote that the observed facts of the matter were generally the following:

> The demand for means of production fluctuates more violently than that for finished consumers' goods, and also appears to fluctuate sooner, taking the lead in a way which would suggest that its changes are a cause, rather than an effect, of the changes in consumers' demand. In point of fact they are both effect and cause. . . . Something similar is true of raw materials as compared to finished goods, while wholesale prices fluctuate more than retail.[49]

Aside from psychological considerations, Clark argued that there seemed to be two main reasons for the more intense fluctuation in the means of production. One was financial and involved the criteria of the market; the other technical – "wholly independent of the money economy." This technical acceleration principle caused fluctuations in investment demand through consumer demand for finished goods. For increases in investment demand to be maintained at a new level, there would have to be periodic increases in consumer demand for the output. A levelling-off of consumer demand would lead to a decrease in derived demand which could be reinforced by the resulting unemployment in the producers' goods industries.[50]

The acceleration principle presupposes the existence of an elastic credit system. Furthermore, Clark wrote, "when demand is strong and increasing, competition between producers takes the shape, not of reducing the price of the finished product, but of offering more for the factors of production." Because input prices lag behind prices for finished goods, employers' expectations rise and firm projections are made for expanding output. Since producers have imperfect knowledge concerning the stage of the business cycle they are presently in, this increase in output is cumulatively reinforced and lasts beyond the turning point.

This contributing cause of business cycles had an interesting corollary in Clark's view. During the upswing, prices actually distort the socially efficient allocation of resources. "When the purchasing power of money itself changes," Clark wrote, "it loses its value as a guide to the most effective use of society's stock of resources. In terms of need, the higher price does not represent the more pressing want; and if it outbids the lower price in the market, the economic system is to just that extent distorted." And as a stabilizing influence, prices functioned at counter-purposes to economic needs:

As a means of distributing production and consumption over the various phases of the business cycle, money values operate in exactly the wrong direction and are directly opposed to the most efficient timing of productive activity.[51]

Another factor in business cycles, closely related to the foregoing, was what Clark called the "shifting and conversion of overhead costs." Constant costs were often converted into variable charges as the product passed through various stages of production and different firms. This converting of constant charges into variable costs distorted the process by which producers decided whether or not it was profitable to produce. That is: "Every producer has an incentive to avoid idleness, but the strength of his incentive is measured by the amount of his own constant expenses, not by the total amount of constant costs involved in the whole process, from beginning to end of the chain of operations and exchanges."[52] The distortion effected by the conversion of overhead costs worked to the opposite end during an upswing. Thus, Clark argued, "whenever constant costs are converted into variable or variable into constant, there is a stimulus either to wasteful overuse or wasteful disuse of our productive facilities."[53]

TOWARDS ECONOMIC STABILIZATION

Clark next turned his attention to the difficult area of remedies for the business cycle and economic stabilization in general. At least three points had emerged from his overall study of overhead costs. The first followed from the fact of the shifting and conversion of overhead costs. That is, "the question [of] how much overhead cost there is *in any particular industry depends largely or entirely on the system of contracts under which industries acquire the use of the factors of production.*"[54] The second point, drawing upon H.J. Davenport's concept of opportunity cost, was that, from the standpoint of society as a whole, "when it is a choice between use and involuntary idleness, the bulk of the ultimate costs of industry are 'overhead costs'."[55] There were no alternative uses for the total stock of productive inputs of society at any given time. From this, Clark argued

> *There is no natural system of prices in the old sense. Cost prices do not mean anything definite any more.*[56]

In short, much of the difficulty lay in the fact that industry as a whole appeared to be unwilling to treat its costs as overhead and continue production in the face of a slackening of prices.[57]

As has been seen, the existence of overhead costs led to cutthroat competition or monopolistic agreements. This resulted, Clark wrote, in "a compromise between actual competition and a spirit of mutual restraint which is essentially anti-competitive in character." It was as if there were a conflict between the social interests and that of private interests, since the former required capacity output while the latter sought to maximize revenue over variable cost and struck a balance between decreased output and decreased earnings.[58]

Initially, Clark thought that part of the solution to this general problem could be achieved as follows:

> If everybody *stood ready* to cut down to the absolute minimum of "variable cost," and if everybody shared such cuts as were made, *nobody would have to cut that low* or anything near it, in order to restore demand to a reasonably normal level. For the chief cause of a falling-off in demand lies in the fact that any unemployment reduces people's purchasing power and so returns on itself in a vicious circle creating more unemployment.[59]

In his last major work, Clark summarized his revised thinking on this question. He noted that "there is a little evidence that moderate price flexibility in particular industries may somewhat mitigate fluctuations of production; but no ground for thinking that full stability" could come about by this process. As things stood, "The balance of economic judgment would surely class this unlimited kind of flexibility . . . as unstabilizing."[60]

As things stand, output is usually cut more sharply than sales because of changes in expectations. This seemed to Clark much like the situation under the National Bank Act of 1863 (amended 1864) which required a fixed ratio of reserves to deposits. When this ratio was not maintained, loans would be cut and cash payments suspended to protect reserves, in spite of the fact that reserves were only wanted in order to maintain cash payments. "All of which," Clark wrote, "irresistibly suggests a man on a rock, jumping into the water for fear the tide will rise and wet him."[61] Clearly, then, remedies must point the way toward creating a frame of mind requisite to a more satisfactory working of the economic machinery.

To begin with, Clark noted that proposals for tempering the peak of the cycle concentrated mainly on monetary actions designed to control the inflationary effects generally experienced at those times. The Federal Reserve System seemed the most obvious institution available with its leverage on discount rates. But this and other tools would probably best be experimented with and discussed by specialists. The timing of any such checks would be considerably aided by the development of accurate and comprehensive statistics – both in the financial and physical dimensions of production.

Another remedy would aim at filling up the troughs of the cycle by giving business an incentive to anticipate demand and postpone non-essential production as far as possible. Clark argued that there was a considerable amount of evidence to support the proposition "that industry actually outgrows itself in terms of physical output, and that part of the growth is unassimilable and does not contribute to the long-run wealth of the country."[62] In order to smooth out the cycle, industry must bear some of the responsibility for the costs incurred to handle peak demand. A salient proposal in this regard by Clark was that labor be treated as an overhead cost. Originally presented in a paper before the American Economic Association in 1920, the full import of Clark's proposal is best viewed against the background of his studies on overhead costs.[63]

Clark argued that labor power, as with other productive inputs, had no alternative use at any given time from the standpoint of society as a whole. Employers had already partially recognized this fact by the customary distinction between salaried employees and wage earners. Salaried employees "expect to adapt their hours to the requirements of the business: to work overtime without extra pay, to receive a vacation with pay, to be kept on the rolls during sickness (within limits), and during dull times."[64] Nor could it be argued, Clark wrote, that vacations or leisure time were the appropriate alternatives to involuntary idleness. This was because when labor was *involuntarily* unemployed as in a depression, it had no alternative uses. Leisure time, for instance, could only be viewed as an appropriate alternative or opportunity cost to an already employed laborer.

As matters stood, the laborer necessarily had to bear the expenses of his own "overhead" in much the same manner as the businessperson was forced to maintain fixed plant and equipment whether it was used or not. However the existing system of contracts allowed the producer to shift and convert his fixed costs into variable costs;

this conversion was obviously not possible for the individual worker. Therefore, just as unused capacity was an overhead charge to society as a whole, so was unused labor a similar overhead charge for which the employer did not necessarily pay an appropriate share – though he freely utilized the stock of labor and capital in handling peak loads. As Clark phrased it: "the overhead cost of labor is a collective burden upon industry in general, but the market does not allocate to each employer the share for which his own enterprise is responsible."[65]

Clark did not, however, argue that all irregularities in employment should be abolished even if this were possible. If all labor were employed on the same basis as salaried employees, the matter would be settled. But "it will probably never be desirable to try to make such a system universal." Humankind probably needs a certain amount of irregularity, and in addition it would be wasteful to require employers who do a highly seasonal business to maintain workers on their payrolls throughout the year. There were really two problems here: one was to reduce waste brought about by the business cycle and producers' attempts to handle peak loads; the second was to mitigate, though not eliminate, the wastes brought about by normal movements of workers between industries.[66] "Nevertheless," Clark wrote, "if we had to choose between two sweeping propositions: one saying that the human cost of labor varies in proportion to work done and the other that it is a 'constant cost,' the latter would be preferable because it expresses those truths of which the present industrial system is most oblivious and around which the constructive effort of the present generation needs to center."[67]

Further remedies for the business cycle would include better coordination of employment offices, making the task of matching employers and the unemployed more effective. Another proposal was Irving Fisher's plan for the stabilization of the dollar. Clark thought this plan ought to be adjusted to concentrate on mitigating long swings of prices, letting short-term movements of particular groups of prices perform their useful allocative function. Also short-term declines in producers' goods prices would encourage building ahead of projected demand in dull times, lending stability to the economy.

Clearly, achieving thoroughgoing remedies for controlling the business cycle and stabilizing production was a complex task, requiring the concerted efforts of business, government, the banking system, insurance industry, and organized labor. The opportunity and power for such action was probably greatest, however, in the business sector, Clark wrote. Any long-term solution must contain some way to properly assess, apportion, and collect overhead costs. Clark mentioned four logical bases for apportioning these. The first was the ability to pay, placing them in a class with taxes. The second was the rather elastic term "causal responsibility." The next, related to the first two, was benefit or use. And the last was on the basis of a stimulus to improved utilization. All of these principles were more or less overlapping, however.[68]

Clark amplified a proposal of Walter W. Stewart by suggesting that the process of bringing all interests to bear upon the problem would "require some means of common and co-ordinated action not less far-reaching and effective in the industrial field than the Federal Reserve System in the banking field."[69]

Proposals for redistributing the burdens of overhead costs, Clark argued, had ample precedent in countries like Germany – and the United States was a far richer country. The role of government was indeed "self-evident" by now for filling up the troughs of the business cycle. It "should plan an elastic schedule for public works of a postponable sort, and should save certain works to be prosecuted only in time of depression and unemployment, or prosecute the entire program more actively as such times." Although government revenues shrink during depressions, such a program could be financed by "the setting aside of funds in good time[s] and the use of banking credit."[70]

Turning from the subject of business cycles, Clark noted that the existence of overhead costs had import for marginal productivity theory. He argued, following Philip H. Wicksteed and A.W. Flux, for example, that payments to factor inputs would indeed equal the value of the total product – Euler's theory.[71] But this was only under static conditions, with no fixed costs and with all costs varying exactly in proportion to output. But fixed costs, Clark wrote, "stand for factors of production which have unused capacity." In this light, increases in inputs might add nothing to output and only serve to deduct a charge from the total. "Thus the marginal product might be everything or nothing." And therefore the payment made to labor, for instance, does not under dynamic conditions rest upon as firm a footing as had been commonly supposed.[72]

Clark's landmark work concluded with the following, appropriate assessment of the relevance of overhead costs:

A knowledge of the laws of overhead costs is not a master key to all the mysteries of our new dynamic-organic economy; in fact, there is no master key; but it opens many doors, and is one of the indispensable avenues of approach to a better and more systematized understanding of the things which static economics does not explain. In such a study, *overhead costs are not exceptions to a general economic law: they are the general law. Dynamic economics must not merely take account of them, it must be built around them*, for they are part of its essential framework.[73]

And, as Clark phrased the matter in 1958:

Cost of some sort is supposed to set a minimum below which sales will not be made. *But cost is not a precise, unambiguous objective fact; it is rather a convention allowing considerable latitude.*[74]

In view of Clark's dissertation, and in retrospect, Overhead Costs appeared to lead to two areas of study: stabilization programs through regularization of the business cycle, and the social control of business.[75] In the middle nineteen-twenties, Clark turned to a study of the control of business enterprise.

4 Control of Industry – By Business and Society

As with his *Studies in the Economics of Overhead Costs*, the earliest source of Clark's *Social Control of Business*[1] is to be found in his doctoral dissertation. As noted earlier, the dissertation contained essentially two sections. In the first part, Clark sought to discover the cost principles upon which railway rates were actually based. It was this track which led Clark into the study of overhead costs and to the proposition that overhead costs were the *usual* rule in modern industry. The second section of his dissertation followed directly from the "fact" of overhead costs and provided the basis for his view that new measures of public control in industry were necessary.

CLARK'S DISSERTATION AND THE CHANGING REQUIREMENTS OF PUBLIC CONTROL

With respect to the railway industry, Clark wrote in his dissertation that there was a fundamental difference between the profit motive which governs all business enterprise and the motive of public service. All firms contain aspects of both motives; that is, they are "both a business enterprise affected by self interest, and a branch of the public service bound to promote the welfare of the community at large. . . ." The degree of public authority varied as well: in the United States and England, for instance, the systems operated with public control at a minimum, while in countries like Germany and Austria, public control was the accepted norm.[2]

Yet, whether the railway system operated with a mode of more or less private or public control, each based their rates on the basis of "value of service" or "what the traffic will bear" in order to cover their fixed charges. These terms, Clark wrote, "are constantly being used by practical men as sufficient grounds for the practices followed in actual rate-making. But the principle is ... quite indefinite. Taken alone as an explanation of rates it does little more than to base rates for the most part on themselves and each other." In Clark's view, the phrase "value of service" was misleading since it suggested "control by natural laws, an involuntary bowing to irresistible outside forces, and an inevitableness, which are for the most part fictitious."[3] Clark was arguing that the pricing mechanism was not a sufficient guide to the allocation of resources in the railway industry or, by extension, in other industries characterized by relatively large overhead investment. He amplified this by noting that "the value principle in its bare form is not a positive but a negative one," because it failed to provide an "external standard for judging rates or adjusting them." He emphasized that "the economic laws of value take on very different aspects according as a business is public or private in character, or as it is monopolistic, competitive, or of mixed nature."[4]

Clark pointed out in this early work that a discrepancy existed between public benefits and costs, and benefits and costs in the private sector. Does the "value of service" principle "contain, incidentally, any strong forces of social benefit?" Often there were social benefits: "free competition in many cases does work for society's good. But no less certainly have the results of private self-interest in many other cases been more than doubtful from a social point of view." Clark was emphatic on the conflict between interests in the case of railroads:

> It does not require long scientific treatises to convince the American public that, while the interests of privately-owned railways may coincide with those of society to a certain extent, they are not identical nor nearly so in practice, and that a laissez-faire policy would expose the American public, consumers of railway transportation, to the risk of serious evils. It may practically be taken for granted that "value of services" under laissez-faire stands for a policy of purely private interest to which any public benefits secured are incidental.[5]

Clark then noted the ethical components of systems of control – a problem with which he was concerned throughout his life. He wrote that "any law of value, to be accepted and acquiesced in, must of course be ethical. The doctrine of free competition has an ethical principle at the bottom of it, but it can be perverted; and if this happens, justice must be restored if possible by some force other than that of private self-interest."[6]

Here, then, was the early source of many of Clark's later works. The investigations of overhead costs, in his dissertation and in the

1923 work on overhead costs, had shown that costs, and therefore prices, were not as definite and immutable as had been assumed by many economists. The legal and institutional structure dictated the extent to which costs would be shifted and converted from constant into variable, and vice versa. Prices were then a function of the institutional framework of society and the way was open, in Clark's view, to an examination of a broader, more relevant, view of the economic machinery of society. *Social Control of Business* was not a primer on how to dabble at correcting the market mechanism here and there. It was an examination of the *institutional roots of resource allocation* in modern society.

THE EVOLUTION OF CONTROL

Clark began the *Social Control of Business* by noting that society was undergoing a process of rapid evolution. This change was "transforming the character of business, the economic life and economic relations of every citizen, and the powers and responsibilities of the community toward business and of business toward the community." He likened the tempo of change to the "Industrial Revolution" and argued that they were "but two phases of one greater revolution, which consists of the development of science and its application to economic life."[7]

Private business "is no longer private" in the sense that most people would have interpreted this term a hundred years ago. The prodigious rise of control of, and inquiry into, large businesses marks a break with the period of individualism which followed the medieval attempts at control. In the United States the new movement began virtually with the Granger laws of the early 1870's which marked "the first serious attempt at state control of railroad rates."[8] Since then, railroads have come under effective control, and the general notion of a public utility, subject to public control, has come to be accepted. The telephone and electricity industries have not only become public utilities, but it has become recognized that these are industries of national importance, with interests going beyond state boundaries. The list of industries considered sufficiently affected with a public interest as to be national in impact has expanded, with radio and air navigation being added to those of irrigation, land reclamation, and flood prevention. Nor does that exhaust the list:

The trust movement and anti-trust laws, conservation, the Federal Reserve System, vast developments in labor legislation, social insurance, minimum-wage laws and the compulsory arbitration of industrial disputes, pure-food laws and the growing control of public health, prohibition, control over markets and marketing, enlarged control over immigration and international trade, city planning and zoning, and municipal control of municipal growth in general, all have come about in this period.

The frontier of control was extending, with movements towards health insurance, control of the business cycle and unemployment, "and the insertion of social control within the structure of industry itself, through the 'democratization of business.'" Beyond these movements were questions of the stabilization of the dollar, and of birth control and eugenics, "while the control of large fortunes and of the unequal distribution of wealth is an ancient and ever new question which is becoming more and more acute as the masses gain a growing sense of their political power."[9] Clark wrote that this movement could not be ignored or forbidden, even by those honestly opposed. "It may be guided and directed," he argued, "its movements may be made more informed and enlightened, but it cannot be stopped, and no one group can dictate its course."

In his view, the drift towards public control was the necessary consequence of the development of three main factors: large-scale enterprise; democracy; and science – all of which have engendered a slowly changing attitude toward social institutions.

> This attitude regards institutions as means to ends, but not as sheer bits of social machinery to be tinkered with and altered wholly at the will of the tinkerer. They are themselves . . . living things, evolving according to their own laws, and these laws the human understanding has not yet mastered. Yet their course is subject to some degree of direction, and man is continually calling on them to justify themselves by their results, and trying to improve them where they do not seem to meet this test.[10]

To clearly understand the nature of this process it was necessary, in Clark's view, to understand what was meant by terms such as "control," "social control," and "business" or the broader term, "economic activity".

Control, of course, meant coercion, though no coercion is absolute, since one could always elect to pay the penalty for failing to comply – indeed the penalty is sometimes so slight that it is less than the profits of the offense. Though this seemed obvious to most people, some tended to view the market mechanism as coercion-free. This was not the case according to Clark. It was simply a question of a less obvious system of controls with the extent and effects depending upon the nature of the market as well as the institutional structure. Clark posed this aspect of the problem in the following way:

> To the common-sense mind individualism appears as the absence of control, and control as the antithesis of individualism. That is, of course, simply the result of the fact that, when things are too familiar to raise problems, we cease to be conscious of them at all. One of the difficult tasks, then, is to exhibit individualism as itself a system of control, and to analyze the institutions of control on which it rests. Legal rights of person and property are at the basis of it, supplemented by the informal controls of morals and public opinion and the many-sided institution of competition.[11]

For example, a monopolistic pricing policy might result in the denial of a commodity to which a consumer had "become accustomed as a part of a well-ordered existence, or even a necessity of life" since there was no alternative but to accept the price or do without (assuming no acceptable substitutes). Thus, even under free contract, control may exist under monopoly. This situation had come to be recognized by most; but what if the market were competitive? Could private control exist then?

Clark clearly believed that it could. Taking an illustration from the labor market, Clark pointed out that a worker with no savings and a family "cannot easily take advantage of the competition by canvassing the market." In addition, the substance of liberty, distinguished from the form, depended upon the knowledge fund of the worker: knowledge of a particular task and skills; knowledge of bargaining techniques; and knowledge of how to canvass the market effectively. Without this knowledge, the person might be "compelled" to accept less than a satisfactory living wage for his particular work: "That person is in a position to be exploited and to be forced to make contracts which are essentially made under duress."[12] Therefore a coercive situation existed in Clark's accounting, which was to be distinguished from the "voluntary bargaining" between equals too often assumed to be the usual situation under perfect competition.

Where a degree of private control does exist in a competitive market, where does the coercion originate? "Does it come from the employer who last discharged him, or from an informal control of the market by the employers in general, or from the customs and habits of the business, or from the 'impersonal and immutable laws' of supply and demand?" To Clark, all of these forces contributed a degree of private control, operating in an impersonal fashion and not as the result of "deliberate oppression." This form of control was felt most strongly when wages fell during a business depression. In such an instance employers, even in a perfectly competitive market, were unable to pay a living wage: the laborer might become unemployed as the result of "a mere failure to cooperate in a purely voluntary arrangement for mutual gain" – a situation for which no individual felt fully responsible. In fact, however, the worker depends upon "the cooperation of *employers in general*" since he has no reasonable alternative given the economic structure of modern business society. Clark also noted that other, intangible, forms of control may be even more pervasive, such as the forces of custom or importunity; "the contempt of one's class;" and, at least formerly, the power of the church.[13]

"Control" – as distinct from voluntary cooperation – thus existed in Clark's view under all types of market conditions, and apart from any "state" activity. Now he turned to a discussion of "social control."

Clark characterized "social control" as control exercised by or in behalf of society, as opposed to control *of* society – a concept he considered not useful for the purpose at hand. Society was held to be "an aggregate of individuals, interests, and groups which, however organically bound together, are still distinguishable. Ideally, it should include all the interests affected by its economic system." Within a nation, various levels of government constituted the most powerful group of control agencies. Thus social control meant, in the large, government control, though Clark emphasized that other agencies and interests also exercise a measure of social control – neighbors, trade unions, newspapers, and so forth. And "whether governmental control is truly social is mainly a question whether the government is truly representative of the various interests and groups in the nation."[14]

A distinction was made between "group control" and "social control." Group control existed when only one group in society exerted control as in a trade union. In general, "the more inclusive the group is, the better socialized is the control which it exercises." Drawing on John R. Commons' *Legal Foundations of Capitalism*, Clark further noted that even when the state acts, it is in fact an individual acting who is more or less in sympathy with a particular law, and which in turn might have been enacted under the influence of a pressure group.[15] Another example of group control is provided by the system of free contract, originally devised as a means of control by the trading community by and for their own class. This system "did not deal with the great conflicts between class and class, but with the relations of traders with traders; *it was primarily a law of contractual relations between equals whose central occupation was bargaining.*"[16] Clark was here noting that in effect there was a sort of comparative advantage in (rational) calculating: businessmen calculate more than other groups.

But it is a different story when the idea of contract between equals is extended to "industrial relations" or to other relations between members of different classes. For here not only is the bargain no longer between equals, but the two parties perform functions which differ more widely than anything found in the dealings of the world of traders. As a result, it becomes far more difficult so to order the system of contract that it will satisfy both sides of its fairness. The situation lacks the saving grace of reversibility, which causes the man who suffers from a given rule today to realize that he may benefit by the operation of the same rule tomorrow. And if the contending parties harmonize their interests at the expense of the public, that also is a form of class tyranny and not to be borne in a self-governing community. The method of allowing a class to build up its own instrument of control is still more unthinkable in the case of trust control or tariff legislation, where the essential question is one of conflicting interests between the class in question and the public.[17]

Clark in effect adopted the hypothesis that there were group interests, in possible conflict with those of society at large, incapable of adequate resolution on the market level with free contract, even given competitive markets. It was this conflict that wanted "social control."

Since it was the social control of business that was being considered, Clark defined business as "the system of social cooperation by mutual exchange." He pointed out that business was "a means to an end rather than an end in itself" and necessarily subject to controls simply because it was a form of organized human activity.

These controls were on three levels. First was the informal kind which the business group developed to fit their own needs. Second were controls developed by courts in settling disputes. And last were the controls instituted by legislation designed to affect the future. "For this reason," he wrote, "when we speak of the 'social control of business,' we must take some pains to avoid the implication that business exists first and is then controlled. Control is rather an integral part of business, without which it could not be business at all. The one implies the other, and the two have grown together."[18] It was the legislative level of control to which most people referred when speaking of the social control of business. Yet Clark stressed that one cannot intelligently approach the legislative area without an understanding of the substratum of law which provides the starting point for legislation and thoroughly pervades it.

The most thoroughgoing system of restraint underlying legislative control could be summed up under the rubric "individualism." The rights of personal security, liberty, and property, as well as the systems of inheritance, contracts, bankruptcy, poor relief, and more recently the business corporation all presuppose the existence of widespread legislation. For this reason, Clark wrote that "under individualism the state does as little as it can in the way of coercive control, but it always had to do a great deal. The ideal of the 'pure' individualist is a state which does nothing but protect property and enforce contracts, *but there has never been any such state and never can be. . . .*"[19] This point was crucial in Clark's view. Elsewhere he elaborated the point, noting that it was "out of date to decry – or praise – all economic legislation as 'socialistic'" yet the view that "complete individualism or complete socialization" were the only two possible end-conditions still prevailed amongst some. On the contrary, Clark noted, the "two conditions are impossible: pure individualism and complete socialism. Everything lies in the realm between; bare of logical anchorages though it may be." He continued:

> There had always been more control than the theory of pure individualism calls for. . . . And one may hazard that . . . there

will always be a large and important place for that principle of free voluntary action and of mutual arrangements for
the mutual advantage of those immediately and primarily concerned.[20]

Thus since control had always existed, the task involved developing
a system of scientific standards for control. For if the present
system of control becomes obsolete, "the whole social fabric may
be shattered by a revolution."

Clark recognized that the present system was "most often
defended on the ground that any available substitute would be even
more wasteful and less efficient." Yet this did not deter him from
arguing that the cure for the "failure of social coordination" in
meeting human needs was "to release enormous powers of production which are now imprisoned and make a greater contribution to
human welfare than any conceivable technical invention could do.
At present, the greatest field open to invention for bettering the lot
of mankind is the field of improvements in our system of social
control."[21]

Against this backdrop, Clark proceeded to a broad amplification
of the development of various systems of control invented by
humankind through time, culminating with an inspection of the
system of business enterprise – the most recent system of social
coordination and control. Social organization from the primitive
clan, the military-aristocratic slave state, the medieval rural economy, the town economy, and the early national system – mercantilism – were each examined as systems of social control. Clark noted
the mercantilist roots of the nineteenth century view of "individualism," "freedom," and "liberty."

Historically, individualism was a reaction against the excessive
and perverted restraints of the mercantile system. It has often
been set forth as a statement of eternal and universal truth by
those who were in the midst of the movement and could not see
it in its historical perspective. Some believed that a benevolent
Creator had so ordered the world that the natural impulses of
men worked together for the good of the whole; and yet few of
them carried this belief to its logical conclusion, which would
mean rejecting all government. The government to which they
were accustomed appeared to them as natural, except for the
restrictions of mercantilism.[22]

Yet all writers during the eighteenth and early nineteenth century found room for some form of legislative controls. "One might conclude," wrote Clark, "That the truth of individualism consisted, at bottom, in the errors of eighteenth century mercantilism." In his Chicago lectures on the sesquicentennial of the publication of *The Wealth of Nations*, Clark spoke of "the well-known system of Mercantilism, which we think of as a system of restrictive control, but which was, . . . based on a transfer to the nation of controls previously exercised locally, in which process most of them were considerably relaxed. Within the boundaries of the nation, the principle and practice of free trade and exchange made great headway, . . . despite the retarding effect of many survivals of earlier restrictions, including apprentice laws, the law of parish settlements in England, and local customs duties in France."[23] Furthermore, early writers on the individualistic system such as Adam Smith and John Stuart Mill wrote at a time when large-scale industry and the modern corporate institution were largely unknown.

In an unpublished manuscript, probably written in 1927, Clark noted: "During this [nineteenth-century] development [of economic theory] the theory of the personal business enterprise was insensibly transferred to the corporation, and the theories of free exchange and competition transferred to the new and evolving forms of these institutions. Such a process inevitably leads in time to need of overhauling." He explained that

> In other words, organization is in the same historical position now that free individual exchange occupied at the time of Adam Smith; and it must occupy the same central place in theory if the theory is to play a pioneer role corresponding to that which Adam Smith's thought played in the life of his time. Even to understand "free exchange" we must study the many changes which organization has brought about in that developing institution.[24]

The nineteenth century was one of rapidly expanding, but piece-meal modification of the basic eighteenth-century system of control, according to Clark. Thus legislation and railway rate regulation, for instance, attempted to follow, rather than depart from, "the competitive-individualistic standard." Depressions were regarded by many as unfortunate accidents and other evils were largely ignored or treated as the result of business excess.

CONTROL IN THE MODERN PERIOD

To this long period of individualism, World War I definitely put a close. "From 1914 to 1918 the economic resources of the combatant nations were marshalled by their governments as never before." Indeed this war-time period could be regarded as one in which wide experiments in various new types of control were undertaken.[25] This is why Clark devoted attention at several other points to the issue of transition from a war-time economy to a peace-time system; he saw in the adjustment period an opportunity for the reexamination of systems of control. In this light, his review of Alfred Marshall's *Industry and Trade* noted that:

It is interesting and significant that the phrase "social endeavor" appears in place of the narrower phrase "functions of government," which was used in the preface to the "Principles." In the last century men naturally thought of private enterprise and political government as the two alternative agencies through which things might be brought to pass. Today such a point of view is obsolete.[26]

Writing of the contemporary business system, Clark saw a definite public or social stake in private business. "The individualistic system of checks and balances, by which it seeks to harness private greed, clearly leaves many and important public interests unprotected or unaccounted for. The effect which business has upon these interests cannot be treated as a matter of purely private concern." Clark further noted:

The effects of business transactions are not limited to the parties directly engaged in them; and therefore they cannot properly be regarded as simply an exercise by those parties of their "natural rights." They can be justified only in so far as they form a part of the most just, workable, and effective system humanly available for organizing the work of creating wealth and distributing it.[27]

Although the economic structure was clearly a legitimate area of public or social concern, this did not mean to Clark that there existed therefore a clear prescription for any degree of legislative intervention. Control was not viewed as an either- or proposition:

market control versus complete, non-market, direction of the economy. Clark had, after all, stressed that control was inherent in the business system as with any form of cooperative economic behavior. This is what he meant when writing "*Complete individualism has never existed*." It was rather a question of discovering in what ways the underlying institutional structure had changed from the late eighteenth-century small-enterprise type, and then devising methods of control appropriate and adequate for dealing with the large-scale enterprise which Clark took to be characteristic of modern times. It was one thing to argue that a new harness was needed for the forces of the industrial system, and quite another to decide upon the *kind* of harness. As he noted elsewhere,

> Economics may play a useful part in this development [of new institutions]. To do so it must study business in the light of the need and scope for these further community-building forces. And it must study these forces, not only in terms of the failures, injustices and conflicts which are all too evident, but also, as Adam Smith studied the forces of free exchange, in terms of the constructive functions which these agencies, however haltingly, serve to fulfill. The interpretation of these agencies and their functions is one of the great tasks of twentieth-century economics.[28]

The proper aim or purpose of social control was a continuously evolving question.

In the United States, as Clark had pointed out, the development of control had been a disjointed affair aiming only to ameliorate specific trouble spots. The protective tariff, public utilities commissions, the Wagner Act, pure food and drug acts, and banking control were among the many examples at hand. Unlike thoroughgoing dictatorships or militaristic states, there were no general goals toward which the nation moved. Instead, the underlying community had usually performed only a permissive or passive role. The nation, as a group, did not know what it wanted: a fact presenting obvious difficulties for the development of control.[29] In fact, there was a real question among several segments of society whether "democracy" – "rule by popular will" – was feasible in modern society because of the difficulty of mobilizing the population for the achievement of specific goals. Those who rejected popular rule, from whatever quadrant, rested their argument "on the idea that the masses are not competent to formulate and pursue their own ideals and aspirations." Clark wrote that if the first requirement of a democracy could not be met, an educated, competent, and responsible people, and if industry could "do no better for the masses than to offer them some modernized equivalent of the Roman 'bread and circuses,'" then "we may expect a corresponding outcome, a downfall paralleling that of the Roman Empire." The drift of economic organization was not pre-determined toward a teleological "progress."[30]

Clark asked what democracy or self-government would mean with respect to industry. The presumption was that the "boss" should be elected.

> Should such election be by the customers or by the workers, and should either group control what corresponds to the nominating machinery? The answer may depend on what we regard as the more important product of industry, goods or men. Giving control to the customers is clearly the thing if goods are the most vital product. But suppose men are; suppose quality of activity means more than quantity of product. Then the answer is not so clear. . . .[31]

Amplifying this point elsewhere, Clark indicated his complete agreement with John A. Hobson's "theme of the positive effects of work and working conditions on the worker as a value coordinate with [the] increase of consumer goods."[32] Additional requirements for democracy in industry were, for example, an absence of social barriers; decentralization in government; the right of revolution by the majority; and a willingness to abide by due process of law.

Aside from the preceding considerations, there was the question of harmonizing the needs of democracy with the modern requirements of large-scale enterprise and the concomitant, enabling, institution of the corporation, the simplest way of harmonizing liberty with efficiency according to Clark "would be to give each person that kind of control we call 'ownership' over the land and materials he works with." This has however been rendered impossible by the efficiencies of scale in enterprise which Clark assumed to outweigh the inefficiencies generated by the utilization of non-owner employees who "do not put their hearts into their work as the proprietor-worker does."[33] It was therefore necessary to develop forms of social control congruous with the requirements of the modern industrial state. He explained:

> The political state is clumsy, rather unhuman, and unduly centralized. More mobile agencies exist in every walk of life; neighborhood, trade, and professional organizations. They control the individual in the interest of a group, but the group is too narrow and its interests are too often in conflict with those of the community at large. These agencies must be used, but they must also be socialized; real organs of common action must be built of the raw materials available in trade unions, employers' organizations, cooperatives, professional associations, and the like.[34]

Clark thought that the development of appropriate types of control might occupy the efforts of several generations. He did not anticipate the quick implementation of nostrums, especially in light of the problems to be resolved. While there was little disagreement on the more general goals of public policy, any attempt to give them a more specific content led to the familiar conclusion that specific programs did not easily harmonize one with the other. To illustrate, Clark suggested that the dominant goals might be grouped under eight headings which would "include 'efficiency' and abundance, liberty, 'equality of opportunity,' equitable distribution of goods, leisure, security, the development of the individual, and 'progress,' or a sense of improving conditions."

An even more trenchant question concerned the premises by which social policy was to be guided. Since it appeared unlikely that people would desire a return to the handicraft level of production, with its concomitant "liberty" in ownership, Clark looked at the current mode of guiding the industrial system: the pursuit of profit by businessmen. Here, he stated two related premises underlying his search for systems of control appropriate to the twentieth century. The first was that

> The most important objective of any right policy is to give human nature a chance to show whatever fitness it may have for the highest and best system of control we can conceive, and the one which appeals most directly to the best motives rather than actually stunting them by placing everyone in a competitive struggle where he is virtually forced to develop a selfish attitude, whether he has it naturally or not.

To this was added the second premise relating to the efficacy of business direction of the industrial system:

> This [policy objective] calls for a system of control which begins within the individual himself, making it his main business to render efficient service, instead of leaving this to be an incidental by-product of the chase after profits. "Production for use, not for profit" must be the ruling principle of any system that hopes for permanence in the modern interdependent industry.[35]

The statement that "efficient service" is only "an incidental by-product" of the profit system would surprise many students of standard economic theory. What Clark had especially in mind were such phenomena as business cycles – an outgrowth of the business system – which at times fell "into a deadlock in which output shrinks because demand has shrunk, incomes shrink because output has shrunk, and demand shrinks because incomes have shrunk."[36] Unless production "directly for needs and not for the balance sheet" can be introduced as a permissible objective of control, other controls limited to the existing institutional framework would be self-contradictory on Clark's premises.

> From the standpoint of those who are impatient for far-reaching reforms, democratic gradualism has one serious weakness. It assumes that business is to go on being an affair of private self-seeking and definitely sanctions the business man in adopting this role and then tries to control him by external force, after it has arrayed against itself the whole power of customary business morals. Under such conditions, control is necessarily ineffective – so runs the criticism – and business remains primarily acquisitive. Any such institution is doomed unless it can somehow be saved from itself, and it can be saved only by something which will change its basic motivating character.[37]

What then were the possible avenues of change? Clark saw three: establishment of a collectivistic system of production by public decree; voluntary experiments in consumers' and producers' co-operation; and "progressive change in the constitution of industry itself." He rejected the first on the grounds that the country was not ready; the second was already assured of a place in guiding social policy. The third was only beginning to be seriously tried: here

Clark saw distinct possibilities. The evolving business corporation would be induced to meet the competition of guilds or consumers' cooperatives, should they come to hold a place in the industrial system. Since the modern corporation is now directed by those who have furnished only a small part of the capital of the enterprise, there existed the unmistakable possibility for far-reaching changes in the terms by which the industrial process was conducted.[38]

TYPES OF PUBLIC CONTROLS

The second part of Clark's study was devoted to a more detailed examination of general instruments of control in modern society. In the order of his treatment, they were: legal, economic or market, state, and lastly, informal controls by most people; the last was often not considered in the economic realm.

With respect to the legal framework of control, Clark summarized aspects of the pioneering work of thinkers like John R. Commons, Richard T. Ely, and Roscoe Pound. Their view was that Sir William Blackstone's theory of natural rights, which assumed the existence of a "natural" moral law set down by a deity, had failed to allow for the cumulative change of economic institutions. Specifically, this meant that absolute concepts needed to be set aside in favor of evolutionary ones. The notions of "rights" and "liberties" furnished an example. Instead of regarding these as absolutes, one must recognize that they defined changing boundaries of obligations or duties as well as areas of freedom. A contractual agreement to transfer property involved a duty to transfer title as well as a duty to pay. A "liberty" to one party required restrictions on the action of other parties, "so that it appears that absolute liberty is a contradiction in terms."[39]

Clark illustrated the legal quandary associated with systems of social control with an examination of some fundamental legal institutions. As he had previously written, personal liberty and personal security could not be viewed as absolute rights. One's personal security may be effectively constrained by the necessity to work in such a hazardous occupation as coal mining. People do not consciously think in terms of a trade-off between so much coal and so many lives, yet the social need for coal permits the industry to operate. Production workers in coal mining thus have a lower level of personal security than others. In the large, personal liberty hinges upon the right of personal security. Even putative liberty may be illusory in practice. Legal justice is often a mere formality yielding no liberty of action: "the costs and delays of the law amount to depriving the poor of equal access to justice."[40]

To Clark, the substance of liberty, as opposed to the form, had an economic basis. In addition to a stock of knowledge a person needs to have sufficient reserve funds "to be able to hold off from the market and see if the second or tenth or twentieth bargain that offers will not be better than the first." In some instances a real canvass of the market may be limited by the costs of transportation. Here " 'liberty and the pursuit of happiness' may require a free ride on the railroad." Real liberty required a certain minimum level of economic welfare to fall back on in order to preclude the compulsion to accept whatever the market offered at the moment. This requirement presented difficulties, "especially in a society where the bulk of industry is in private hands and where there is a settled fear of undermining the initiative and responsibility of the individual."

Finally, there was the commonplace fact that the liberty of each must be restricted in the interests of all: so that no one may impinge upon the liberty of an individual. This principle can be interpreted in two ways, however, each resulting in quite different economic effects. "One way is to make the *same rules for all* and to maintain them even when there is so much inequality between man and man and so much difference between their functions – the things they desire to do and the ways in which they affect each other's interests – that the same rules no longer have any real equality about them." Clark illustrated by paraphrasing a French writer: "The law in the majesty of its equality alike forbids rich and poor to sleep on park benches."[41]

The second way of interpreting this rule, Clark wrote, was to recognize that our modern specialized society calls upon people to enter into relationships with each other in which the part played by one is essentially different from the part played by the other, the things one can do to injure the other are essentially different from the things the other can do to injure the first, and therefore each must be subject to *different* limitations in order to prevent abuses and produce essential fairness. A rule of literal equality would only serve a homogeneous society; this hardly characterizes modern industrial conditions. To promote "social justice" it might be necessary to enact a piece of one-sided legislation in favor of labor to offset a situation which would otherwise favor the employer.

"But the search for a differentiated social justice, while unavoidable," Clark noted, "is unavoidably dangerous." It is quite easy to fashion rules of formal equality. But rules which discriminate tempt class legislation or political favoritism. Although the judiciary can serve as a useful check, a large discretionary power must remain with the legislature.

Turning to the institution of private property, Clark wrote that "ownership" had continually undergone evolution. With respect to the public weal, for example, changing attitudes toward public health – which change with industrial technique – gave rise to new restrictions on ownership rights and liberties. Compulsory spraying of orchards, building regulations requiring certain air or light specifications were one type of resulting modification of "ownership." These examples – many more could be adduced – served to convey Clark's notion that this fundamental institutions was "a many-sided and elastic thing," rather than the fixed legal or natural-right entity understood by the popular mind. This being the case, then, what can be said of the justification of private property?

"Some kind of private ownership in some kinds of things," he wrote, "appears to be absolutely indispensable." This says little however with regard to the essential matter.

> The chief question lies in the private ownership of land and industrial capital; and here the answer depends a great deal on the *limitations imposed* on the owner's use of such property, *in the interests of the community*.[42]

Here was an evolutionary approach to property rights in pronounced contrast with the "eternal" or static view of such matters. Clark noted that the natural rights view of private property referred mainly "to the fact that it is natural for a man to have complete control of the tools of his work and to receive the whole fruits of it; and furthermore, that this gives him the greatest possible incentive not only to work hard, but to conserve his own capital assets." The small farmer was a proverbial example. "But this justification of private ownership clearly does not justify ownership by an absentee landlord or by any other kind of landlord, for that matter." In the social interest of economic efficiency, however, legislation permitted absentee ownership while giving rights to the tenants.

Large-scale industry was one important area where property rights were modified for the sake of efficiency. Apparently it was necessary to obtain some manner of centralized control in large concerns in order to direct production. The corporate device was the familiar solution to the problem of raising sufficient masses of capital. Shareholders' representatives were appointed to supervise and direct the work force on the assumption that the workers or their representatives were not suitably disciplined to manage their own labor.

> Nevertheless, this right of corporate management of industry is not by any means an absolute or natural right. It rests on special grants from the state and is naturally subject to the ultimate power of the state to impose whatever limitations are necessary to prevent abuses. . . . The fact that the laborer does not own the product of his own work will never cease to be a serious disadvantage, . . . But this condition is capable of being reversed at any time when labor develops the ability to organize industry under its own direction and still maintain discipline and efficiency.[43]

Clark turned now from his discussion of legal institutions to a brief consideration of his second general instrument of control: competition. In the first part of the book he had already established the proposition that competition *was* an instrument of control in his sense. Although not completely rejecting the traditional analytic view of competition, Clark was primarily interested in examining the many-sided relation of competition to control. Thus he saw competition as an exception to the rule that one may not use one's property to injure another. This was permitted on the assumption that the consumer gained somewhat in relation to the loss of any specific producer.

This rivalry was not unqualified in practice: many varieties of competition existed. Excess capacity led to cut-throat competition; the desire to force out competitors and establish a monopoly led to predatory competition; there was discriminatory or localized competition; and various types of "unfair competition." Finally, there was "partial or imperfect competition and competition modified by agreements, informal understandings, or a sentiment against 'spoiling the market' by unsound or cut-throat tactics."[44] Even this brief listing of various grades or varieties of competition was enough to suggest, in Clark's words, that "the public cannot afford to rest on a simple belief that all competition is good." Clark wrote that "careful differentiation" between the various types was necessary.

Such distinctions as might be made between the types of competition led to no obvious or a priori guidelines for regulation. "Unfair competition" was a case in point. It seemed easier for most to decide which practices were unfair than to indicate the basis for such judgement. Bribery, industrial espionage, intimidation, control of raw materials, even advertising by certain professional groups as physicians or lawyers, were all considered "unfair." Which rules should be established? Here Clark adduced his standard:

> We must fall back on the purpose of the game from the point of view of the community, namely, the selection of servants to organize and carry on its production who can – and will – serve it most efficiently and on the lowest terms of ultimate expenditure and sacrifice. . . . It is one of the tasks of control to attach the sentiment of unfairness to all practices which violate the social purpose of the game of competition.

But was the system of competition itself capable of adequately achieving the economic goals of the community in this new era?

Clark saw the evidence as mixed. On the one hand, he noted that "under a competitive system industry has been revolutionized at an incredible pace and tremendous increases in physical productiveness have been forthcoming, proving that competition has not been a wholly unfavorable influence." On the other hand, there was the fact of widespread waste under competition: "not the 'ideal' competition of economic theory, but the actual institution with all its inherent crudeness." He put the problem in the following way:

> Though no evidence could be irresistibly conclusive – not even a protracted trial of an alternative system – it seems fairly clear that while competition has produced a great deal of waste, it has – let us say, up to 1929 – more than made up for it by a stimulus to productive efficiency. The most serious question remaining is whether it can continue to work with dominating effect under the changing conditions of large-scale industry; and whether the hybrid system now in force, with many elements of rigidity in prices and wages, can continue to show equally favorable results.

The next general instrument of control considered by Clark was the state. Clark enumerated two lists of grounds of the public interest which constituted the basis of the government's right to interfere in business, all under the heading "An Economic Constitution for the State." The first was the usual one allowed for under "strict individualism": national defense, protection of person and property, regulation of natural resources in the public domain, inheritance and bequest, and the raising of public revenues.

The major thrust of Clark's thinking in this area, however, was to be seen in his second list. This list arose from the fact that conditions necessary for strict individualism were lacking – and always had been.[45] Here Clark included the following:

1 Government should prevent or control partial or complete monopoly and maintain a level of competition in service to the public.
2 Public action is necessary in all cases where the individual is not able to effectively acquit the responsibilities imposed by individualism.
3 Amelioration for the victims of economic change and natural catastrophe must be provided, and a policy of the "social minimum" followed. Here certain principles have been evolved by society: (a) Prevention is better than relief; (b) Rehabilitation of victims is the only sound goal; and (c) Industry must bear its full responsibility.
4 State guidance in research and education in sound farming or efficiency in any other industry are appropriate policy objectives, as are controls in labelling, truth in advertising, and impartial testing to benefit consumers.
5 The government must secure and maintain effective equality of opportunity. Here, in the interests of the general welfare, it may be necessary to restrain individualism by control of land distribution and tenure, access to bank credit, and the concentration of inherited wealth.
6 The state has an interest in seeing to it that industry is charged various costs which characteristically go unpaid, such as pollution or adequate compensation to the worker for the risks of injury or unemployment. Also the state should provide compensation in instances where "inappropriable services" are produced which benefit the general public though not the agent responsible; unpatentable knowledge being one example.
7 Society has a clear interest in avoiding the wastes of unused capital and labor: unemployment constitutes a valid ground for governmental interference. Additionally, the state has a duty

regarding the conservation of natural resources and in cognate areas.

With equally careful attention, Clark examined the limits which should properly be placed on the role of government in economic life. To Clark, the "paramount human value" was liberty; therefore only limitations which increase liberty should be sought. His basic framework here included a strong predilection for voluntary, non-coercive controls which allowed the individual "to decide his own destiny just as far as he is capable." Again he cautioned that the substance of liberty could be limited as much by ill-health or poverty as by actual servitude. Aside from these general considerations, Clark wrote that government controls should be limited to specific situations. Also where wages, prices, or other production costs are regulated, "some safeguards must be imposed in order to see that the public is not deprived of the quantity and quality of goods and services which it needs and is willing to pay for, under guise of protecting it from the extortionate exactions of the producers." Of vital importance, however, was the fact that there was a zone within which the law of supply and demand was indeterminate. Within this range, it is difficult to appraise the economic impact of specific controls and legitimate controversy may be expected by the interested parties.

Characteristically, Clark warned of serious handicaps under which the American political system operated "which in themselves created a presumption against the exercise of coercive controls:"[46]

First, its resources are limited in comparison to the "interests" it strives to control, and its experts are typically pitted against higher-paid experts, presumably of greater ability. Second, the ultimate control lies in the hands of people who are not specialists: cabinet officers, legislators, and especially judges. The legislator receives plenty of expert guidance (or pressure) from interested testimony but no disinterested counsel. . . . Third, and as a result of this, questions are likely to be settled by popular clamor, by judicial conservatism leaning on an outworn economics, or, worse yet, by the political process of "log rolling," in which each group of legislators buys support for the measures in which its own constituents are interested, and no measure receives the benefit of an impartial and courageous judgment of what the common interest demands. . . . Fourth, the game of politics is one in which a good issue is an asset not lightly to be sacrificed; and it may be better politics to keep it unsettled and go through the motions of fighting for the public interest and shifting the blame for failure on the opposition or the courts, rather than to bring about a reasonable settlement which, precisely because it is reasonable, does not carry a spectacular victory for the financial interests of the majority of voters . . .

As a result of these and other weaknesses, the actual working of political control is full of fakes and perversions, and the arguments which furnish social justification for control too often become mere pretexts to cover the conferring of privileges on some private interest.[47]

To round out his detailed examination of controls, Clark turned to the nature of informal controls. These were so important "that there are some who believe that we should get on better if we employed no others." He noted that "direct control by group opinion" was inexpensive and prompt, unless it forgot to act at all. Further, it examined each case as a particular. Against these advantages were weighed the fact that "public opinion often discriminates on personal or sentimental grounds which have little to do with the economic seriousness of the act. It is swayed by the spectacular." One's own group may be quite effective, yet "it is often too little interested in the code of the community at large." As examples of these informal controls, Clark listed codes of ethics, both personal and professional; codes of business conduct stressed service to the community as well as profit making and adherence to the variegated canons of conduct of a "businessman." Labor had ethical codes as well; revolutionists had standards of "revolutionary morality"; and all were affected by what Thorstein Veblen had termed the "instinct of workmanship."

Studies in the Economics of Overhead Costs and *Social Control of Business* became the wellspring which nourished all of Clark's subsequent contributions. As it happened, the drift of business enterprise was to occasion novel opportunities to examine the "failure of social coordination" and "unused capacity" in great detail.

5 Problems of War, Depression, and Effective Competition

Clark's own last estimate of his "chief published works" listed *Studies in the Economics of Overhead Costs*, *Social Control of Business*, and his final book *Competition as a Dynamic Process.*[1] The two earlier works might have served as the foundation for a subsequent treatise on economic dynamics.[2] There is sufficient evidence in the J. M. Clark Papers to indicate that Clark was thinking of a general treatise on economics as early as the 1920s; in view of his prodigious output this can hardly be taken as wishful thinking.[3] Furthermore, this desire persisted into his mature years as Clark indicated at several points. For example, in response to Professor Ray B. Westerfield's suggestion that Clark join him in a joint petroleum industry study, Clark wrote in 1949:

> The question is: what is the one most important thing I can do? I have long wanted to do a general treatise of a sort. I can't tell just what it would look like – not much like the one I had outlined twenty-five years ago. At least it would bring together disconnected parts of my remarkably-scattered work. I had thought of it as my main job – still undone. To do it, I should have to refuse the tempting bribes that special projects offer. I suspect that is a case in which the dollar yardstick is an imperfect measure of the most useful direction in which to turn one's efforts – and I hope that isn't just a case of personal vanity. Another way of looking at it is: if I don't do the oil industry job, it will still be well and competently done; . . . If I don't do the general treatise, nobody else will do just the job I would do; the approaches I want to try out won't get tried out in a systematic way.[4]

Three years earlier, Clark had written that the second World War, and by implication, the depression of the 1930s, had caused him to postpone his task:

It may be a little late to start the job of integrating and supplementing it [his scattered works] in a major general treatise. I was ready to start doing this in 1940, but Hitler willed otherwise. Now there is less time and less strength, but I still think I can do the job on my present basis, although I do not expect to finish it before reaching 65. It is a queer thing for a man to start his major theoretical work at the age of 62, but these are queer times, and if the thing had been done before the war, it would necessarily have been, to some extent, "dated".[5]

In his own later estimation, *Competition as a Dynamic Process* was not the "major general treatise" he had spoken of, as will be seen below. In retrospect, then, John Maurice Clark's "scattered" contributions may be seen as the consequence of his attempts to develop constructive responses occasioned by the drift of business enterprise in the United States: War and Depression. That all of these contributions were not systematically woven into a comprehensive general treatise points to the further importance of Clark's variegated works subsequent to *Overhead Costs* and *Social Control of Business*. Furthermore, one should avoid the conclusion that a synthesis of his work is contained in *Competition as a Dynamic Process*, important as that work is in Clark's overall contribution.

THE COSTS OF THE WORLD WAR

Clark's first major work after completing *Social Control of Business* was *The Costs of the World War to the American People*.[6] The economic issues raised by a wartime economy had long occupied Clark's thinking.[7] The controls and regulation of production in World War I furnished examples of national efforts to mobilize the economy. Postwar demobilization brought with it the opportunity – and challenge – of bringing economic organization more in line with the economic requirements of the twentieth century. As early as 1917, Clark had indicated his interest in the forthcoming peacetime adjustments of the national economy:

How much of the near-socialism of this war [WWI] is temporary and how much, if any, will be permanent? Some of the needs that have given rise to collectivist policies have been created by the war, but others have been merely revealed. The net result is to give social policy a definiteness of objective it has not had before in America, and this effect will not quickly evaporate. The need of a more coherent social organization is probably not less great in times of nominal peace, merely less obvious and less immediate, and it tends to be met by methods which, because they are more leisurely, involve less centralization and less compulsion.

During time of war, he noted, one principle was operating: "our society, as an organization, knows what it wants and can draw up specifications." Further, Clark continued, "the social product of industry is no longer always reckoned through the accounting of private acquisition, and its function of social service is no longer incidental to profits, but has become the dominant fact, and independently determined."

Society, in the interests of national efficiency, had chosen to regulate the economy by means other than the system of prices and markets; this raised questions concerning the peacetime structure of the economy:

> It may well be asked, indeed, just how and why the individualistic system is organized as it is in time of peace, and whether it is, as a matter of fact, just as unsuited to the highest efficiency in ordinary times as it appears to be, if left to its own devices in time of war. It is a system for giving society the things it wants, but what does society want?

This question of the goals of society was a theme to which Clark was to return in later years. For the time being, he noted that "the existence of objective standards by which to judge the things society wants, as distinct from the subjective standard of price, tends to make an increased degree of social control tolerable and wieldable by furnishing a considerable safeguard against the danger of degenerating into tyranny or log-rolling."[8] Again, in 1944 he noted that "Laissez faire is in fact a movable milestone, though probably only within limits." It was a question of which controls the business community had come to take for granted, especially after the experience of the 1930s.[9]

The immediate history of *The Costs of World War* began in 1911 when the Division of Economics and History of the Carnegie Endowment for International Peace proposed to undertake a scientific study of the effects of war upon modern life.[10] With the outbreak of World War I, it was decided to modify this proposal and produce a broad, international, "Economic and Social History of the World War." Clark's was the final volume in the American series, though it had originally been conceived that others would supplement by detailed studies the various problems treated by him.[11]

Clark began the volume by noting that a broad topic such as the costs of war "is either a relatively simple matter of tabulation and fiscal allocation, or else it is an economic problem of insoluble difficulty, one which no volume can master and no series of volumes exhaust."[12] Although he dealt with "tabulation and fiscal allocation," Clark characteristically chose to probe the areas "of insoluble difficulty" as well. "Social-economic costs," Clark wrote, "may be greater, or less, than is indicated by governmental fiscal outlays." He emphasized that

> In this volume, the fiscal payments are regarded as of little significance in themselves, their chief importance being as evidence of the outpouring of goods, the divisions of productive power from peace to war uses, and the sacrifices of the people, all of which constitute the more important realities behind the various sums of money which serve to call them forth.[13]

Clark noted that the American experience must be differentiated from that of other belligerent nations, since the war had affected the United States relatively lightly. This compounded the problem of trying to separate the effects of war on the United States from those resulting from the existence of war in Europe, whether America had entered the war or not. "We profited greatly as a neutral country," he wrote, "and after the War we profited by serving the needs of Europe's reconstruction. But Europe would have needed reconstruction whether we entered the War or not; and we must try, at least, to distinguish gains due to other people's wars from the costs of our own."[14]

Contemporary interpretations of the effects of war on the United States needed review as well. In addition to the comparatively light effects on America, the war saw us shift from a debtor to a creditor nation on a large scale, which caused some observers to argue that 'a profit was made out of the War': the increased stimulus to industry and trade more than outweighed the war costs. Another view had it that 'the War called forth its own means of support' since consumption demand and the power to produce suffered no appreciable setbacks. Nor could the longer-term effects be ignored. As Clark put the matter:

> we are now, over twelve years after the signing of the armistice, in the depths of a major depression which is almost certainly, to some unmeasurable extent, not only a sequel of the War but a result of the chain of consequences which trace their origin back to it. Moreover, this depression involves a shrinkage of income, measured from the peak reached in 1929, which is quite certain to bulk larger, before recovery is fully achieved, than the whole immediate cost of the War itself to the national economy. If the previous post-war prosperity had canceled the cost of the War, the present depression may more than cancel the cancellation. This can, of course, never be definitely known, since the normal level with which to compare our actual post-war record must remain in the conjectural realm of what might have been had the world remained at peace. This is an uncertainty which cannot be fully resolved.[15]

Similar questions applied to Europe, where the world-wide depression had called into question the soundness of the post-war recovery program.

Clark devoted the first several chapters to a narrative description of some major social and economic trends before, during, and after the war. In addition to "the bare bones of statistical tables,"[16] he made mention "of financial conditions and institutions, of education, of the state of the labor movement and of economic radicalism, of business organization and the relation of government to business, and of prevalent attitudes and issues bearing on international economics."[17]

In dealing with the gains stemming from the war in Europe, Clark introduced a rough foreign-trade multiplier. "It is a fair assumption that the main precipitating cause of our general prosperity in the neutrality period was the increase of our exports, as shown in the trade balance." He continued:

> But the resulting increase in national income was several times as large as the excess of exports. . . . It appears that the additional goods we sent to Europe were not a substraction from

home production, but added to it so much that they left a remainder larger than before, by more than the amount taken away. It is not orthodox arithmetic to take one from ten and leave eleven and one-half, but it seems to be possible economics, if the ten represents income at the worst point of a depression, and the one is a new "effective demand" for goods.

Noting that this multiplier effect was contingent upon an elastic credit system, Clark went on to add a domestic multiplier concept:

Another essential feature in the cumulative piling-up of prosperity was the fact that demand was created for extraordinary additions to productive equipment. Steel was needed, not only for munitions to be exported, but even more for buildings and plant with which to make them, and for increased capacity in the steel-making industry itself, with which to make both the goods for export and the plants to make them, also the increased amounts of goods which prosperity enabled home consumers to buy, and the increases in plant capacity which these demands called forth. Thus the effects of the war demand were cumulative in multiple fashion, virtually up to the limits set by capacity to expand in those industries on which the resultant increase in demand was most sharply concentrated.[18]

These multiplier concepts, with suggestions of accelerator interactions, were to be more fully developed in his *Economics of Planning Public Works* (1935), discussed below.

This raised the question noted earlier and accepted by many: was a profit made from the war? As Clark put it, the question was "whether disasters which consume or destroy wealth can be, after all, advantageous to the social economy because the demand they create is 'good for business' and leads to increased production and circulation of wealth." The answer of traditional economics was in the negative asserted Clark, and he used as an illustration the breaking of window panes: "The breaking of windows, for example, can never be anything but destruction of wealth, no matter how far its effects may be traced as they ramify through the economic system." More specifically, Clark asked: "is the effective demand for other things, and the consequent production of other things, necessarily cut down by exactly the amount that is spent on replacing the broken panes?" Clark asked this of a temporary, war-induced situation, since "the establishment of a permanent habit of breaking some thousands or millions of panes every year might be expected to have substantially this effect." He concluded that "the effect seems to depend on the character and extent of the disaster, on the attitude with which it is met, and on the state of the credit system and of business activity in general." As he explained further:

> A disaster which does not cripple the machinery of production, of an extent which spurs people to increased efforts rather than reducing them to helpless despair, coupled with a credit system and an industrial system each of which has some unused capacity for expansion – these conditions enable a disaster to be self-repairing in part at least, through stimulus to productive activity.[19]

This was not the only aspect of the problem of profits, however. There was, for example, the question of the redistribution of income resulting from war-time inflation and the increased rewards accruing to producers of war goods. This "is a social cost, not because it is a reduction of the total income serving private ends, but because it is a maldistribution of that income. That is," continued Clark,

> provided we could agree that it *was* a maldistribution; certainly we could never agree as to just which gains and which losses deserved this term and just how serious the matter was. How many dollars transferred from A to B are equal as "social costs" to one dollar sunk in the sea or burned up in the Argonne offensive? Only an arbitrary answer could be given: the two are not commensurable quantities.[20]

Furthermore, this war-induced inflation, which "was in itself one of the heavy costs of the War," created distortions in the types of goods and services produced. Indeed, "inflationary borrowing . . . does not postpone the sacrifice of goods and services, but distributes the burden more unjustly that any other method of financing, and leaves more disturbing consequences in the way of subsequent financial adjustments. It may be justified if the immediate command of goods and services cannot be secured in any other way, but it is a deplorably expensive method of securing such command."[21] This, combined with the subsequent unemployment after the war, created additional difficulties.

Clark referred to the more general acceptance of the philosophy "that wages must be high to provide industry with the demand for its products which is essential to the prosperity of large-scale mass production." He noted that it was necessary to distinguish this proposition "from the fallacy which results from ignoring the fact that money distributed as profits is spent for goods, and spent just as much even if it is saved and invested. This is true," he noted,

> and yet the distribution of the income does have an effect on the kinds of goods for which the money is spent, as well as on the promptness of the expenditures. And the modern mass production must be able to market its products to the many and not solely or chiefly to the few, or the whole basis of its large and cheap production is undermined.

Clark posed the question of "just how is the beneficence of the principle of high wages affected when they are accompanied by large amounts of unemployment . . ? Such a condition may be more favorable to the sale of automobiles, radios, and possibly rayon, than a condition of lower wages paid to more people; but it is not easy to show that it is better for industry in the aggregate, on the score of wider demand. Whether it is favorable to general business 'propensity' depends on other factors; chief of which are probably the effect of sustained wages on productivity, and the ultimate incidence of unemployment."[22]

Clark was unambiguous concerning the argument that the war had called forth its own means of support:

> by no stretch of the methods of statistical comparison is it possible to sustain the claim that the War paid for itself while it was being fought. The only possible basis for such a conclusion, in the face of the sober evidence of statistics, is the extremely dubious assumption that the War caused the whole of our post-war "prosperity" but did not cause the present depression. It was probably in some measure responsible for both, but to what extent can never be proved.[23]

In addition, he had pointed out elsewhere that "during the war the violent shifts of production caused wasteful utilization of capital and dilution of labor with green workers, and other unfavorable conditions tending to prevent full employment from having its usual effect."[24]

In assessing costs of the war, Clark undertook an estimate of the economic costs incurred by the surviving dependents as a result of the death and disability of the service personnel. Here he differed from other estimates which had included costs incurred by *potential* dependents as well. Part of Clark's figures were discounted at four per cent for the purpose of comparison. However, he argued that "the whole principle of discounting is of doubtful appropriateness as applied to such social totals" since these sums did not necessarily represent "industrial capital destined to be put to uses increasing the measurable flow of economic goods."[25]

Clark's work was much more than the sum of several theoretical contributions or particular observations of events. It was a searching and wide-ranging effort to portray the ramifications of that ultimate disaster, modern war. As he noted, we have learned things from the experience, but "too often we seem to have learned the wrong things. And we might have had better experience to learn from. Perhaps all we can be sure of is that nothing has remained untouched by the War. Everything that has happened differently because of it."[26]

In the wake of the First World War and the 1920s came the depression and the Second World War. The special problems occasioned by these events were to occupy Clark for nearly the remainder of his life.

STRATEGIC FACTORS IN BUSINESS CYCLES

During the 1930s, several works appeared by Clark dealing with the depression. *Strategic Factors in Business Cycles* was an attempt to probe further into the factors of basic significance in recent business cycle history.[27]

Clark defined "strategic factors" as those which were amenable to some degree of control. He attempted to chart a course between the extremes of theoretical study which gave causes too far and too simple on the one hand, and inductive studies which revealed "so many factors at work, so completely interrelated, that we are likely to come to the conclusion that everything is both cause and effect" and present too many complications to be of practical use. Finally, Clark wrote that he intended to interpret the business cycle rather

broadly though drawing heavily upon the definitions given by
Wesley Clair Mitchell and the staff of the National Bureau of Economic Research.

His interest in business cycles and problems of economic change
were long-standing. Clark's pioneering article on the accelerator
had already been noted, and business cycles had played a role in his
thinking on *Overhead Costs* and *Social Control of Business.* Clark
had long given attention to more heterodox thinkers in this field;
Thorstein Veblen was a clear influence. As Joseph Dorfman has
documented, Clark as well as J.M. Keynes were stimulated in their
thinking on the multiplier concept and its relation to the overproduction fallacy by N.A.L.J. Johannsen.[28] In his 1931 *The Costs of
the World War*, Clark had written:

> The attitude of economists toward the problem of over-produc-
> tion has changed radically since the days when it was dismissed
> with the statement that supply of one thing constitutes demand
> for something else, and therefore general overproduction is an
> impossibility. The economist no longer endangers his profes-
> sional standing if he expresses doubt as to the finality and all-suffi-
> ciency of this dogma of the older school, or even if he admits
> that under certain conditions demand rather than technical
> power to produce goods may be the strategic factor limiting the
> amount of goods that is actually produced.[29]

Further, Clark noted that Keynes had paid tribute to some precursors of this line of thinking in his *General Theory.* Clark wrote that
"Keynes pays his respects to" those who criticized J.B. Say's
strictures against overproduction of goods: Mandeville, Malthus,
Gesell, John A. Hobson, C.H. Douglas and John M. Robertson. To
this, Clark added his own list of precursors: "the Earl of Lauder-
dale (1804), Rodbertus (1850), . . . H. Abbatti (1924), P.W. Martin
(1924) and Foster and Catchings (chiefly 1923-8)." As noted
earlier, N.A.L.J. Johannsen had been a clear influence on both
Keynes and Clark.[30] And in 1932, Clark wrote that "it seems fairly
evident that the real overproduction is not of consumer's goods in
general but of productive equipment and construction; and, at
times, of certain basic materials." He continued:

> As to consumption, it appears probably that *actual shrinkage* of
> consumption is mainly a result and not a primary cause, arising

from the shrinkage of incomes when production declines and workers are laid off.[31]

In *Strategic Factors in Business Cycles*, Clark examined the concept of theoretical equilibrium or "balance" in the economic process. He noted, if one asks "Why does business *not* run smoothly?" only "one glaring gap in the conditions of [a theoretical] equilibrium is sufficient for an answer which will carry conviction to many, however inadequate it may be to explain the full phenomenon of the actual cycle in all its complexity and variety." On the other hand, as noted earlier, it was necessary to do some simplifying and arranging of the mass of factual data in order to provide useful explanations.

One necessity in his view was "a more adequate attempt at the specification of the conditions of economic stability" in order to present a more manageable picture. Here Clark wrote that

> The idea of balance seems to have as its point of departure the idea of approximate equality of supply and demand, so far as this is consistent with movement and incentives for movement. But supply and demand for *goods* may reach momentary balance at very varying levels of price and of volume of production and employment. In that sense the present condition of depression might be said to be one of balance . . .

More basic uses of the term "balance" might be a balance between costs, prices and profits in some sustainable manner. "More fundamental still, perhaps, is a balance between supply and demand for *productive forces, especially labor*; in other words, freedom from undue amounts of unemployment."[32] Indeed, Clark was clear on his understanding of what the requirements for a "balanced" economy would be:

> A fundamentally balanced economy would be one in which the business cycle as we know it would have ceased to exist, or would be limited to rather mild fluctuations. It would be a state in which productive powers and productive opportunities would be reasonably well matched, and there would be no great discrepancies between supply and demand, and no great wastes of productive powers for lack of opportunity to use them.[33]

Clark admitted that it was difficult to define balance in the labor market and that there were difficulties in actually achieving such a condition. Still, "fairly regular employment for all reasonably qualified workers seems, however, not a fantastic standard to set in the long run." To achieve this would require, among other things, "a reasonably steady rate of production in general."[34]

He was doubtful about the "Individualist Prescription" for gaining full employment: "do not maintain prices." The "logical individualist" would "slash them [prices] without limit until full production is restored, for all except the high-cost producers who may fall by the way-side. If there is 'technological unemployment,' do not maintain wages. Slash them until the worker can compete with the machine and the employer can afford to hire him." Such "cut-throat" wage policies might not in fact do the job.

> If prices, wages and profits all fell in harmony, nothing might be accomplished. And if wages fell more than the other shares, might there not be a cutting-off of markets for consumers' goods which would defeat the purpose of the whole process? There is need of a balance between the portion of income spent for consumption and the portion saved, and this will be disturbed by any sudden shifting of incomes from wage and salaried workers, who spend most of their incomes, to profit-takers, from whom the bulk of the savings comes.[35]

To Clark, one of the most promising areas in controlling the business cycle was the stabilization of consumer incomes. He wrote that the fact "that expenditure for consumption is steadier than production and income may represent one of the forces setting limits on the cumulative effects of disturbances. . . ." Thus:

> If every reduction of productive activity at any point caused an equal reduction of expenditures, diffused throughout the economic system, resulting in further reduction of production and so on, there would be no logically assignable limits to the lengths to which such contraction could go. . .

> But if a reduction of production, and of income, is followed by a *smaller* reduction of expenditures, then the series of derived effects is a dwindling series of the type which should have a finite, not an infinite sum.[36]

The question of the most effective means of stabilizing incomes, however, raised the question of which aspect of the cumulative process would be most amenable to social control. Here Clark noted that "it does seem significant that, for a given class of goods, it is at the stage farther removed from the consumer that the initiatory movement takes place – that is, at the stage of production rather than retail selling – if the available figures are representative."[37]

Repeatedly, Clark emphasized the "organic interrelations" of the business process. "The business cycle is a vicious circle with no beginning this side of the origin of capitalistic production and no end until a way is found of breaking into the circle at some point and controlling its hitherto-endless sequence." This involved much more than merely creating a more informed business community and correcting errors of judgment on the part of businessmen. Clark wrote that his study "yielded relatively little support" for the thesis "that cycles are due to the mistakes of judgment made by individual business men" and that the solution lay in adducing additional data for more successful prediction. Obviously more data were needed, but Clark argued that the "actual interests" of businessmen "lie in doing the things which bring on the cycle, so long as they are acting as individual business men or representatives of individual business interests." He continued:

> A business man who refused to expand his sales on the up-swing would gain nothing, and one who refused to retrench on the down-swing would probably go bankrupt. One who stabilized his individual construction program would incur some risks by building ahead of demand or by being caught with inadequate reserve capacity in an expansion. . .

Clark emphasized the results of this following of individual business interests as follows:

> It seems to be a case in which the best policy for an individual to follow in adjusting himself to the existing bad conditions is not the same as the policy by which the business community as a whole may hope to get rid of the evil. It is only from a change in these customary reaction patterns that we may hope for real changes in the result.[38]

In addition, another danger lay in the possibility that the business community could become "hardened to living through cyclical depressions" and accustomed to holding on until a revival of business conditions by restricting output in the interim. This would pose a further obstacle to prompt action.

Thus the shorter cyclical fluctuations of industrial activity are not merely in themselves examples of lack of balance; they also tend further to obstruct the action of the longer-run forces. If prices are pegged – meaning always certain particular prices – this tends to perpetuate a state of over-equipment, as well as to prevent a recovery of demand, and keeps the price system at large unbalanced.[39]

More than prompt action was needed in the task of finding solutions to the general problem of fluctuations, however. Clark brought his accelerator analysis to bear on the problem when he wrote that:

The tendency to intensified fluctuations of derived demand, including the demand for the work and materials involved in producing durable consumers' goods, as well as producers' goods, is of basic importance, in the judgment of the writer. If it could be controlled in all its manifestations, the primary result would be a great stabilization of the average rate of productive activity by cutting off those fluctuations of production which exceed the fluctuations of consumers' current expenditures. As a secondary result, consumers' expenditures would themselves be made far more stable than they now are. Thus the effects of stabilization would be cumulative, and the back of the business cycle would be broken.[40]

He noted that "any very close approach to complete stabilization is probably out of the range of possibility so long as we retain even the main elements of the present system of private enterprise," but much could be accomplished with "sufficient resolution and open-mindedness."[41]

Much of Clark's treatment of business cycles stemmed from the influence of Wesley Clair Mitchell's work. He noted in 1928 that Mitchell's study of business cycles "has implications for general economic theory and method which may be even more far reaching" than the specific impact on a "special field" of business cycles.[42]

Many of Clark's specifics in *Strategic Factors in Business Cycles* were presaged in the *Report of a Subcommittee of the Committee on Unemployment and Industrial Stabilization of the National Progressive Conference*. The report, entitled "Long-Range Planning for the Regularization of Industry," was "genuinely a joint product" of the committee members. While Clark was the committee chair and assumed the responsibility for writing the document it was noted that "it seems certain that the substance of the report is different from what any one member would have drafted if working by himself."[43] The subcommittee report advocated "an elastic system of organization for planning" which relied "on voluntary action to the fullest extent consistent with ensuring that whatever action is taken is guided by the interests of the whole community, and that these interests are adequately protected." The proposal for a National Economic Board staffed by people "chosen for their capacity to represent the interests of the public at large" which would assemble a national plan for production was to be developed by Clark in a fuller manner in his *Economics of Planning Public Works* in 1935.[44] Clark noted that "coordination" might better express the concept he had in mind rather than all-out national planning. This was a theoretical and descriptive work designed to provide the basis for such coordination in the American economy.

THE ECONOMICS OF PLANNING PUBLIC WORKS

Some of the greatest interest in this work, however, stems from Clark's comprehensive discussion of the "Cumulative Effects of Public Expenditures." Here he examined in detail the theoretical impact of public expenditures from both the standpoint of the multiplier approach and the monetary approach. Each should yield the same provisional results, he noted, since each would be expected to take account of all factors considered by the other. With the multiplier or "successive-spendings" approach, Clark wrote that the question was one of the limits to an expansion imposed by initial spending. If there were no limits or leakages out of the consumption process into savings, one dollar spent by the government would lead to an endless series of successive spending chains. Two general facts seemed clear: "(1) That economic expansions and contractions have cumulative effects; and (2) that these cumulative effects tend either to exhaust themselves after going a certain distance or to give rise to counter-acting forces." The main questions were "why" and "how".

Noting that J.M. Keynes and R.F. Kahn had developed multiplier theories as well, Clark characteristically felt that "no such mechanical formula can do justice to the many variable conditions affecting the problem."[45] To begin with, only inflationary expenditures could rightfully be considered expenditures which would otherwise have remained idle. If this were not the case, it would simply mean a redistribution of the types of spending taking place, not new spending. Here a first set of limits becomes apparent. There are limits on the public borrowings which can be made and limits on the extent of expenditures that can be undertaken in this manner without resulting in a loss of confidence in the credit of the government. This presupposed of course that the credit system had room for expansion as in a severe depression. If this were not the case, expenditures of this nature might have no stimulative effects at all.[46]

Turning to the problem of leakages, Clark estimated a national leakage at about one-third, giving a multiplier of three which he noted coincided with Keynes' independently produced estimate. One source of leakages was of course found in expenditures for imported goods. Another source was savings. This was higher in the depression than it might be in better times when people felt less the need to escape pressing problems of indebtedness. Still another factor which might be taken up under the question of leakages was that of price increases. Arguing that "if a public-works program is so handled as to result in a material increase in prices, it will largely defeat its own purpose," since the loss in confidence on the part of businessmen or the weakened credit structure of the government would put an end to all further stimulative effects, either primary or secondary.

"Another conjectural factor," Clark wrote, "is the effect of the program on private capital expenditures." Public works expenditures might increase or decrease domestic investment. An increase was usually assumed, but if the consumption expenditures resulting from governmental expenditures came to be viewed as temporary, investment might fail to increase as much as it would have otherwise. Businessmen would be likely to wait and see what happened when the government spending ceased. Furthermore, public works expenditures might drive construction costs up to the point where it would have an inhibitory effect on private investment. "Thus the secondary and tertiary effects may be extremely great or may be nothing at all, depending on conditions which cannot be reduced to a formula."[47] Years later, Clark amplified this point:

> But perhaps the chief vagueness [in Keynes' system] is as to what determines investment. The formula assumes that conditions outside it determine a schedule of different amounts that will be invested at different rates of interest. Actually, investment reacts to factors included in the formula, but in a complex way, of which time and recent change are of the essence. If spending and income increase or decrease, the whole schedule of investment expands or contracts for a time, until productive equipment has become adjusted to the new volume of demand, after which the schedule may revert to something like its former magnitude. In this way changes may tend toward endless oscillation rather than toward any level of equilibrium. Keynes hints at these matters in his incidental comments, but does not take them into his formula.[48]

Turning to the monetary approach toward public works expenditures, Clark wrote that "Those who are studying problems of business fluctuations from the monetary angle tend to be distrustful of the results of the type of theorizing followed by Keynes in dealing with this problem." To those of this persuasion, assuming a constant income velocity of money,[49] "then stimulation of business requires an increase in the volume of money, and the government expenditures, in order to produce a stimulative effect, must be inflationary in the literal sense of increasing the volume of the circulating media." Pointing to James W. Angell's estimates of income velocity, Clark wrote that

> A given volume of money poured into the circulation continues to circulate and to maintain the increase it has brought about in the total financial volume of the national dividend at the rate of 1.6 times its own amount every year. . . . Thus the "multiplier," in Keynes' terms, would be infinity limited only by time. The only essential feature which this very much simplified . . . [exposition] does not show is the distributed lag by which the successive effects follow the original impulse.[50]

However, "one of the crucial points is obviously what is likely to happen to the velocity of circulation." Here Clark noted that "the evidence indicates that velocity varies greatly, decreasing with business depressions and increasing with revivals." Even with the shorter cyclical movements, "there is every reason to suppose" that income velocity "fluctuates very materially." Thus,

> While there may not be any logically necessary difference between the two approaches, there seems to be a very real difference of attitude between the theorists who follow them. This shows itself especially in the attitude toward velocity of circulation.[51]

He noted that Keynes assumed velocity to be a passive factor which automatically adjusted itself in order to finance the number of transactions and that other monetary theorists took velocity to be "an independent governing or causal factor." This last view did not preclude changes in velocity, only that they came about because of forces other than the volume of government spending, such as a desire for people to turn their funds over more quickly. Here Clark took issue and noted that this "attitude appears definitely wrong": "Circuit velocity of money is not an independent entity like the velocity of sound: It is a ratio between total production (or total income) and volume of circulating media." It was clearly possible to explain an increase in velocity along the lines of the Keynes and Kahn approach simply because an increase in the volume of business without an increase in the volume of means of payment must lead to an increased velocity by definition.

On the other hand, this multiplier approach was not necessary to explain changes in velocity. Clark wrote that increases in factor payments typically come about before increases in the volume of finished goods have taken place. Factor payments increase within a week or so of renewed activity; finished goods may take a year or more to work their way through all the stages of production from raw materials on up. Since this process calls for money payments, the abnormally high ratio of cash balances to business volume is drawn down. Further, borrowing will call into use some of the leakages described in the Keynesian system. Clark also noted that

> there is nothing in this process to indicate a serious drawing down or exhausting of the total volume of balances possessed by

business as a whole, even though that might happen at certain points, and there might be some net shifting of balances from business to personal accounts. Most of the funds will circulate within the business community; using them faster will not exhaust them, and business as a whole will always have funds available to make payments. These considerations seem to furnish ample cause for an increase in the velocity of circulation.

Therefore, Clark concluded "that there is no absolute necessity at any stage of the process for government outlays to take the form of an increase in the supply of purchasing media. If the attitude here taken toward changes in velocity is correct – and of that the writer has no doubt – this necessity disappears."[52] Thus as Keynes had maintained, there was no essential difference between the two approaches. In either case, "The increased flow of incomes is the essential thing."[53]

Economics of Planning Public Works contained a comprehensive analysis of the uses and difficulties involved in public expenditures. Clark argued that a properly constructed program which was projected "as an organic whole in which single projects are viewed as parts" could go far toward ameliorating business fluctuations. And as he noted: "Systematic planning is at least no worse than no planning." Systematic planning involved coordination at all levels however, from the federal, through state and regional down to local areas. He saw limitations involved in such an undertaking if the goal was to enable private expansion to come about more fully. "If public expenditures are so handled as to tend to bring about a condition in which the volume of production and employment will become dependent on a perpetual continuation of such expenditures, then it will defeat the end of revival as that is commonly conceived, and will tend to bring us that much nearer the point at which the task of producing goods and maintaining the livelihood of the population could not be successfully handled by private business as now constituted."[54]

In June 1936, Clark reviewed *Public Works Policy* by the International Labor Office and noted that their main thesis, "that the regular budgets of public works and public purchases in general can and should be so planned and scheduled as to be carried out more slowly in prosperous times and more rapidly in times of depression; and [that] this may mitigate the severity of these movements" was "one of the most logical and defensible public policies for mitigating the severity of economic fluctuations."[55]

INFLATION AND THE NEW DOGMA OF "KEYNESIANISM"

Among the problems which came to concern Clark increasingly were those of inflationary effects of government expenditures, especially as a result of the Second World War. It became clear that Clark saw grave dangers in the uncritical application of a supposedly "orthodox Keynesian" doctrine – a doctrine which seemed to be in the process of becoming dogma with potentially disastrous results. After a high level conference with Keynes in Washington on 23 July 1941, Clark wrote to Keynes:

> It has seemed to me that what I call the "income-flow analysis," of which yours is the most noted presentation, has done something which has not been done in comparable degree since Ricardo and Marx: namely, constructed a coherent logical theoretical system or formula having the quality of a mechanism, growing directly out of current conditions and problems which are of paramount importance and furnishing a key for working out definite answers in terms of policy. On this a "school" has grown up. All that has tremendous power; and is also exposed to the dangers of too-undiscriminating application, from which classical economics suffered, and of which I think the [Richard V.] Gilbert-[Don] Humphrey attitude is one illustration.

> I am myself enough of an "institutionalist" (whatever that may mean) to have more than a lurking distrust of formulas and equations! But not enough of an institutionalist to ignore their importance: merely to want to think all round them and reckon with the imponderables that modify their action; and the other factors which no single formula can comprehend – for instance, the long-run incidence of continued large deficit spending.[56]

Keynes' response was: "As you will have gathered the other evening, I agree with what you say about the danger of a 'school,' even when it is one's own. There is great danger in quantitative forecasts which are based exclusively on statistics relating to conditions by no means parallel. I have tried to persuade Gilbert and

Humphrey and [Walter S.] Salant that they should be more cautious. I have also tried to persuade them that they have tended to neglect certain theoretical considerations which are important, in the interests of simplifying their statistical task."[57]

Clark was concerned that the "followers" of Keynes were transforming his insights into a narrow orthodoxy which omitted the breadth of Keynes' original thought. In an unpublished note in 1950, Clark compared the fate of Keynes with that of Ricardo in this regard:

> Both selected problems that sprang from practical conditions of the time; conditions of disturbance or malfunctioning making their issues of policy. . . . Both evolved general theories: "Abstract" laws related to these problems but in the form of strictly-operational theorems or models, . . . distinct from the policy implications they carried. Both left "values" out of their models. Both died in the height of their powers, while adjustments were still going on in their theoretical systems, & too soon [(] R, 6 years [;] K, 10 years of war and reconstruction [)] after the publication of their major works for their adjustments to find expression in revisions of these works.
>
> Both founded schools, with disciples more orthodox than the master: ready to use their doctrines as bibles, & bases of policy.[58]

And in a 1949 review of a collection of essays, Clark commented that the one by Paul A. Samuelson

> exhibits what happens to the Keynesian theory when it is simplified by isolating the central mathematical formula and its corollaries from the context of factors that do not lend themselves to this treatment, and which Keynes handled in "literary" fashion. . . . To the reviewer, it seems that the relation of investment to incomes varies with time and past changes of income, and therefore breaks down the whole static-equilibrium formula; which thus comes to constitute the chief error in the current simplified exposition of Keynesian theory.
>
> The upshot seems to be that investment cannot be treated as a simple rising function of current income alone, without doing violence to the essential facts; and that a more realistic (and dynamic) treatment inevitably introduces instability. Even without allowing for this, equilibrium comes to depend on the inter-

section of two lines which are so nearly parallel that the determinateness of the outcome becomes dubious (current graphic representations sometimes grossly exaggerate the angle of intersection).[59]

At the end of 1941, Clark warned of his forebodings in an address before the American Economic Association:

Among other things, we appear to be in for a period of government by statistics and econometrics. This is little better than chartless fumbling with essentially quantitative [qualitative?] problems; . . . There is real danger that, in certain sectors, government's immediate objective will be not a realistic picture of the lives of its citizens but figures in tables or lines on charts which leave out vital imponderables and are not even accurate as figures. . . .

An enormously important element in the attitudes of government will consist of certain economic consequences of Mr Keynes (for which Mr Keynes himself should not be held too closely responsible). These consequences include a propensity to intervene at any point short of something called full employment on a chart, representing a condition probably quite unattainable in actual life by the measures advocated. They also include a propensity to obliviousness of the importance of wage and price adjustments . . . [and] a dogma, the purport of which appears to be that deficit spending will take effect in sustaining or increasing physical output and employment, and will not tend to be dissipated in increased prices and wage rates, until "general full employment" is reached. . . . [T]his doctrine . . . is unsupported by reason and flies in the face of experience. My conjecture is that in any attempt to approach full employment by this route, the tendency of money wages and prices to swallow up a major part of the benefits would prove to be one of the chief difficulties.[60]

Clark's work in the Office of Price Administration served to underscore his views on this fundamental question. In 1943, he wrote: "The history of OPA has been a succession of crisis [*sic*], in which the force of inflationary pressures, and of the efforts to resist them, have been progressively increasing." He noted that "The base figures of the 'inflationary gap' do not afford a very revealing picture of the real pressures at work." Clark's specific suggestions to deal with this problem included "A combination of taxes, and of savings which are either compulsory or sufficiently assured to be dependable. . . ." He argued that "It is out of the question to levy taxes enough to close the 'gap' at a time when war expenditures are rapidly moving up to more than half of the total national income, in addition to normal Federal, state and local outlays." An attempt at reducing the "inflationary gap" by taxes alone

> would create inequities comparable in kind to the inequities resulting from inflation itself. Thus all that can be done by the most drastic possible fiscal policy is to reduce the inflationary pressures so that they shall not be irresistible. They will still be considerable in any case.

Further proposals included stabilization of farm prices, "concentration of production and, where desirable, of distribution," and subsidies.[61]

The changed attitude towards deficit spending was becoming so ingrained that in writing of the removal of war-time controls in 1944, Clark wrote that "if any general policy is adopted which insists upon public deficit spending up to a point of 'full' or extremely high employment and without regard to the removal of monopolistic and other obstructions which may exist in the structure of the system, then general inflationary pressures are certain to result, and, if progressive inflation is to be avoided, indefinite continuance of direct control of prices and wages will probably be necessary."[62]

COMPETITION AS A DYNAMIC PROCESS

In December 1939, Clark presented a paper suggesting a line of analysis which was to culminate in 1961 with the publication of his last major work, *Competition as a Dynamic Process*.[63] The paper, "Toward a Concept of Workable Competition,"[64] "was an attempt to find an escape from the negative conclusions stemming from the Chamberlin-Robinson group of theories, in which it appeared that all feasible forms of competition in industry and trade are defective in the same direction in which monopoly is defective, from the standpoint of the services competition is supposed to render."[65]

Clark had long argued that "perfect competition" as viewed in standard theory "does not and cannot exist and has presumably never existed." This left an unrealistic analytical structure with which to view competitive conditions and as a standard by which to judge them. The reification of the model of perfect competition had inhibited theoretical developments.

Clark's efforts to expand the frontiers of economic theory spanned his entire life and may be seen as early as 1912, when he undertook a modernization of the elder Clark's *The Control of Trusts*. As the historian of American economic thought has pointed out:

> In this work, according to J.B. Clark, the son was primarily responsible for the modernization. Particularly noteworthy was the beginning effort to convert the traditional ideal of perfect competition into the more usable concept of 'workable competition' in the real world.[66]

In *The Control of Trusts*, it was pointed out that

> It cannot be said too early or too emphatically that the supreme test of measures for regulating trusts is that which tells us whether they will accelerate technical progress or retard it – whether they will make the world as a whole grow richer or poorer, and so better able or less able to afford good pay to its workers.[67]

In order to accomplish this goal, it was necessary to steer a course between the hopeless policy of laissez-faire small units and trusts:

> Unless a tolerant and healthy competition between great corporations is possible, then our regulative policy is going in the wrong direction, and the sooner we reverse it the better. But if competition, though working badly in many cases, can be made to work better – if the source of the trouble can be found and removed – then we may still succeed in our attempt to check monopoly by restoring healthy business rivalry as a regulating agent.[68]

The device by which they expected to be able to set this course was potential competition.[69]

Potential competition had never been far from the younger Clark's thinking.[70] In "Workable Competition," Clark developed this notion in an attempt to more explicitly revise the standard analytical structure of economic models. As he put it, a contribution might be made

> by attempting to formulate concepts of the most desirable forms of competition, selected from those that are practically possible, within the limits set by conditions we cannot escape. . . . For some of the features listed as "imperfections" in our present theoretical scheme may turn out to have some positive use in actual situations. . . . [I]t will mean something if we can find . . . that some of these forms do their jobs well enough to be an adequate working reliance – more serviceable, on the whole than those substitutes which involve abandoning reliance on competition. And it will be useful if we can learn something about the kinds and degrees of "imperfection" which are positively serviceable under particular conditions.[71]

Clark argued that if, say, five conditions are necessary for perfect competition to exist, the absence of any one of these does not mean that economic conditions are more competitive because of the presence of the other four. Indeed, it could mean that competition works less efficiently unless some degree of "imperfection" in the other factors may be realized. Thus if perfect mobility of productive factors is not present and demand declines, a "sick industry" might result. Or the absence of many producers may lead to oligopoly, and so forth.

Clark held "that long-run curves, both of cost and of demand, are much flatter than short-run curves, and much flatter than the curves which are commonly used in the diagrams of theorists."[72] He wrote further that "there is typically no definite 'optimum size' " of plant and that "imperfections in competition arising from the slopes" of the long-run curves, "so far as these curves affect actual policy," are "relatively unimportant."[73]

Drawing on his *Studies in the Economics of Overhead Costs*, Clark argued for "the abandonment of the idea that competition and discrimination are mutually inconsistent." He had noted earlier that with large fixed costs, either discrimination or cut-throat competition would be the normal outcome. What this meant with regard to "Workable Competition" was that with the modern conditions of relatively large fixed costs, a tangency solution which equated marginal costs to demand would mean bankruptcy. "Instead, the requirement is an individual demand curve with sufficient slope to bring price, on the average, far enough above marginal cost so that average cost may be covered, over the run of good times and bad." Price flexibility was needed of course, as well, though this "contains no guarantee of ideal prices."

Against all this the main forces working were those of potential competition and substitute products. "Both potential competition and substitution have the effect of flattening the slopes of individual demand curves." Clark argued that "neither is a perfect check; but both together may come near it under favorable conditions."[74] As The Attorney General's National Committee to Study the Antitrust Laws, of which Clark was a member, declared in 1955:

> The basic characteristic of effective [or workable] competition in the economic sense is that no one seller, and no group of sellers acting in concert, has the power to choose its level of profits by giving less and charging more. Where there is workable competition, rival sellers, whether existing competitors or new or potential entrants into the field, would keep this power in check by offering or threatening to offer effective inducements, so long as the profits to be anticipated in the industry are sufficiently attractive in comparison with those in other employment, when all risks and other deterrents are taken into account.[75]

Thus " 'workable' or 'effective' competition supplies no formula which can substitute for judgment." However, in contrast to the theory of perfect competition, workable competition does seek "to provide a method for making necessarily less exact but more practical realistic judgments of actual market conditions."[76] As Clark noted at another time: "The first thing that seems to be needed is to supply the missing conception of competition: one that covers different degrees and is not limited to impossible perfection or destructive rigor."[77]

In order to develop this line of thinking more fully, Clark turned in the late 1950s to what was to be his last major work: *Competition as a Dynamic Process*. Although this was a work containing the broad sweep which had come to be typical of Clark's writings, it was not the General Treatise which he had envisioned at several points in his life, as indicated earlier. As he wrote in the month following the publication of this work in a letter to Robert D. Calkins, President of the Brookings Institution:

> When I undertook the project on competition for Brookings, I was abandoning a more general project: an attempt to map the essentials of 'social economics', as I conceive it, related to social 'values' and not limited by market valuations to the extent that economics regularly is. The whole of that job is presumably too big for me to tackle at present; but the second of your suggested topics fits in with it: that is, the public interest as economists look at it, and as they need to look at it in order to treat it adequately, without [added in Clark's hand in the margin] stultifying their contribution to social judgements, *or* [end of Clark's insert] forfeiting their character as scientific students. Economics seems to me to be full of unduly-limiting misconceptions as to the restrictions required by 'scientific' standing in economics.[78]

A key point in this work was that "some departures from 'pure and perfect' competition are not only inseparable from progress, but necessary to it. The theory of effective competition is dynamic theory." Clark noted: "From the standpoint of this volume, the crucial question is: What is the proper place of competitive forces in promoting innovation or dealing with it, and how may they take their proper place and render effective service?"[79] Several years earlier, in a letter, Clark had indicated the direction of his thinking on this matter:

> My present view is that this price-cost-equilibrium theory focuses on the less important of the benefits competition has to offer, the more important being dynamic – ample assortment of products with qualitative differences, new products in which to embody increasing productive power, and cost-reducing improvements. Further, that it is essential to the dynamic processes that the static equilibrium should never be reached – which makes it a little queer to call it "perfect."[80]

In *Competition as a Dynamic Process*, Clark pointed out that Alfred Marshall's faith in "the superior inventive force of a multitude of small undertakers"[81] had slackened by the time his *Industry and*

Trade was published. And Joseph Schumpeter had entirely shifted his emphasis "to huge organizations" because of their assumed efficiency in innovation. In 1961, in dealing with the issue of innovation, including product differentiation, Clark wrote:

> While product differentiation is treated in theory as a special case, it is actually the most general case, or the most comprehensive class of cases, since nearly all the products and services in industry and trade involve some differentiation between competing sellers. . . It follows that most of the defects of competition, as well as most of its virtues, are to be found in competition of this sort. It is an inseparable feature of the most essential operation of the freely progressive economy: the operation of constantly finding new products in which to embody its constantly increasing productive power. . .[82]

The question thus arose: what was there in this process which brought about product differentiation and innovation in general?

To this Clark responded that "competition as an activity (as distinct from a state of hypothetical equilibrium) may be viewed as a series of initiatory moves and defensive responses; and much of the explanation of the basic competitive paradox in this field resides in this sequence, and is to be explained in terms of the character of the moves, the character and timing of the responses, and the uncertainties of their timing and their efficacy."[83] Defensive responses were understandable enough, though it was not as clear in the case of initiatory moves. As Clark saw the matter, it was not a simple case of considering whether the rival would respond immediately to neutralize any gains or not respond at all.[84] "This simplification misses the really characteristic cases, which lie between the extremes and need more to explain them than can be represented in a curve on a diagram."[85] Indeed, "the outcome . . . is neither a perfect equilibrium nor an oligopolistic stalemate, but a continuing give-and-take of moves and responses." Initiating firms have the best change with differentiated products since it takes time for competitors to develop responses and the initial firm can gain in the interval, and has "a fair chance for a continuing gain" after this. In general,

> initiatory moves may be made by firms that see opportunities for a particular gain, are aware that they are starting a game of

moves and responses, if it has not been started already by others, and who have enough self-confidence to expect to be able to keep ahead in the game, or at least to be better off than if they neglect the game and thus let others get ahead of them in it.[86]

Clark presented several types of conditions which might arise from these typical circumstances, using what he termed a "descriptive analysis," a term borrowed from Wesley Clair Mitchell. Clark maintained that this view of the matter had, still, more in common with Alfred Marshall's *Principles of Economics* "than the more recent emphasis on rigorous equilibrium models."[87]

Clark also devoted attention to the problems of competition over distance, in line with his view "that this was the largest and most conspicuous neglected area of problems in the theory of competition. . . . ever since Cournot set the precedent of bypassing it."[88] Clark's sustained interest in this question had led him to conclude that this area involved "a complex of inter-related problems" covering the policy goals of "avoidance of discriminations injurious to competition between customers, bringing about competitive pressures on sellers which are effective without being destructive or demoralizing, and reduction of wastes of 'cross-freighting.' " No static analysis could adequately cover this area however, since in his view the sequence of moves and responses over distance made it necessary to understand that "where transportation costs are a decisive factor," problems "are not solved, they evolve."[89] Some years earlier Clark had written that he was "semi-seriously wondering if there's something to be said for changing trade-practice rules every ten or fifteen years for the sake of changing them, on the theory that competitive pressures are likely to stalemate with the passage of time whereby everybody learns just what to expect." Clark's contact with basing-point problems in the cement, steel and potash industries had led him to conclude that he did not "think the diagnosis and prescription are the same in any two of those three cases – that is, there are differences that seem important enough to make a difference."[90] In *Competition as a Dynamic Process*, Clark suggested "moderation and flexibility in restraints" for the Federal Trade Commission owing to the complexity of the issue. Clark was firm on the question that, especially when sales over distance are concerned, the static concept of "price" needed to be 'broken in two': "price paid at destination and net amount received at point of origin." For this reason, questions of "discrimination in price" as used in the Robinson-Patman Act needed to be viewed in a much more thoroughgoing, descriptive fashion.[91]

In *Competition as a Dynamic Process*, Clark had tried "to treat the subject in a way that could be understood by a serious and intelligent reader who is not an economic theorist, and still show what difference it makes to, let's say, the Chamberlinian type of theory, and in what respects that body of theory is barking up the wrong tree." He was well aware of the difficulties involved in utilizing a new and unfamiliar type of theory

> ... from my standpoint, my biggest and most difficult job is to establish that the dynamic approach *is* theory; and to show how existing theory is biased and limited by built-in static preconceptions in ways that most exponents probably don't realize. Hence Chap. VI, also Chap. V, which belong in the larger project for a general economic treatise.[92]

In the book itself, he further noted that "the threat of failure looms large, in that readers whose conception of theory is identified with models of determinate equilibrium are likely to decide that no theory has been produced.[93]

That this concern was not without foundation is indicated by the mixed nature of the reviews of his volume. A reviewer in the *Economic Journal* called it "unsatisfactory and disappointing" and wrote that "the analytical framework of the book is difficult to discern."[94] In *The American Economic Review*, Myron H. Watkins noted that "Clark's new study confirms his reputation for keen observation, subtle analysis and rare detachment. Nevertheless it is a disappointing book."[95] On the other hand, the reviewer for the Indiana Law Journal wrote: "His analyses are ... extremely valuable guides to argument and decision in particular situations under that laws; and his conclusions as to over-all policy should become widely influential in discussion and legislation."[96] And Donald Dewey called it Clark's "finest book." Noting that "the chapter on innovation [is] the more original in the book," Dewey wrote: "If this book is judged for what it is – a treatise on competition for professional economists – praise can hardly be too high.[97]

In a paper some years earlier, Clark developed three sets of constructive suggestions for freeing theory from its static mold:

First, as to our dealings with ultimate human values. . . . Instead of attaching great importance to a formal analysis of choice in the abstract, devoid of content, I suggest that we deal with the content of values the system inherently tends to promote or neglect.

It is time we abandoned the idea that an individual can always choose for himself better than anyone else. . . . If my doctor does not know better than I do about the needs of my internal workings, then medical science is a failure. And economists need not assume that they alone, of all people in the society, are ignorant of that fact. . . .

The second suggestion relates to the kind of theoretical analysis, generally of conditions of equilibrium, commonly expressed by lines in graphs, centering on maxima, minima, and points of intersection. The suggestion is that for lines we substitute bands or zones with a width gauged to represent the indeterminateness which the hard lines conceal. This would turn a maximum or an "optimum" into a range, not a point, and would make it incumbent on the student to do something about the question how wide this range is likely to be. . . . This would force attention to a fresh group of problems: namely, within this range in which results are indeterminate by the factors entering into the curve, what other factors determine the actual result, and how do they act?

One of the neglected variables is time. . . .

My third and last suggestion concerns what can happen to "economic law" when its field is pre-empted by power-enforced decisions. . . . To make it harder for those who tend to retreat from reality, one might stipulate that the aim be something that could conceivably throw light on some actual decision: for example, on the question what would be an economically correct wage for producers of steel, automobiles, or bituminous coal. Or, instead of refining formal utility curves or indifference curves, . . . the question would be: "What should a wise government do about consumers' freedom of choice? . . ."[98]

Competition as A Dynamic Process went far to implement Clark's own constructive suggestions and contribute to the formulation of a dynamic economic theory.

No view of Clark's work, however, can be considered complete without an examination of the ethical thread which ran throughout all of his writings, and which became more pronounced during his later years, in his treatment of the relationship of economics to ethics.

6 Economics and the Bridge to Ethics

Throughout his life, Clark gave explicit attention to the question of ethics in economics – a concern which he also found rooted in the elder Clark's work. In the mid–1950s, in his notes for the revision of a sketch of John Bates Clark written by Alvin Johnson for the *Dictionary of American Biography*, John Maurice Clark observed: "I could always count on him [John Bates Clark] to find a place for anything I might do in the field of 'dynamics.' After writing my 'Alternative to Serfdom' [1948], I reread his 'Philosophy of Wealth' [1886], and was delighted to note the basic similarity, allowing for some 70 years of historical change."[1] By stressing what he considered the inescapable links between ethics and economics, Clark placed himself outside much of the conventional thinking in modern orthodox economics. To better understand Clark's contribution, a brief essay into the accepted view will be helpful.

THE ORTHODOX VIEW

Modern economic thought sprang in great measure from the field of moral philosophy, and ethical considerations were seldom far from hand in the classical world. By the end of the nineteenth century, the situation had changed. In 1890, John Neville Keynes distinguished a "positive science of political economy" from "a normative or regulative science." Positive economics dealt with "what is"; normative with "what ought to be." Thus, "political economy, regarded as a positive science, may . . . be said to be independent of ethics." Keynes held that ethical considerations entered in the "art" of applied or practical economics.[2]

In his course of Moral and Political Philosophy given in 1873–1874, Alfred Marshall is reported as saying: "I have argued that not only is ethical well-being a portion of that well-being which any reasonable utilitarian system urges us to promote, but that it is much the most important element of that well-being." Yet Marshall dropped the brief references to "ethico-economic problems" in his *Principles of Economics* in the 2nd and 5th editions.[3]

In the twentieth century, theoretical welfare economics had attempted to make the ethical judgments in economic analysis explicit. The type of ethical valuations permitted, however, had been constrained by the requirements of the mathematical method favored by most theorists in this area.[4] And, writing in 1952, Paul A. Samuelson noted: "At some point welfare economics must introduce ethical welfare functions *from outside of economics*. Which set of ends is relevant is decidedly *not* a scientific question of economics."[5]

Finally, Lionel (later Lord) Robbins wrote in his influential 1932 work:

> Economics deals with ascertainable facts; ethics with valuations and obligations. The two fields of enquiry are not on the same plane of discourse. Between the generalisations of positive and normative studies there is a logical gulf fixed which no ingenuity can disguise and no juxtaposition in space or time bridge over .... Propositions involving the verb "ought" are different in kind from propositions involving the verb "is." And it is difficult to see what possible good can be served by not keeping them separate, or failing to recognize their essential difference.[6]

With most of orthodox economics, the matter stands substantially as J.N. Keynes and Lord Robbins framed it: ethics is not susceptible of treatment within the province of scientific ("positive") economics. In remarkable contrast, Clark viewed ethics as central to economic analysis.

CLARK: ECONOMICS AS THE BRIDGE TO ETHICS

Primarily in a trio of works spanning the period 1940 through the late 1950s, Clark articulated "a broadening of the traditional economic problem."[7] In so doing, he wove together many strands of his earlier thought, dating as far back as 1912.

Clark noted the usual dichotomy between causal analysis and value judgments while at the same time discerning a bridge between them. He wrote that

> there are two worlds, the world of impersonal investigation of cause and effect, and the world of desires, ideals, and value judgments. The natural sciences deals with the first; ethics deals

with the second. In these terms, the peculiarity of economics is that it is called upon to bridge this gap. It is a science . . . and its subject matter consists of desires and values. If "science is measurement," the measures that give economics its claim on that score are of the sort in which things are measured, not in terms of their weight or any physical quality, but in terms of their "value" or their cost. Economics simply cannot report those relations between phenomena which are most characteristic of it without translating physical quantities into terms of value or cost.[8]

Illustrating this with what was apparently closest to a physical law in economics, he pointed to the "law of diminishing returns." Upon inspection, however, he noted that there was no way to determine optimum inputs of the variable factor without having recourse to cost principles. "Thus the nearest thing in economics to a purely physical principle turns out on analysis to be a principle of economical choice in terms of cost." This clearly recalls one of the principal conclusions of his pioneering work on *Overhead Costs*. That is, that costs do not mean anything definite without regard to the institutional structure. As Clark phrased this in 1958: "cost is not a precise, unambiguous objective fact; it is rather a convention allowing considerable latitude."[9] But the present institutional structure deals in terms of market valuation.

THE BIAS OF THE MARKET

Clark wrote that "an economist can hardly escape asking what this value means and what lies behind it, or whether the market yardstick is a safe and dependable guide to the organization of a country's resources. Does it lead us to produce the right things in the right amounts, or not? Could any other system, or any modification of this one do better?"[10]

In the first instance, it was clear to Clark that the market mechanism did not remove the ethical question from the economist's realm; it merely clouded the issue. In a volume dedicated to Charles Horton Cooley, he pointed to Cooley's "excellently analyzed" treatment of the bias of the market. Clark declared that economic mechanisms were not neutral. "The economist's chief mechanism – the market – cultivates certain kinds of needs and

neglects others. It is biased; and if the economist limits himself . . .
[to the market], he is accepting the bias of his mechanism. The
correction of the bias is then left to others, without the help economists can give in what is properly a joint undertaking."[11]

Putting the matter in another fashion, Clark elaborated in a letter:

> Judgments of what ought to be done, as distinct from ideas of
> particular desirable ends, depend on knowledge of the alter-
> natives, and ethical standards in this sense evolve with changing
> understanding of what the alternatives are. So study of facts and
> ethical judgments mutually influence one another. That is, they
> do when there is a chance for them to make working contacts.
> But if one proceeds on the hypothesis that these are separate
> planes which can never touch, the working contacts are barred.
> This tends toward the attitude that judgments of what ought to
> be done are not based on facts or reason.[12]

If these working contacts were to be established, Clark believed, the
matter would have to be framed differently.

Thus, in the second instance, it became clear that the more logical
treatment was to ask at the outset: "What are our ends? What do
we want, or what should we want?" If these – ethical – questions
are not asked at the outset we are led to "judging the system by *its*
ends, nor ours; by the ends it is best adapted to serve, those it tends
to promote and cultivate."[13]

The ends of economic activity did not warrant discussion in
earlier periods simply because the goals were given by "the powerful few", whether kingly or ecclesiastical. Only "when the many
gain power" does the question, and the need, for discussion of goal
and purpose necessarily arise.[14]

Indicative of the gap between the necessary discussion of goal and
purpose and the absence of such treatment within the confines of
standard economics was the confusion encountered by newcomers
to the study of economics: the student. If thoughtful people,
unfamiliar with the discipline of economics were asked "What is the
most important product of a country's structure of industry?,"
Clark held that "there is little doubt that the prevailing answer
would be, not 'material' goods and services, or objective or market-
able gratifications, but people" and the total effect of industry upon
them. "Now," he continued, "put these same thoughtful observers
in a class in economics."

They find themselves in a different and restricted world. Here the final word on values is what individuals or businesses (or other economic entities, including government) are willing to pay for them in markets . . . It is not that the student is expected to change his former beliefs about what is most important; he is merely told that those beliefs are out of place in an economics classroom, and *as an economist* he is expected to measure the total value of chewing gum, patent medicines, and erotic perfumes as greater than that of boy-scout camps or classic literature, if people pay more for them. . . . The broader questions are alleged to be the business of sociology or ethics, or both.

The student may also find that his existing ethical judgments are called into question "as not being based on sound and adequate economic analysis." Or, the student who wishes to evaluate his ethical judgments in light of economic analysis may discover that the most important evidence has been excluded. To Clark, the necessary connection between economics and ethics was missing. With characteristic restraint, he concluded, "Surely, there is some confusion here."[15]

To put the matter another way, Clark wrote that "a purchase in a market is a 'fact'" which is the position taken by standard economic theories:

But if one goes no farther than that, it has no more economic significance than the specific gravity of a piece of rock. The real question arises when it is accepted as evidence of preference, in somebody's scale of preferences, while other evidences are ruled out. As evidence of this kind of preference, a purchase in a market is insufficient to be the sole basis of what claims to be an authoritative "scientific" judgment. *That conclusion* is not a fact but an hypothesis, along with hypotheses about the relative importance of things to different people. (Incidentally, most purchases in markets are made by somebody on behalf of a household, and therefore involve interpersonal comparisons.)[16]

The ethical questions, those involving judgment are definitely *not* removed by the usual treatment of theory: taking preferences as "given."

If the findings of economic theory based on the confines of "abstract utilities and disutilities (or indifferent rates of 'substitution')" were restricted solely to market phenomena, there might be less cause for concern. But as these findings are used to gauge social efficiency and afford guides for community policy," the absence of explicit ethical treatments leaves only those norms implicit in the market system itself as Clark had noted earlier. For the classroom, one way out of this dilemma would be to introduce descriptions of the "human values involved in purchases of goods and in the doing of a day's work." Other methods of exploring the ethics in economics were necessary, though.

AN ECONOMIC CONSTITUENT ASSEMBLY FOR RECONSTRUCTION

The broadened economic problem with which Clark was dealing here was "the question how our economic mechanisms operate to serve, to disserve, or to neglect the wants and needs of the people as a whole."[17] This demanded that a more accurate picture of "the wants and needs of the people" be rendered. The narrow 'rational economizing person' of traditional theory[18] would have to give way to a realistic version of actual behavior as Clark had urged from the beginning of his career.[19]

Against this background one could be invited to explore the various agencies available for meeting these needs of human nature. What were the strengths and drawbacks of these agencies? The market was one. "The main alternative agency – but not the only one – is political government. Co-operative, private organizations for educational, research, or civic purposes, all are significant variants, having their . . . characteristic biases. . . ."[20]

Or one might imagine oneself as part of "an economic constituent assembly" designed to amend the economic constitution. Here it would be necessary to ask what people needed and wanted, and strive to achieve a reasonable balance in the process – not with the goal of setting up priorities for all time, but for the time being, subject to change and modification. As Clark explained in a 1960 letter: "I'd be shy of using a perfectionist work like 'Utopia' in connection with it [*Economic Institutions and Human Welfare*]. I'm an evolutionist, and feel rather strongly that criteria of perfection are irrelevant for a dynamic and evolutionary society."[21] However, some priorities might be international peace; domestic peace; employment – "ample and stable"; and security, both in its quantitative and qualitative or psychological aspects. Indicative rather than exhaustive, this list underscored Clark's concern with the search for "a balanced society": balanced in terms of reconciling the rights of people in a new and changed setting from that of earlier times. "For the community needs rebuilding – nothing less."[22]

A rebuilding, "an adventure in reconstruction, for which no happy outcome can be guaranteed," is needed, comparable to the reshaping of society which followed the shattering of the medieval community in order "to make possible the development of modern science, industry, and democracy." This "long and gradual process" saw the customary rights of the medieval community give "way to the institution of a class dependent on wages, fixed by contract. With this went the expansion of markets for commodities. Over it all stood the early national state, representing not a community, but dynastic or class interests."[23] This development brought the conception of "the community as an arithmetic sum of separate, rationally calculating individuals, whose economic requirements were fully met by unmitigated self-seeking under free contract. Community status was replaced by market mechanisms.

But self-interest was no longer, if it had ever been, an adequate guide to social relationships, including those called "economic." Current economic policy indicates that we do not really believe that consumer free choice is infallible. Society does "not leave individual consumers entirely free to decide whether to buy narcotics, to quarantine contagious diseases, to attend school or not," or any number of other actions which have social consequences. In point of fact,

> our [economic] policy is not explained by any conviction that there is something so sacred about free individual choice that it must not be interfered with, right or wrong; or that people have a supreme right to make their own mistakes, and profit from them – if they can. This last principle breaks down where choices have irrevocable effects, and mistakes can be disastrous.[24]

Clark added that people "need protection from the impossible burden of full application of the doctrine of *caveat emptor*, which would be crushing in an age when every year brings in a bewildering assortment of new foods, medicines, gadgets and synthetic substitutes."

Parenthetically, Clark noted that this approach constituted

> a denial of all the main assumptions that have been relied on by general or abstract theoretical economics dealing with utility or individual choice, from Bentham through Jevons and down to and including the assumptions which are implicit, though unavowed, in the currently-favored "indifference-curve approach. . . . [T]he position taken is at variance with the further view that economists must abjure all "interpersonal comparisons" – except, be it noted, those that are embodied in the existing distribution of incomes and existing purchases, which are largely made for family units, not for individuals. This appears to be a theorist's perversion of the valid principle that economists, as "scientists," should be neutral in these matters, and should be guided by actual prevailing valuations. In practice, this perversion leads to acceptance of market valuations, which are notoriously biased, in ways easily demonstrable. I maintain that there are other actual valuations which have more validity for this purpose, and that need to be taken into account by an economist who really wants to be neutral.
>
> Obviously, detailed establishment of these negative criticisms would require a treatise, and would be out of place here. The main point I am suggesting is a substitute method of dealing with these problems, which may not be easily recognized as "theory," but is based on theoretical analysis, and which, with all its indefiniteness, appears to come nearer the goal of objective neutrality which economists have set for themselves.[25]

Shedding these restrictive assumptions in theory might then enable economists to go on and develop an adequate, instrumentalist, theory of social-economic needs.

Clark himself suggested that the reconstruction of society would have to differ from the medieval conception of community in three essential ways:

> It must be largely voluntary rather than based on authority. It must be largely built on quasi-federative relations between groups rather than solely on direct relations between individuals and a supreme power. And its structure of rights must maintain flexibility.[26]

In 1927, Clark had put the matter in these words:

> [T]he progress of methods has made us so interdependent that
> we are in process of being forced . . . to organize our economic
> life into the form of a real community again. This new com-
> munity is large, transcending the bounds of nations, and its
> morals cannot be merely customary, for it is making new
> customs every day. They must be democratic, voluntaristic,
> elastic enough to adjust themselves to rapid and unforeseeable
> change; and yet they must contain more binding standards of
> economic conduct and more positive mutual obligations than
> *laissez-faire* could furnish.[27]

These strivings for a new theory of social economics were the
substance of Clark's life work.

AN INDISPENSABLE FACTOR OF PRODUCTION

Concern with ethical questions in economics cannot be seen as the
ruminations of an elder statesman of economics, since they simply
summarize, as well as expand, themes which Clark had expressed
throughout his life.[28] The early concern with railroad rate-setting
and methodology as well as his work in *Overhead Costs* are of one
piece with his thoughts on ethics. Changed theory was needed to
keep up with changed practice. As he noted: "We can no longer rely
on reaching economically correct results automatically, as an un-
intended by-product of what individuals do in pursuit of their
private interests." What was clearly needed, in Clark's view, was
"some understanding of what economically correct adjustments are
and a will to promote them rather than to pursue self-interest
irresponsibly. This element of practical ethics had become an
indispensable economic 'factor of production.'"[29]

7 J. M. Clark – An Evaluation

Clark's work placed him in the highest rank of American – and world – economics and provided a substantial basis for the reconstruction of economic thought along the cumulative, dynamic, lines appropriate for the twentieth and twenty-first century.

That his contribution was of the highest order was formally recognized by the American Economic Association in 1952 when Clark was chosen to become the second recipient, after Wesley Clair Mitchell, of the Francis A. Walker Medal. This award was given "not more frequently than once every five years to that living American economist who . . . has made over the course of his life the most distinguished contribution to economics. . . ."[1]

The reconstruction in economics which Clark sought with unflagging labor has not yet been accomplished, however. In large measure this is because the extent and depth of his contribution require such thoroughgoing changes in the patterns of standard economic thought. His work on *Overhead Costs*, published nearly seventy-five years ago, demonstrated conclusively that costs could not be taken as precise and unambiguous items in the modern era of large-scale organization and joint products. In fact, costs were "rather a convention allowing considerable latitude"[2] reflecting the institutional arrangements of society. As a result, in order to obtain a meaningful analysis of the process of economic life, it became necessary to examine the principal social forces involved. These social forces included those of law and custom; the various types of voluntary organizations; and the several spheres of public influence through governmental activity. Clark's *Social Control of Business* went far in pulling together diverse currents of thought in many "fields" and suggesting how these social forces affected the fiber of economic activity in point of fact.

In addition, Clark provided convincing arguments for restructuring the behavioral assumptions of economic analysis in light of modern psychology and sociology. His contributions included specific and constructive examples of how a dynamic economic analysis would be applied in such areas as business cycles, public works planning, and the theory of competition. Furthermore, many of his later works stressed the dangers of a new orthodoxy arising from a narrow interpretation of a "Keynesianism" in which the requirements of plane geometry and algebra edged aside those of the underlying real forces at work. To this end, from the time of his 1914 review of A.C. Pigou's *Wealth and Welfare* onwards, Clark cautioned against the reification of mathematical abstractions. He urged mathematical economists to communicate with others rather than give way to a mistaken conception of the requirements of science.

He sought to counter another erroneous view in some scientific work by bringing ethical questions to the forefront of economic analysis rather than leaving them hidden, implicit, in the recesses of economic thought. He demonstrated that, if ethics were not considered in the open, necessary consideration of the vital and urgent questions of social policy would be truncated by limitations of mathematical methods. What, for instance, was the effect of the job on the worker's welfare, or the economic system on social morale? Clark undertook a constructive approach here as well, by asking 'What do we want from our economic system?' The question, and the responding guidelines he developed, were undertaken with the hope that other scientists would follow his lead and build upon these foundations.

Clark's point of view, also, was deeply influenced by the intellectual inheritance provided by his father, and a strong sense of continuity with his New England heritage. As a result, he retained a life-long "prejudice," as he once termed it, for seeking constructive solutions to social ills within the framework of an evolving system of business enterprise. Yet there was an element of ambiguity here. He was not a socialist, but he was strongly aware of the early Christian Socialist influence upon his father, and made reference to this influence in his last autobiographical note published the year of his death. He rejected Marx's technical analysis of exploitation in favor of the ethical implications of Euler's Theorem which, in static theory, showed that the owners of the factors of production, including laborers, were paid according to their marginal contribution to the joint product and were therefore not "exploited." But Clark noted: "it is the ethics of the parable of the talents, not that of the workers in the vineyard."[3] And, in his papers, he once ranked Marx as an institutionalist. While the shadow of his father's marginal productivity analysis might be perceived in this regard, Clark never contented himself with the static explanation of distribution as sufficient. In his development of dynamic analysis, he suggested that labor be made an overhead cost and urged "a true relation of partnership between labor and the other parties in industry."[4]

In any case, Clark was never a sanguine apologist for the business system. His writings contain a striking sense of urgency and doubt concerning the likelihood of peaceable transformation of the institutional structure to one freed from group and class domination. One cannot find in Clark's writings an analogue to the presumption of John Stuart Mill – and John Bates Clark – that the system of private property has not yet had a fair trial. It may be fairly concluded that the issue was far more pressing to Clark and the outcome far from certain.

Clark's work not only significantly enriched the dynamic theory of institutional analysis, but, in addressing itself to matters of fact rather than *a priori* doctrine, it also serves as a link to all analyses of economic process concerned with fact. "Economic theory," he wrote, "wherever it speaks of 'supply and demand,' is likely to be transferring ideas of market to industry and trade, where they do not fit the facts."[5] His dynamic analysis was a *different type* of economic theory designed to fit the changing facts of industry and trade. Some of the work which has won him high acclaim, such as the accelerator and multiplier analysis, was acclaimed because it appeared to be consistent with static patterns of model construction. But Clark's contribution does not rest merely upon these techniques, and a preoccupation with them would serve only to obscure the nature of his much broader and deeper contribution to economic analysis. His substantial addition to the analysis of cumulative process clearly pointed the way for relevant contributions to come.

Notes and References

1. BACKGROUND AND ORIGINS

1. Joseph Dorfman, "John Bates and John Maurice Clark on Monopoly and Competition," Introductory Essay to John Bates Clark and John Maurice Clark, *The Control of Trusts*, Rewritten and Enlarged Edition [1912] (New York: Kelley, 1971), 5.

2. Both John Bates Clark's great-grandfathers served in the Revolution: his paternal great-grandfather, Daniel A. Clark, serving under his maternal great-grandfather, General Jedidiah Huntington. Daniel Clark was a founder of the village of Plymouth Kingdom in Vermont. General Huntington was "one of the eight original brigadier-generals appointed by Washington." See Frances A. Toyer, "The Economic Thought of John Bates Clark," unpublished Ph.D. dissertation (New York University, 1952), 4; and "John Bates Clark" in *The National Cyclopaedia of American Biography*, vol. 13 (1906), 48.

3. The reference is to Daniel Clark. See *Economic Essays, Contributed in Honor of John Bates Clark*, edited by Jacob H. Hollander ([Published on behalf of the American Economic Association] New York: Macmillan, 1927), 365.

4. The evidence for this is ample and will be presented in following chapters. Two examples may serve here. Towards the end of his life (probably in 1955) Clark made the following notes on an envelope:

    "About 75 years ago, J.B.C[lark] called for truer 'anthropology' as basis for ec[onomics].

    "40 years ago (1915) [*sic*] I was writing 'Changing basis of ec[onomic] respons[ibility]'."

    And in a letter to John C. Schramm, Director of the Calvin K. Kazanjian Foundation in 1955, Clark wrote: "For the purpose in hand, I like to think that I am continuing the tradition of my eminent father, who some 75 years ago began to stress ethical elements in economics." The "purpose in hand" was the forthcoming Kazanjian Foundation Lectures delivered in 1955 and published as *The Ethical Basis of Economic Freedom*. Clark to Schramm, 10 March 1955. Copy and envelope in J.M. Clark Papers. None of this, however, is to be interpreted as suggesting that the efforts of the younger Clark were *limited* to those originally undertaken by his father.

5. Joseph Dorfman, *The Economic Mind in American Civilization*, 5 volumes (New York: Viking, 1946–1958) V: 440.

6. *John Bates Clark: A Memorial* (Prepared by his children and privately printed, 1938), 5.

7. Thomas le Duc, *Piety and Intellect at Amherst College, 1865–1912* (New York: Columbia University Press, 1946), 27–28.

8. Alan Simpson, *Puritanism in Old and New England* (Chicago: The University of Chicago Press, 1961), 39.

9. A converter is a device for transforming energy from one form to another. The steam engine transforms heat energy into mechanical energy. Carlo M. Cippola adopts the useful term "inorganic converter" in order to distinguish technological advances beyond the use of animal or "organic" converters. See his *The Economic History of World Population*, rev. ed. (Baltimore, Maryland: Penguin Books, 1964), esp. Chapter 2.

10. See, for example, Joseph Dorfman, *The Economic Mind in American Civilization*, volumes I and II (especially chapters 25 and 34), and volume III.

11. Simpson, 33.

12. *John Bates Clark*, 5.

13. John R. Everett, *Religion in Economics: A Study of John Bates Clark, Richard T. Ely, Simon N. Patten* (New York: King's Crown Press, 1946), 26. This work, Everett's dissertation at Columbia University, benefited from the suggestions of John Maurice Clark and Joseph Dorfman. The elder Clark, however, "was the third American figure to attain outstanding international importance." See Joseph Dorfman, *The Economic Mind in American Civilization*, II: 804; III: 102, 188.

14. Hollander, 5. Professor E.R.A. Seligman placed him "on a level with Ricardo, Senior, John Stuart Mill, Jevons, and Marshall." See *Essays in Economics*, 151. Allan G. Gruchy notes that "textbooks are still largely written in the pattern sanctioned by Alfred Marshall and John Bates Clark at the turn of the century." *See Modern Economic Thought: The American Contribution* (New York: Prentice-Hall, 1947), 13.

15. J. M. Clark was to later recall that his father commented "that when he was young, Hell was a very real thing . . . but he was reserved about discussing such matters." John Maurice Clark to J.R. Everett, 17 September, 1944. Cited in Everett, *Religion in Economics*, 1953.

16. Toyer, 5.

17. *John Bates Clark*, 6, 7.

18. The patents were No. 86210 (26 January, 1869) and No. 571511 (17 November, 1896). "One was a 'new apparatus for heating houses of all kinds' which was purported to save money in the initial installation of a heating apparatus and also in the use of fuel; the second was a machine for converting wave motion into [mechanical] power." Toyer, 6. Other "Patents in the attic" were "Bridge across the Atlantic," "similar idea for mid-ocean airports," "Rope fire-escape," and "2-story streets for N.Y." See notes in John Maurice Clark's hand in J.M. Clark Papers.

19. Everett, 28.

20. Toyer, 7.

21. *John Bates Clark*, 8.

22.   Of the ten clerical members of the first Board of Trustees, Claud M. Fuess writes: "with one or two exceptions, they were all aggressively Calvinistic." Amherst was appropriate in another way for Clark since his paternal great-grandfather, the Reverend Daniel A. Clark, was on the original Board of Trustees. The Reverend Clark was "a vigorous, original personality, who had made himself unpopular in the town [Amherst] because of his energetic espousal of the temperance movement and who was evidently a consistent trouble maker, moving rapidly from one pastorate to another . . . ." See Fuess' *Amherst: The Story of a New England College* (Boston: Little, Brown, 1935), 42, 43.

23.   Fuess, 170, 179.

24.   Friedrich August Gottreu Tholuck (1799–1877) was the son of a goldsmith who rose to become a leading defender of evangelical religion and Calvinism. In 1819 he was appointed professor at Berlin; in 1826 he became a professor at Halle where he remained the rest of his life.

25.   Fuess, 209, 211, 219. Seelye had studied at Amherst under Henry B. Smith, who persuaded him to spend a year in Germany following his graduation. Smith himself had studied Kantian philosophy at Halle and Berlin and theology under Tholuck. See Le Duc, 42. As one student of the class of '71 remarked, "the atmosphere of that senior lecture may at times have been highly rarefied, but we did think, and we thought about God, freedom, and immortality." Yet another student described the lecture "as mainly an exposition of the Westminister Catechism . . . ." Fuess, 217, 219. Still, Amherst produced men like Francis A. Walker, Herbert B. Adams, and Richmond Mayo-Smith in economics.

26.   Fuess, 213, 215. In his campaign for Congress, Seelye "refused to make speeches or to spend money. His only expenditure, in fact, during the campaign, was the postage stamp which he placed on his letter of acceptance." *Ibid.*

27.   From the manuscript, cited in Le Duc, 98.

28.   *John Bates Clark*, 8, 9.

29.   See, for instance, Veblen's "Professor Clark's Economics," *The Quarterly Journal of Economics*, 22 (February 1908), reprinted in Thorstein Veblen, *The Place of Science in Modern Civilisation and other essays* (New York: Russell & Russell, 1961). The opening paragraphs clearly indicate Veblen's high regard for his former teacher.

30.   See "J.B. Clark, 1847–1938" in J.M. Clark Papers.

31.   Much of this was as a Latin teacher. See Joseph Dorfman, *Economic Mind*, III: 189.

32.   Maurice (1805–1872) was a professor of English literature and history at King's College, London and, later, Cambridge. This earlier, English "movement was composed of 'social conservative critics' of capitalism and classical political economy. It attempted at the same time to meet the challenge of the 'un-Christian socialism' of the French revolution of 1848." See Joseph Dorfman, *Economic Mind*, III: *xxiii*.

33. Donald O. Wagner, *The Church of England and Social Reform Since 1854* (New York: Columbia University Press, 1930), 110. See also Peter D'Arcy Jones, *The Christian Socialist Revival, 1877–1914: Religion, Class and Social Conscience in Late-Victorian England* (Princeton: Princeton University Press, 1968).
34. James Dombrowski, *The Early Days of Christian Socialism in America* (New York: Columbia University Press, 1936), 3.
35. *Ibid.*, 15.
36. The article later became Chapter 10, "The Principle of Cooperation," of his *The Philosophy of Wealth: Economic Principles Newly Formulated* (1st ed., 1886; reprint of 2nd ed., 1887; New York: Kelley, 1967), 198. The original article appeared in the *New Englander*, n.s., 2 (July 1879): 565–600.
37. Joseph Dorfman points out that the three sons pursued as careers the three main interests of the elder Clark: Religion, Engineering, and Economics. Clark's sister married Henry Carrington Lancaster on 11 June 1913. At that time, he was professor of French Literature at Amherst College.
38. *John Bates Clark*, 13.
39. J.M. Clark Papers. Understandably, in light of this recollection, the younger Clark's copy of John Stuart Mill's *Autobiography* was heavily underlined.
40. He also joined his father's fraternity, Sigma chapter of Delta Kappa Epsilon.
41. London: James Clarke [1896], 350, 354.
42. (Boston: Houghton, Mifflin, 1898), 12. *Looking Backward* was published in January 1888.
43. Le Duc, 144.
44. Fuess, 224.
45. Fuess, 239. Garman also took some illustrations from theology, but they were relatively few.
46. In the posthumous *Letters, Lectures, and Addresses of Charles Edward Garman*: A Memorial Volume, prepared with the cooperation of the class of 1884, Amherst College by Eliza Miner Garman (Boston: Houghton Mifflin, 1909), 343. This excerpt is from stenographic notes made by a student in 1893, and is entitled "The Right of Property." Garman published little in his lifetime, but seems to have been a remarkable teacher. His volume is filled with imagery such as the following:

> "To recur to Kant's illustration. We know that no effort at flight can ever take the bird beyond the atmosphere of the earth, because when we know what it is to fly we see that it is merely to receive support from the air. So when we investigate what it is 'to think,' 'to judge,' 'to get science,' we see that it is to weigh accurately the evidence concerning the data in consciousness, and to do it according to the *constitution of consciousness* (= law of thought). So all our science is merely a knowledge of the world of consciousness."

"Ultimate Problems – Two Letters to an Alumnus," in *Ibid.*, 110–111 (emphasis in original).

47.   Le Duc, 102, 106. Among Garman's students were Walter Francis Willcox ('84), "dean of American demographers"; Professor Robert Sessions Woodworth ('91), the behavioral psychologist at Columbia University; and the Columbia University philosopher and one-time dean of the Graduate Faculties, Frederick J.E. Woodbridge ('89). On Willcox, see Dorfman, V, 566. One tribute to Garman was *Studies in Philosophy and Psychology*, by Former Students of Charles Edward Garman (Boston: Houghton, Mifflin, 1906).

It is interesting, in light of J.M. Clark's early criticisms of the hedonistic psychology in economics, to note the following from Garman's course in psychology. Citing E.B. Titchener, William James, and Paul E. Flechsig, Garman pointed out: *"Thought is a function of the brain."* He continued:

"Our work begins with the law of association as explained in terms of brain action. This involves a study of habit as resting upon a physiological basis.

"We next take up physical action or what might be called volition. . . . The old view of thought might be [illustrated by]. . . . a modern thermostat for regulating our furnaces. Formerly intelligence would be compared to the thermometer which informed us of the temperature of the room. But the furnace would be ineffectual until the fireman should intervene and open or close the dampers. But the modern thermostat is ideo-motor action, and the fireman has no function aside from feeding the coal and supervising the setting of the thermometer."

In "A General Survey of the Course [in Psychology]," *Letters Lectures, and Addresses of Charles Edward Garman*, 129–132; 133–134. See chapter 6 for Clark's views on ethics. In poor health by 1900, Garman died in 1907.

48.   His dissertation was *German Wage Theories: A History of their Development* (New York: Columbia University Press, 1898). Interestingly, Crook's teacher at Columbia was John Bates Clark, the man he had replaced at Amherst in 1895 when Clark moved to Columbia.

49.   Clark later recalled that his earliest contact with an economic problem came when he was two or three years old: he wondered why the carpenter received $2 per day while his father's salary was around $3500 per year. See "J.M.C.'s recollections of his earliest contacts with economic problems," 8 June 1949, J.M. Clark Papers. Initially, he didn't fare too well at Amherst, however; Crook assigned him a "C" in the course. Clark noted later: "Crook said he 'didn't get hold' of me. He was correct." *Ibid.*

50.   Here he read William Z. Ripley's *Transportation* (1902); Emery R. Johnson's *American Railway Transportation* (1903); and Edward S. Mead's *Trust Finance* (1903) (Mead at an earlier time spelled his name *Meade*).

51.   He was elected to Phi Beta Kappa and graduated *Magna cum laude*. At the commencement, Carrol D. Wright was presented with an honorary LL.D.

52.   "A Study of the Principles of Railway Rate-Making, with a view to ascertaining the possibility of establishing correct rates." Unpublished Master's thesis, Department of Economics, Columbia University, 1906.

53.   At Columbia, Clark attended the economics lectures of his father, E.R.A. Seligman, Henry R. Seager, Henry L. Moore, and Alvin S. Johnson. He also took courses with Franklin H. Giddings (Sociology), John W. Burgess (Political Science and Constitutional Law), and William A. Dunning (History and Political Philosophy). He attended the seminars of his father, E.R.A. Seligman, and H.R. Seager. In 1907 he held a University Fellowship in Economics.

54.   Clark to Joseph Dorfman, 18 June 1951, Copy in J.M. Clark Papers. "The other half [of the second minor] I elected with Dunning – 'History of the Civil War and reconstruction' – or maybe just reconstruction; at any rate, that was the part I remembered." *Ibid*. Burgess' course was "Private Rights and Immunities under the Constitution of the United States." Dunning's was "The United States from 1850, with special reference to the Civil War and Reconstruction." Clark also recalled of his Columbia days as a graduate student: "Veblen: slow infiltration of its [*sic*] logical and pragmatic relation to the abstractions of J.B.C." A note in Clark's hand, J.M. Clark Papers.

55.   He described Colorado College during his teaching days there as " . . . a privately-supported institution and one of those outposts of New England Puritan culture that were sprinkled across the country, outstanding examples being Oberlin and Carleton." Clark to Joseph Dorfman, 6 November 1957. Copy in J.M. Clark Papers.

56.   See Joseph Dorfman, "John Bates and John Maurice Clark on Monopoly and Competition." Tarbell was in some ways atypical of the leading muckrakers. She believed in a deity; the others were agnostics, though all were Social Christians. She thought that trusts should be broken up while the others argued for their nationalization. See Harold S. Wilson, *McClure's Magazine and the Muckrakers* (Princeton, New Jersey: Princeton University Press, 1970), 253 ff; 264; 300–306.

57.   *Standards of Reasonableness in Local Freight Discriminations* (New York: Columbia University Press, 1910).

58.   Clark came to Amherst in 1910. Meiklejohn was elected to the Presidency of the college in 1912.

59.   It was at the University of Chicago that Clark met the daughter of a Latin professor and "Dean in the Junior Colleges," Winifred Fisk Miller. They were married in Chicago on 17 June, 1921. Winifred Miller's father was Frank Justus Miller (1858–1938), a graduate of Denison University in 1879. His A.M. and Ph.D. degrees were from Yale. He served for some time as the managing editor of the *Classical Journal*.

60. Clark had been reading William Hope Harvey's *Coin's Financial School,* "the famous free-silver tract." Notes in Clark's hand, dated 8 June 1949, J.M. Clark Papers. On Harvey see Joseph Dorfman, *Economic Mind,* III: 226 ff.

2 AN "EXAMINATION OF PREMISES"

1. Clark to Joseph Dorfman, 12 May 1956; extracts in Dorfman, *Economic Mind,* V: 440. The title of Cooley's book was *Human Nature and the Social Order* (1902; 1922). Cooley's *Social Organization: A Study of the Larger Mind* was published in 1909.

2. "Davenport's Economics," *Political Science Quarterly,* 29 (June 1914), 315–323.

3. "The Prospects of Economics," in *The Trend of Economics,* edited with an introduction by Rexford Guy Tugwell (New York: F.S. Crofts, 1930), 19; reprinted in *The Backward Art of Spending Money, And Other Essays,* compiled and edited by Joseph Dorfman (New York: McGraw-Hill, 1937), 342–385. John Bates Clark had written: "If the Ricardians had recognized that their study was only partial, and had followed it with a separate study of dynamic forces, they would have given to their science a realistic character." See *The Distribution of Wealth* (New York: Macmillan, 1899), xvi.

4. Angell received his Ph.D. under James at Harvard in 1892. See Edwin G. Boring, *A History of Experimental Psychology,* 2nd ed. (New York: Appleton-Century-Crofts, 1957), Chapter 22, esp. 552–559. Also Boring's *Sensation and Perception in the History of Experimental Psychology* (New York: Appleton-Century-Crofts, 1942), Chapter 1. The behaviorist John B. Watson received his Ph.D. under Angell at Chicago in 1903.

5. Although James "was not by temperament nor in fact an experimentalist," he nevertheless stimulated the field. Boring, *A History,* 508.

6. *The Principles of Psychology,* in two volumes (New York: Dover, 1950 [1890]), II, 550. At another point James wrote: "It is of the essence of all consciousness (or of the neural process which underlies it) to instigate movement of some sort. That with one creature and object it should be of one sort, with others of another sort, is a problem for evolutionary history to explain. However the actual impulsions may have arisen, they must now be described as they exist; and those persons obey a curiously narrow teleological superstition who think themselves bound to interpret them in every instance as effects of the secret solicitancy of pleasure and repugnancy of pain." *Ibid.,* 551.

7. "Economics and Modern Psychology," *The Journal of Political Economy,* 26 (January, February, 1918). Reprinted in *Preface to Social Economics,* edited with an introduction by Moses Abramovitz and Eli Ginzberg (New York: Farrar & Rinehart, 1936), 92–169. Several of these early articles are found in this collection.

Cp. Wesley C. Mitchell, "Human Behavior and Economics: A Survey of Recent Literature," *The Quarterly Journal of Economics*, 29 (November 1914), 1–47.

8. *Preface to Social Economics*, 92, 93.
9. *Ibid.*, 96 (the emphasis has been supplied).
10. *Ibid.*, 96–97.
11. Indicative of the discussions on the relationship of psychology to economics in this period, are, for example, Rexford Guy Tugwell, "Human Nature in Economic Theory," *The Journal of Political Economy* 38 (June 1922), 317–345; Wesley Clair Mitchell, "Human Behavior and Economics: A Survey of Recent Literature," *Quarterly Journal of Economics*, 29 (November 1914), 1–47; Mitchell, "The Prospects of Economics," in *The Trend of Economics*, edited by R.G. Tugwell (Crofts, 1924) – reprinted in Mitchell's *The Backward Art of Spending Money and other essays* (New York: Kelley, 1950 [1937]), 342–385; Mitchell, "Bentham's Felicific Calculus," (1918) reprinted in *The Backward Art*, 177–202; Mitchell's "The Role of Money in Economic Theory," (1916) reprinted in *The Backward Art*, 149–176; Albert B. Wolfe, "Functional Economics," in Tugwell, *The Trend of Economics*, 443–482, and particularly 461–469; and Zenas Clark Dickinson, *Economic Motives: A Study in the Psychological Foundations of Economic Theory, with some references to other Social Sciences* (Cambridge, Mass.: Harvard University Press, 1922).

It was not to be expected that these criticisms would go unanswered. Jacob Viner, for instance, wrote in 1925: "In the scientific periodicals . . . in contrast with the standard treatises, sympathetic expositions of the utility theory of value have become somewhat rare. In their stead are found an unintermittent series of slashing criticisms of the utility economics. Its psychology, it is alleged, is obsolete; its logic faulty; its analysis and conclusions tainted with class bias; its service to economic enlightenment nil. The critics vie with one another in finding terms sufficiently vigorous to express to the full their dis-satisfaction with it." "The Utility Concept in Value Theory and its Critics," reprinted in *The Long View and the Short: Studies in Economic Theory and Policy* (Glencoe, Illinois: The Free Press, 1958), 179.

12. "Adam Smith and the Currents of History," (1926, 1928), reprinted in *Preface to Social Economics*, 171; and, another version, "Adam Smith and the Spirit of '76," in Carl Becker, J.M. Clark, and William E. Dodd, *The Spirit of '76 and Other Essays* (New York: Kelley, 1966 [1927]), 88–89.
13. *Preface to Social Economics*, 97–98.
14. *Ibid.*, 98. Royall Brandis has shown that nearly all basic assumptions of nineteenth-century physical science are disputed today. Yet much of contemporary economic theory was developed with these assumptions in mind. See his "Systems of Thought and Economic Systems," in R.S. Smith and F.T. de Vyver (eds.), *Economic Systems and Public Policy: Essays in honor of Calvin Bryce Hoover* (Durham, N.C.: Duke University Press, 1966), 19–36.

15.   *Ibid.*, 101–102, 106. He also pointed out that motives "are sometimes spoken of as commensurable in the sense of being ranked in
order of preference. *If these scales of values had stability* there would
be no quarrel with this usage, save that the establishing of the scale
is not done by a process of measurement." *Ibid.*, 102 (emphasis
added). See below where Clark refers to Wicksteed in pointing out
that preference systems are not transitive.

16.   *Preface to Social Economics*, 98–100 (emphasis added).

17.   The English-born Edward Bradford Titchener (1867–1927) took his
B.A. degree at Oxford in Philosophy and Psychology and his
doctorate at Leipzig under Wilhelm Max Wundt, an early inter-
preter of Darwin. He came to Cornell University in 1892 where he
remained until his death. His extensive writings and criticisms of
John Dewey and the Chicago functional psychologists helped establish modern psychology in the United States. See Boring, *A History*,
410–420 and *passim*. Among the students of Wundt at Leipzig were
Frank Angell and Lincoln Steffens. Wundt's works also stimulated
William James.

18.   *Preface to Social Economics*, 98–100, 103, 104–105.

19.   Clark to W.C. Mitchell, 21 April 1927. In W.C. Mitchell Papers,
Columbia University Libraries.

20.   *Ibid.*, 119, 121. Clark is not referring here to the notion of opportunity costs; his concept of "alternative cost" is considered later in
this chapter.

21.   *Ibid.*, 123. He noted here that Henry Walgrave Stuart takes a similar
position in Creative Intelligence, by John Dewey *et al.* (New York:
Holt, 1917), 282–353.

22.   *Preface to Social Economics*, 108–109.

23.   *Ibid.*, 109–111.

24.   *Ibid.*, 127. Wicksteed's treatment of the intransitive nature of wants
is in *The Common Sense of Political Economy, And Selected Papers
and Reviews on Economic Theory*, edited with an introduction by
Lionel Robbins (2 vols., London: Routledge & Sons, 1946), I,
Chapter 1, esp. 33–34. On the related point of Wicksteed's change
of mind on the marginal productivity theory, see Joseph Dorfman,
"Wicksteed's Recantation of the Marginal Productivity Theory,"
Economica 31 (New Series), 294–95, and Chapter 3 below.

25.   For instance in the familiar form of the Cobb-Douglas production
function, $Q = AL^aK^{1-a}$; "A" is the index of total factor productivity.
Here, only labor and capital are measurable contributors to production; all else is lumped under "A". Cf. Leo Wolman, "The Theory
of Production," *American Economic Review*, 11 (March 1921), 42,
and Evsey D. Domar, "On the Measurement of Technological
Change," *The Economic Journal*, 71 (December 1961), 709–29,
reprinted in *Capitalism, Socialism, and Serfdom* (New York: Cambridge University Press, 1989), 49–72.

26.   *Ibid.*, 128.

27.   *Preface to Social Economics*, 128–129. Compare Wesley Mitchell's
statement on business cycles: "Since the processes of a nation's

business life never cease or begin afresh, no natural starting point for the descriptive analysis to which we are committed exists. It is necessary to plunge *in medias res* by breaking into the unceasing processes at some arbitrarily chosen point." *Business Cycles and Their Causes*, reprint of Part III of *Business Cycles* (Berkeley: University of California Press, 1959 [1913]), *xii*. And, Charles Horton Cooley: "There *is* no beginning; we know nothing about past beginnings; there is always continuity with the past, and not with any one element only of the past, but with the whole interacting organism of man." In *Social Process*, reprint edition (Carbondale, Illinois: Southern Illinois University Press [1918], 1966), 46.

28. *Preface to Social Economics*, 129–130.
29. "Value," as Clark used the term in this context, was "used to mean human [or social] value, implying a 'utility' sufficiently scarce or expensive to have economic importance." And he emphasized: "The values immediately in question *have no adequate measure in price*, though all values take some effect on prices." *Ibid.*, 133 (emphasis added).
30. *Ibid.*, 131.
31. Compare Alfred Marshall, *Principles of Economics*, 9th ed. (London: Macmillan, 1961), Book II, Chapter 2.
32. *Preface to Social Economics*, 132 (earlier emphasis in original).
33. *Ibid.*, 133; see also 132. The notion of the "power to withhold" is used in an identical sense by John R. Commons in *Legal Foundations of Capitalism* (Madison, The University of Wisconsin Press, 1968 [1924]), 32. Neither author mentions the other in this context.
34. *Ibid.*, 133–134. These notions were to play a large role in Clark's *Social Control of Business* (1926). See Chapter 4 below.
35. *Preface to Social Economics*, 104–105; 139–140; 161–165.
36. *Ibid.*, 140–141 (some emphasis added).
37. In his *Social Choice and Individual Values*, Cowles Commission Monograph No. 12 (New York: John Wiley & Sons, 1951), Chapter 1, and 89–91.
38. *Preface to Social Economics*, 142, 143.
39. *Ibid.*, 142 (emphasis supplied). This notion is clearly suggestive of Clark's later work.
40. *Ibid.*, 142. On the subject of quality, see Lawrence Abbott, *Quality and Competition: An Essay in Economic Theory* (New York: Columbia University Press, 1955), esp. Chapter 14. This was a revised version of his Columbia Ph.D. dissertation done under Clark's guidance.
41. *Preface to Social Economics*, 143.
42. *Ibid.*, 144.
43. *Ibid.*, 146.
44. *Ibid.*, 169.
45. "The Empire of Machines, *The Yale Review*, New Series, 12 (October 1922), 132–143.
46. See "The inspiration of this sketch. . . ." in *The Yale Review*, 12 (October 1922), *xxviii*, where Clark writes "Some three years ago the

chapter on machines in 'Erewhon' seized upon my imagination and demanded a sequel."

This published version may be a revision of one submitted to *The Yale Review* on 6 April 1920. See Clark's letter to the editors of *The Yale Review*, 6 April 1920, in the Beinecke Rare Book and Manuscript Library, Yale University. In Clark's papers are a number of notes on this theme. Among them is a clipping of "The Machine as Slave and Master," by Herman George Scheffauer in *The Freeman* (12 May 1920), 208–210. One outline, wrapped in the *Boston Globe* of 6 August 1921, is entitled "Empire of Machines: Erewhon version" with a projected 8 chapters. Of this Clark wrote: "Est[imate] 115–20 pages." Another note in Clark's hand states: "Living things are habits of thought: Butler: Cooley [.] Sci[ence]:Veblen." Clark experimented with "Rewop" (power) and "Ecneics" (science). J.M. Clark Papers.

47. "The Empire of Machines," 133. See Butler's article in *The Press*, Christchurch, New Zealand (13 June 1863): the original part of Erewhon. Here Butler wrote: "Day by day ... the machines are gaining ground upon us; day by day we are becoming more subservient to them. . . . The upshot is simply a question of time, but that the time will come when the machines will hold the real supremacy over the world. . . ." Entitled "Darwin among the Machines," the article is signed "Cellarius" and is reprinted in Arthur O. Lewis, Jr. (ed.), *Of Men and Machines* (New York: Dutton, 1963), 183–187.

48. "The Empire of Machines," 133–134.

49. *Preface to Social Economics*, 40.

50. "The Empire of Machines," 135, 136, 140.

51. "Economics and Modern Psychology," in *Preface to Social Economics*, 94 (the emphasis is Clark's).

52. The Relation Between Statics and Dynamics," in *Preface to Social Economics*, 196, 199.

53. Note in Clark's hand, J.M. Clark Papers. No date given: probably around the 1950s.

54. "The Relation Between Statics and Dynamics," in *Preface to Social Economics*, 203 (emphasis added).

55. *Ibid.*, 204–206.

56. Clark's admiration for Cooley is revealed in his review of the third of Cooley's trilogy, *Social Process*. In *The Journal of Political Economy*, 27 (March 1919), 218–221.

     Clark dedicated a book to the memory of Cooley in 1948: *Alternatives to Serfdom*: See Chapter 6, below.

57. Cooley's major works are: *Human Nature and the Social Order* (1902, Rev. and enlarged ed., 1922); *Social Organization* (1909); and *Social Process* (1918). See also his "Political Economy and Social Process," (1918) reprinted in *Sociological Theory and Social Process*, Selected papers of Cooley with an introduction and notes by Robert Cooley Angell (New York: Holt, 1930), 251–159.

     On Cooley, see Edward C. Jandy, *Charles Horton Cooley: His Life and His Social Theory* (New York: Dryden, 1942), and Joseph Dorfman, *Economic Mind*, III, 401–407; IV, 137–139.

58. *Social Process*, 48–49; 294–295. Compare Wesley C. Mitchell's "The Role of Money in Economic History," *Journal of Economic History*, Supplement, 4 (December 1944), 61–67, and "The Role of Money in Economic Theory," (1916) reprinted in his *The Backward Art of Spending Money, and other essays* (1937), (reprint; New York: Kelley, 1950), 149–176.

59. "The Relation between Statics and Dynamics," 196–197.

60. A fundamental distinction between induction and deduction is logically untenable. Clark adopts common usage by using these terms in the sense of an *emphasis* on one or the other approach. For a first-rate discussion of the problem, see E.H. Carr's *What is History?* (London: Macmillan, 1961), especially 16–18. Clark wrote that "the core of scientific method lies, not in induction nor in deduction, but in taking account of all relevant facts and excluding none." In "The Socializing of Theoretical Economics," 6.

61. "Clark to Mitchell, 13 January 1944. In W.C. Mitchell Papers, Columbia University Libraries.

62. Clark's rejection of this dichotomy and his insistence on treating ethical matters explicitly are discussed in Chapter 6, below.

63. "The Socializing of Theoretical Economics," 10–11 (emphasis supplied).

64. *Ibid.*, 6 (Clark's emphasis). This is, of course, his principle of alternatives.

65. "The Relation between Statics and Dynamics," 197–198. "The work of J.B. Clark includes examples of both the narrower deductive and the broader qualitative modifications of statics. The former are found in his *Essentials of Economic Theory* [1907], while the most challenging fragments of the broader type of study are contained in his earlier work: *The Philosophy of Wealth* [1886]." *Ibid.*, 198.

66. *Ibid.*, 197.

67. "The Socializing of Theoretical Economics," 4, 5.

68a. "The Socializing of Theoretical Economics," 11–12.

68b. "A Contribution to the Theory of Competitive Price," 274. There is the related question, of course, as to why the "simplicity of a well-formed hypothesis" should seem "beautiful" compared to "amorphous facts." For a penetrating historical insight into the origins of the prominence of the deductive emphasis in economic thought, see Wesley C. Mitchell, *Types of Economic Theory, from Mercantilism to Institutionalism*, edited with an introduction by Joseph Dorfman, 2 vols. (New York: Kelley, 1967), I: 312–374.

69. "The Socializing of Theoretical Economics," 3, 5 (the emphasis is Clark's).

70. "The Changing Basis of Economic Responsibility," 80.

71. John Maurice Clark and others, *Adam Smith, 1776–1926* (Chicago: The University of Chicago Press, 1928), 55.

72. "Economics and Modern Psychology," 94–95.

73. Clark's system is sometimes referred to as "Social Economics." Joseph Dorfman described it as a "constructive synthesis."

3. THE EMERGENCE OF OVERHEAD COSTS

1. Published by The University of Chicago Press, it remained in print for fifty years.
2. *Ibid.* Clark's Master's Essay foreshadowed the dissertation: "A Study of the Principles of Railway Rate-Making, with a view to ascertaining the possibility of establishing correct rates" (Unpublished Master's thesis, Department of Economics, Columbia University, 1906). See also Chapter 1, above, for further background on his interest in the problem of railroads.
3. *Standards of Reasonableness*, 19.
4. *Ibid.*, 20.
5. *Ibid.*, 21. It could be asked whether the basic industries, transport, and wholesale and retail industries were, in this regard, fundamentally different from the railway sector. If not, they too could exert a similar power over the economy. In this context, it is not difficult to understand Clark's interest in the social control of business enterprise.
6. See below. Clark refers to this as the gradual "discovery" of overhead costs.
7. Clark notes that Francis A. Walker made a similar distinction in the United States, and that Dionysius Lardner also distinguished fixed and variable expenses in his *Railway Economy* (1855).
8. *Standards of Reasonableness*, 24 (emphasis supplied).
9. Marshall later preferred the terms "common" or "allied" costs. "When two things, say locomotives and stationary engines, are made in the same works, and in a great measure by the same labour and plant, it is often said that their costs are 'joint'; but, this term has a special historical association with groups of things, such as wheat and straw, which cannot be produced separately and it seems better to speak of such groups as having 'common' or 'allied' costs." See his *Industry and Trade* (London: Macmillan, 1920), 193. Clark reviewed this volume in 1921; his copy was heavily marked.
10. In *Overhead Costs*, Clark indicated that he now preferred to use "joint cost" in the strict sense, as Marshall had done. Clark instead used "overhead costs" in a generic sense. See *Overhead Costs*, 58–59.
11. A.C. Pigou subsequently joined the debate (May, August 1913).
12. *Standards of Reasonableness*, 28–29; chapter 2. See also *Overhead Costs*, 58–59.
13. *Standards of Reasonableness*, 30. "Special" costs are, today, variable costs. In a modern formulation: "the optimal contribution to overhead will vary with the operating rate; actual pricing behavior looks not only to the short-run cost curves, but also reflects the relationship between the existing capital stock and the current rate of production." See Otto Eckstein and Gary Fromm, "The Price Equation," *American Economic Review*, 58 (December 1968), 1163.
14. *Standards of Reasonableness*, 40–41 (emphasis supplied).

15. *Ibid.*, 41. Other portions of the dissertation will be considered in the next chapter on the social control of business.
16. *Overhead Costs*, ix, 1.
17. *Overhead Costs*, 90–91. George Stigler, for example, preferred to define capacity output as that output at which short-run marginal cost equals long-run marginal cost. See Stigler's *The Theory of Price*, 3rd ed. (New York: Macmillan, 1966), 156–158.

On the influence of scale, Clark shifted his emphasis further in his last book, *Competition as a Dynamic Process*. Here he wrote:

> The shape of the long-run cost curve, as presented in [orthodox] theory, becomes an issue because certain theories hinge on the use of a U-shaped curve with a definite optimum scale of production, and a curvature such that departures from this optimum entail in either direction materially increased costs. *This is contrary to the limited available evidence*, which seems typically to indicate no clearly marked and precise optimum scale of production. . . . the curve seems typically to flatten out over most of its length; and most of the productive capacity seems to be spread over a range in which. . . . trends traceable to scale of production are too small to be of controlling effect.

See 60, and 58–59. (Emphasis supplied).

18. *Overhead Costs*, 1–2 (emphasis supplied). Morris A. Copeland, a student of Clark's, put the matter in the following words: "A good deal of what has been written about the theory of the firm has assumed . . . two conditions that were closely approximated . . . [under the putting- out system]: zero costs when production is zero; and with only one product, no costs except those directly attributable to producing that product. When Clark spoke of the 'gradual discovery of overhead costs' he had in mind partly that we have come gradually to recognize the need to waive these two assumptions. But he had in mind also that as the domestic system has been replaced by highly integrated businesses with large capital investments, fixed and overhead costs have become more and more important." See his *Our Free Enterprise Economy* (New York: Macmillan, 1965), 144–145.
19. *Overhead Costs*, 107. Adams helped found the American Economic Association and was the first statistician for the Interstate Commerce Commission. See Dorfman, *Economic Mind*, III, esp. 164–174, *passim*. For a contemporary view of the "geometrical progression," see Jay M. Gould, *The Technical Elite* (New York: Kelley, 1966).
20. "The traditional version of the classical theory of the firm calls for no direct influence of the size of the capital stock on short-run, profit-maximizing, price-output decisions; the capital stock makes itself felt through the short-run cost curve." See Eckstein and Fromm, "The Price Equation," 1163.
21. *Overhead Costs*, 2.

22.   *Economics* (1896), 151–154. Quoted in *Overhead Costs*, 12. Hadley's volume was one of the texts used by Clark as an undergraduate. On Hadley see Dorfman, *Economic Mind*, III, 259–264.

23.   *Overhead Costs*, 13.

24.   *Ibid.*

25.   *Ibid.*, 17–18.

26.   *Ibid.*, 18–19 (emphasis added).

27.   The combination of technological exigencies and fluctuations in demand characteristically result in excess capacity in the industrial system, in Clark's view. These fluctuations in demand are the usual state of affairs, however, and are not to be thought of as *only* originating with business depressions; except in so far as business fluctuations are thought to be the usual state of affairs. Thus E.H. Chamberlin, for instance, missed the mark when he wrote that Clark "is concerned, for the most part . . . with the phenomena of the business cycle . . ." See *The Theory of Monopolistic Competition* (Cambridge, Mass.: Harvard University Press, 1956 [1933], 109.

28.   A loss in the sense of an opportunity cost. Clark referred to H.J. Davenport's use of the term "opportunity cost" in *The Economics of Enterprise* (1913). *Overhead Costs*, 49.

29.   *Overhead Costs*, 416.

30.   *Ibid.*, 433 (emphasis supplied).

31.   *Ibid.*, 417. Joan Robinson, for instance, gives a summary of the standard view: "Under conditions of perfect competition price discrimination could not exist even if the market could be easily divided into separate parts. . . . But if there is some degree of market imperfection there can be some degree of discrimination." *The Economics of Imperfect Competition* (London: Macmillan, 1954 [1933]), 179, 180.

32.   *Ibid.*, 24, 417–418.

33.   " 'Administered Prices' in their Relation to Competition and Monopoly," in *Administered Prices: A Compendium on Public Policy*, Subcommittee on Antitrust and Monopoly, Committee on the Judiciary, U.S. Senate, 88th Congress, 1st session (Washington, D.C.: U.S. Government Printing Office), 90–91 (emphasis added).

       While to Clark differences in quality, brands and so on were part of the competitive structure, to E.H. Chamberlin they were indicative of "monopolistic competition." Chamberlin also wrote: "Large numbers are a sufficient requirement for the market to produce competitive results [one price], without retarded action or any other type of imperfection." See his *Monopolistic Competition*, 49–50.

       Clark's interest in product quality persisted throughout his life. At least one of his Ph.D. students did a dissertation on the subject. See Lawrence Abbott, *Quality and Competition: An Essay in Economic Theory* (New York: Columbia University Press, 1955).

       Eckstein and Fromm noted: "some elements of locational or product differentiation attach to the sales of most companies in sufficient degree to create some uncertainty in pricing. When operating rates are high, a firm can feel more confident that an increase in price will not be able to establish new supply connections and will therefore be more likely to pay the higher prices." Eckstein and Fromm, "The Price Equation", 1163–64.

34. *Overhead Costs*, 419–420.
35. Clark pointed here to Jacob Viner's *Dumping: A Problem in International Trade* (Chicago: The University of Chicago Press, 1923).
36. *Ibid.*, 424. Further work by Clark on the basing point system will be considered below in Chapter 5.
37. *Ibid.*, 431–432.
38. *Ibid.*, 432–433.
39. *Overhead Costs*, 434–435.
40. *Ibid.*, 140.
41. *Ibid.*, 142, 147.
42. *Ibid.*, 144–146.
43. *Ibid.*, 444. Clark pointed here to the elder Clark's *The Control of Trusts* (1901) which contained "an early discussion of the force of potential competition."
44. *Ibid.*, 445 (emphasis supplied).
45. *Ibid.*, 445–446; 447.
46. *Ibid.*, 156–157, 166, 386. Clark illustrated: "It would typically be more expensive to run a plant where the output constantly fluctuated between 60 per cent and 120 per cent of its normal capacity than to run steadily at about 90 per cent." *Ibid.*, 94.
47. In a note, Clark wrote: "If the reader wishes to make a thorough study of this subject, he cannot adopt a better guide than W.C. Mitchell's *Business Cycles*. This book not only marks an epoch in the study of the business cycle but is a landmark in the progress of inductive methods of economic study." *Overhead Costs*, 386, 387. Clark first met Mitchell in 1913. Mitchell's influence on Clark is also discussed below. See the "Memorial Address" by Clark in *Wesley Clair Mitchell: The Economic Scientist*, edited by A.F. Burns (New York: National Bureau of Economic Research, 1952), 140.
48. "Business Acceleration and the Law of Demand: A Technical Factor in Economic Cycles," *Journal of Political Economy* 25:3 (March 1917), 217–235; reprinted in *Preface to Social Economics*, 327–354 (which includes an additional note by Clark in 1936).
49. *Overhead Costs*, 389. "Clark became explicit on the acceleration principle in good part through his reading of Wesley C. Mitchell's *Business Cycles* (1913). In a letter to Mitchell, 24 January 1915, Clark wrote that the book had helped him in the analysis of why costs vary and the true order of events as shown by the figures. Mitchell, in turn, accepted Clark's principle as one of the strands in his own later discussion of how prosperity brings a recession." Joseph Dorfman, *Economic Mind*, V, 452.
50. *Overhead Costs*, 390–393; "Business Acceleration," in *Preface to Social Economics*, 330–334. Clark mentioned most of the now familiar qualifications and restrictions: time required to produce equipment; limited capacity of producers' goods industry; varying rates of depreciation; producers' expectations; size of inventories;

role of autonomous investment; changes in the capital-output ratio; and so forth. These assumptions were further clarified in response to criticism by Simon Kuznets and others. See "Additional Note on 'Business Acceleration and the Law of Demand' " in *Preface to Social Economics*, 349–354. For additional references to the acceleration principle, see *Readings in Business Cycle Theory*, edited by Gottfried Haberler, *et al.* (Homewood, Ill.: Irwin, 1951), 460–462.

51. *Overhead Costs*, 396–397; 400–401.
52. *Ibid.*, 398–399.
53. *Ibid.*, 26.
54. *Ibid.*, 27, (emphasis supplied).
55. *Ibid.*
56. *Ibid.*, 32, (emphasis supplied).
57. For a stimulating account of the shifting of business costs onto third parties and society at large, see K. William Kapp, *The Social Costs of Private Enterprise* (New York: Schocken, 1971 [1950]). The volume is explicitly indebted to Clark's works; Clark read portions of the manuscript.
58. *Overhead Costs*, 28–29.
59. *Ibid.*, 29.
60. *Competition as a Dynamic Process*, 435–438. In 1946, Clark noted in a letter: "I have not read it [*Overhead Costs*] myself for many years, but I seem to recall that I expressed more confidence in flexible pricing as a means of insuring full employment than I would be inclined to feel at the present time." Clark to Paul A. Samuelson, 4 October 1946. Copy in J.M. Clark Papers.
61. *Overhead Costs*, 29.
62. *Ibid.*, 408.
63. "Some Social Aspects of Overhead Costs," *The American Economic Review* (Supplement) 13 (March 1923), 50–59. Here Clark went much further than the proposal made by Edward A. Ross in 1918 that workers should be given only two weeks severance pay. See Edward Alsworth Ross, "A Legal Dismissal Wage," *The American Economic Review*, Supplement, 9 (March 1919): 132–136.
64. *Overhead Costs*, 370. On labor as a supplementary (fixed) cost, see Alfred Marshall, *Principles*, 360–361.
65. *Overhead Costs*, 372.
66. *Ibid.*, 156–157.
67. *Ibid.*, 365–366.
68. *Ibid.*, 31–32.
69. *Ibid.*, 30.
70. *Ibid.*, 410.
71. Clark wrote Wicksteed in 1915 that he had a geometric proof of Euler's theorem. But Wicksteed's response to Clark, dated 14 February 1916, indicated that Wicksteed no longer considered the marginal productivity theory a *sufficient* explanation of distribution. See Joseph Dorfman, "Wicksteed's Recantation of the Marginal Productivity Theory," *Economica*, New Series, 31 (August 1964), 294–295. Clark's proof is in the J.M. Clark Papers.

72.   *Overhead Costs*, 473–477. In his review of Clark's book, F.Y. Edgeworth continued his questioning of Euler's Theorem by devoting most of his comments to criticism of Clark's position that "If all costs were variable . . . the sum of the marginal products of the different factors . . . (each multiplied by the amount of the factor) would always equal the whole product." (*Ibid.*, 471–472). Edgeworth wrote:

> No doubt there is a point of view from which, the entrepreneur's service being regarded as a factor of production and his remuneration as a portion of the cost, the . . . statement is admissible . . . But here, where we are considering an entrepreneur or Directorate marshalling the factors of production so as to realise the greatest possible difference between the produce of those factors and their cost, it would not be proper to treat that difference as an element of the subtrahend cost.

See his review in the *Economic Journal*, 35 (June 1925), 245–251.

73.   *Overhead Costs*, 479, (emphasis supplied).
74.   "The Uses of Diversity: Competitive Bearings of Diversities in Cost and Demand Functions," *The American Economic Review*, Supplement, 48 (May): 476; emphasis supplied.
75.   In the Spring of 1918, Clark began teaching a course in the Social Control of Business at Chicago.

4. CONTROL OF INDUSTRY – BY BUSINESS AND SOCIETY

1.   (New York: McGraw-Hill.) The first edition appeared in 1926. A second, somewhat revised and expanded version, in 1939. All references that follow are to the 1939 edition, and are substantially the same as the first edition unless otherwise noted.
2.   *Standards of Reasonableness in Local Freight Discriminations*, 12–13.
3.   *Ibid.*, 14, 52. "The value of any service may be defined as that charge which will in the long run bring in, over and above the special cost of the traffic involved, the greatest clear return possible under the special circumstances of each particular case. French writers express this by a beautifully simple diagram showing the curves of operating expense and gross earnings and the point of maximum difference." *Ibid.*, 55–56.
4.   *Ibid.*, 14.
5.   *Ibid.*, 55–56.
6.   *Ibid.*, 15. See Chapter 6, below.
7.   *Social Control of Business*, 3. Compare another statement: Carlo M. Cipolla, *The Economic History of World Population*, 3rd ed. (Baltimore: Penguin Books, 1965), especially chapters 1, 2, and 3.
8.   *Social Control of Business*, 4, 277–279. Also, the report by Minnesota Senator William Windom's committee attacking railway evils seems

to have been significant in the creation of the Interstate Commerce Commission in the following decade. See U.S. Senate, *Report of the Select Committee on Transportation Routes to the Seaboard*, 43d Congress, 1st session, Senate Report No. 307, Part 1 (Washington, D.C.: Government Printing Office, 1864). For a different view on the extent of governmental involvement in the U.S. economy before the Civil War, see Carter Goodrich, *Government Promotion of American Canals and Railroads, 1800–1890* (New York: Columbia University Press, 1960).

9. *Social Control of Business*, 4.
10. *Ibid.*, 5.
11. *Ibid., xi* (from the preface to the first edition).
12. *Ibid.*, 5–7, 90–92, 115. In Chapter 2, above, Clark's emphasis on the "power to withhold" or "exclusion value" was discussed. In his view, an individual without this power does not fully possess an item of property since he can be made to dispose of it under duress.
13. *Ibid.*, 5–7.
14. *Ibid.*, 7–8.
15. Clark found considerable inspiration in the writings of Commons. In the summer of 1909 he studied at the University of Wisconsin; there is no evidence that Commons was a teacher of his. Commons reviewed the first edition of *Social Control of Business* and after noting that it rested upon the insights in *Overhead Costs*, wrote: "I think these two books should be made the foundation of all elementary courses in economic science." In *The American Economic Review*, 17 (March 1927): 97–98.
16. *Ibid.*, 9 (emphasis added).
17. *Ibid.*, 10. Compare John R. Commons, *Legal Foundations of Capitalism* (New York: Macmillan, 1924), 303–306.
18. *Ibid.*, 11–12.
19. *Ibid.*, 14–15; emphasis added.
20. "Government Control of Industry," *The World Tomorrow*, 12 (February 1929): 75.
21. *Ibid.*, 18. This sentence appears in the 1926 edition as well. That is, Clark spoke of the "failure of social coordination" before the 1930's.
22. *Ibid.*, 27.
23. "Adam Smith and the Currents of History," in J.M. Clark *et al.*, *Adam Smith, 1776–1926* (Chicago: The University of Chicago Press, 1928), 61.

    Cf. *Institutional Economics: Its Place in Political Economy*, by John R. Commons (1934; reprint in 2 vols.; Madison, Wisconsin: The University of Wisconsin Press, 1961), 1: 110–111, 163 ff.

    See also Jacob Viner's statement in *Adam Smith*: "The modern advocate of laissez faire who objects to government participation in business on the ground that it is an encroachment upon a field reserved by nature for private enterprise cannot find support for this argument in *The Wealth of Nations*", 149.
24. "Economic Conditions and Economic Thinking," J.M. Clark papers. The 1927 date is Clark's estimate. Pp. 10, 16–17.

25. *Social Control of Business*, 30. Compare Clark's "The Theory of National Efficiency in War and Peace," in J. Maurice Clark, Walton H. Hamilton, and Harold G. Moulton (eds.), *Readings in the Economics of War* (Chicago: The University of Chicago Press, 1918), 556–587. This article was adapted from his "The Basis of War-Time Collectivism," *The American Economic Review*, 7 (December 1917): 772–790.
26. *The Journal of Political Economy*, 29 (October 1921): 684.
27. *Social Control of Business*, 45. These sentences do not appear in the original edition.
28. "Economic Conditions and Economic Thinking," 22.
29. Clark was to devote considerable effort in later years to the problem of goals. Many of these essays are found in *Economic Institutions and Human Welfare* (New York: Knopf, 1957), a collection of his writings during the period 1940–1955. See Chapter 6, below.
30. *Social Control of Business*, 54.
31. *Ibid.*, 55–56.
32. Clark to E. Ronald Walker, 26 February 1951. Copy in J.M. Clark Papers. In the letter, Clark continued: "Counting John Hobson, yourself, the other economist you referred to, and myself, that makes four who have committed themselves strongly to that position. If we can do something to make it look like an integral part of economic theory, there ought to be a great many more." *Ibid.* Clark was referring in the letter to Walker's *From Economic Theory to Policy* (Chicago: The University of Chicago Press, 1943).

    Cf. Clark's review of Hobson's *Work and Wealth*, *Quarterly Journal of Economics*, 29 (November 1914): 177–180; and his obituary of Hobson: "John A. Hobson: Heretic and Pioneer, 1858–1940," *Journal of Social Philosophy*, 5 (July 1940): 458–460.
33. *Ibid.*, 60–61.
34. *Ibid.*, 60.
35. *Ibid.*, 65.
36. *Ibid.* Although these sentences are not in the 1926 edition, they recall Clark's earlier work on "Overhead Costs and the Business Cycle." See *Overhead Costs*, 390–396, and Chapter 5, below.
37. *Ibid.*, 64. The assumption of profit maximization is a necessary condition to effect Pareto optima in modern theory. At least one writer has defined this assumption as being "a matter of mental attitude." An absence of "neighborhood effects," or externalities, is also necessary for Pareto optima. And the orthodox view of reform is indicated by the following: "Where the actual economic system fails in some respect to correspond to the assumptions of the hypothetical system, comparison of the two may indicate what changes to make in the actual system in order to improve its operation." See William S. Vickrey, *Microstatics* (New York: Harcourt, Brace & World, 1964) 212–221.
38. *Ibid.*, 66. The non-optimization of profits hypothesis has been referred to under the "soulful corporation" heading. For some views on this thesis see Leonard S. Silk, "The Role of the Business

Corporation in the Economy and Society," in R.S. Smith and F.T. de Vyer (eds.), *Economic Systems and Public Policy: Essays in honor of Calvin Bryce Hoover* (Durham, N.C.: Duke University Press, 1966), esp. 83–88; and the comments by James S. Earley in *The American Economic Review*, 47 (May 1957): 330–335.

Clark's later thinking on profit maximization is indicated by his use of the phrase "profit minded" – chosen "deliberately, to avoid the implication that business is solely and uniquely governed by an unrealistically precise "maximization of profits." See *Competition as a Dynamic Process*, 9.

39. *Ibid.*, 71, 77–80, 86.
40. *Ibid.*, 91.
41. *Ibid.*, 91–92. The reference is to Anatole France, who wrote that the poor "must labor in the face of the majestic equality of the laws, which forbids the rich as well as the poor to sleep under the bridges, to beg in the streets, and to steal bread." In *Le Lys Rouge* (1894), Chapter 7.
42. *Ibid.*, 97 (emphasis supplied). Clark's thinking in this area is inconsistent with the hypothesis that the pattern of ownership is irrelevant to the determination of resource allocation. Cf. Ronald Coase, "The Problem of Social Cost," *The Journal of Law and Economics*, 3 (October 1960): 1–44; G. Warren Nutter, "The Coase Theorem on Social Cost: A Footnote," *Ibid.*, 11 (October 1968): 503–507; and George J. Stigler, *The Theory of Price*, 3d ed. (New York: Macmillan, 1966), 110–114.
43. *Social Control of Business*, 99.
44. *Ibid.*, 130–131. The terms "partial or imperfect competition" do not appear in the first edition.
45. Clark noted that much inspiration here was drawn from John Stuart Mill's *Principles of Political Economy*, Book V, Chapter *xi*; and from Henry Sidgwick's *Principles of Political Economy*, Book III, "The Art of Political Economy."
46. The phrase is Joseph Dorfman's. See his *Economic Mind*, V: 460.
47. *Social Control of Business*, 165–166. Cf. Dorfman, *Economic Mind*, V: 460–461.

5. PROBLEMS OF WAR, DEPRESSION AND EFFECTIVE COMPETITION

1. Biographical note prepared by Clark in "'Administered Prices' in Their Relation to Competition and Monopoly," 86.
2. The fact that the elder Clark had given thought to a dynamic treatise undoubtedly stimulated J.M. Clark: "On accepting a post with the Carnegie Endowment for International Peace in 1911, [J.B.] Clark wrote: 'The plan for a fairly large treatise on Economic Dynamics will have to give place to more modest ones, though I hope to make a few contributions to such a science, if life and health

permit" (Clark to Anson D. Morse, 28 September 1911 [in Amherst College Archives])." See Joseph Dorfman, "The Department of Economics," in R. Gordon Hoxie, *et al.*, *A History of the Faculty of Political Science, Columbia University* (New York: Columbia University Press, 1955), 179.

3. See, for instance, the large folder entitled "Raw Material for 'Social Economics' " Which contains material from the 1920s; in the J.M. Clark Papers. Clark's own yearly reports on his current research at Chicago and Columbia demonstrate a consistent correlation between projection and achievement. He did not, however, project a general treatise in writing until the post-World War II period, and this was done in letters.

4. Clark to Ray B. Westerfield, 20 December 1949, copy in J.M. Clark Papers. Cf. Clark's handwritten "Notes for general treatise. . . ." dated 19 May 1946 and "General Treatise: Questions of Strategy" dated 22 May 1946, in J.M. Clark Papers. Also, a note dated 5 December 1951 on "Articles that [I] could use [for] parts of a gen treatise" in J.M. Clark Papers.

5. Clark to Carter Goodrich, 13 December 1946, copy in J.M. Clark Papers. See also Clark to Frederick C. Mills, 30 March 1949, in *ibid.*

6. New Haven, Conn.: Yale University Press, for the Carnegie Endowment for International Peace: Division of Economics and History, 1931. Reprint, with an introductory essay, "Some Documentary Notes on the Relations Among J.M. Clark, N.A.L.J. Johannsen and J.M. Keynes," by Joseph Dorfman (New York: Kelley, 1970).

7. See J.M. Clark, Walton H. Hamilton, and Harold G. Moulton (eds.), *Readings in the Economics of War* (Chicago: University of Chicago Press, 1918).

8. "The Basis of War-Time Collectivism," *The American Economic Review*, 7 (December 1917): 772–774, 790. The same problem was taken up by Clark after World War II. See "Basic Problems and Policies," in Donald H. Wallace, *Economic Controls and Defense* (New York: The Twentieth Century Fund, 1953), 242–256.

9. *Demobilization of Wartime Economic Controls* (New York: McGraw-Hill, 1944), 48–49.

10. A cognate to the Carnegie Institution of Washington's economic history of the United States begun in 1902. John Bates Clark was on the original advisory committee on economics and later became the Director of the Division of Economics and History. See also, Dorfman, *Economic Mind*, III: 349–351.

11. See the "Editor's Preface" by James T. Shotwell in *The Costs of the World War*, v–x.

12. *The Costs of the World War*, xi.

13. *Ibid.*, xi, 3.

14. *Ibid.*, 1–5.

15. *Ibid.*, 4, 5.

16. For these he drew heavily upon the work of the National Bureau of Economic Research, especially that of Willford I. King's *The National Income and Its Purchasing Power* (New York: NBER, 1930). King

was a former student and colleague of John R. Commons and a member of the original staff of the National Bureau. Other sources utilized by Clark included Leo Wolman, Paul H. Douglas, E.E. Day, and Morris A. Copeland. Good data were scarce however: "in 1921 the Joint Statistical Association recommended, unanimously, that all future collection of capital statistics be discontinued by the United States Census." See Paul H. Douglas, "Comments on the Cobb-Douglas Production Function," in Murray Brown (ed.), *The Theory and Empirical Analysis of Production* (New York: NBER, 1967), 21.

17. *Ibid.*, 17.
18. *Ibid.*, 24–26; see also page 83.
19. *Ibid.*, 81–85.
20. *Ibid.*, 113–114.
21. *Ibid.*, 81.
22. *Ibid.*, 60–61.
23. *Ibid.*, 122.
24. "Inductive Evidence on Marginal Productivity," *The American Economic Review*, 18 (September 1928): 449–467; reprinted in *Preface to Social Economics*, 315. This article was a review of Charles H. Cobb and Paul H. Douglas' "A Theory of Production," *The American Economic Review*, Supplement, 18 (March 1928): 163–165. Although Clark severely questions the device of holding "technical progress" constant, he called the article "a bold and significant piece of pioneer work in a hitherto neglected field." *Preface to Social Economics*, 325.
25. *Costs of the World War*, 93–94; 222; Appendix B.
26. *Ibid.*, 290. Forty years later, commenting on the reprint of Clark's volume by Augustus M. Kelley, a member of the editorial board of *The New York Times* noted the significance of Clark's book for the present day. See Leonard S. Silk, "The Postwar Economy," *The New York Times*, 14 April 1971.
27. New York: The National Bureau of Economic Research in Cooperation with The Committee on Recent Economic Changes, 1935; (reprinted: New York: Kelley, 1949). The Committee on Recent Economic Changes was formed under the chairmanship of Secretary of Commerce Herbert Hoover in 1927; it was an outgrowth of the Conference on Unemployment formed in 1921 to deal with some pressing postwar problems.
28. See Joseph Dorfman's "Some Documentary Notes on the Relations Among J.M. Clark, N.A.L.J. Johannsen and J.M. Keynes," introductory essay to the reprint edition of Clark's *The Costs of the World War to the American People* (New York: Kelley, 1970 [1931]), 5–12. See also below.
29. *The Costs of the World War*, 166.
30. *Alternative to Serfdom*, (New York: Knopf, 1950), 95.
31. "Business Cycles: The Problem of Diagnosis," *Journal of the American Statistical Association*, Supplement, 17 (March 1932): 215.
32. *Ibid.*, 129–130. The emphasis is Clark's.

33. *Ibid.*, 131.
34. *Ibid.*, 134.
35. *Ibid.*, 134–136.
36. *Ibid.*, 84–85.
37. *Ibid.*, 52–53.
38. *Ibid.*, 88, 163–164.
39. *Ibid.*, 155–156.
40. *Ibid.*, 191.
41. *Ibid.*, 192.
42. See Clark's "Wesley C. Mitchell's Contributions to the Theory of Business Cycles," in Stuart A. Rice (ed.), *Methods in Social Science: A Case Book* (Chicago: The University of Chicago Press, (1931), 662–73. Appended to Clark's essay are letters between Mitchell and Clark which reveal much about the formation of Mitchell's thought. Reprinted in *Preface* to *Social Economics*, 390–416.
43. See Hearings on S. 6215, 72nd Congress, 1st session, "Establishment of National Economic council," 737–752; Oral Testimony, 210–220. Printed in *The New Republic*, 69 (13 January, 1932), Part 2; reprinted in *Preface to Social Economics*, 229–269. Besides Clark, the committee members were J. Russell Smith, Edwin S. Smith and George Soule.
44. Washington, D.C.: Government Printing Office; (reprinted, New York: Kelley, 1965). See also "Productive Capacity and Effective Demand," in *Economic Reconstruction: Report of the Columbia University Commission* (New York: Columbia University Press, 1934), 81, 105–25; and "Economics and the National Recovery Administration," *The American Economic Review*, 24 (March 1934): 11–25.
45. *Economics of Planning Public Works*, 86. See R. F. Kahn, "The Relation of Home Investment to Unemployment, *Economic Journal*, 46 (June 1931): 173–98; and J.M. Keynes, *The Means to Prosperity* (London, 1933). On the multiplier, see Hugo Hegeland, *The Multiplier Theory* (New York: Kelley, 1966 [1954]).
46. *Economics of Planning Public Works*, 83–87.
47. *Ibid.*, 89–90.
48. *Alternative to Serfdom*, 104–105.
49. Clark's term was "circuit velocity of money" which he defined as "the ratio between the total amount of circulating media in the country and the total net volume of production, or the total national income, which those media of exchange serve to finance." He understood by "money," "all forms of media of exchange." See *Economics of Planning Public Works*, 96.
50. *Ibid.*
51. *Ibid.*, 100.
52. *Ibid.*, 100–101, 102.
53. In light of the foregoing, it is difficult to make factual sense of the following: Clark "failed, however, to show how they [his 'many other interesting insights into the working of the economic system'] were related to each other – he made no use of the multiplier, for

example – or which were of major and which of only incidental importance." See Alan Sweezy, "The Keynesians and Government Policy, 1933–1939," *The American Economic Review*, 62 (May 1972): 118–119. The statement that "Qualified support for Keynesian policies came from J.M. Clark and Arthur Gayer" suggests a lack of familiarity with Clark's own work in this period, as well as his earlier writings. Finally the statement that "Clark and [Arthur] Gayer were still very much under the dominance of the traditional business cycle pattern of thinking" appears meaningless unless the work of Wesley Clair Mitchell and the National Bureau of Economic Research are construed as belonging to the "traditional" pattern.

54.　*Ibid.*, 112.

55.　Review of *Public Works Policy* by the International Labor Office [Geneva], *Political Science Quarterly* 51 (June): 295.

56.　Clark to J.M. Keynes, 24 July 1941; copy in J.M. Clark Papers. Quoted in Joseph Dorfman, "Some Documentary Notes on the Relations Among J.M. Clark, N.A.L.J. Johannsen and J.M. Keynes," introductory essay to reprint of J.M. Clark, *The Costs of the World War to the American People* (1931; New York: Kelley, 1970), 14.

Also quoted in *Activities 1940–1943: External War Finance*, edited by Donald Moggridge, vol. 23 of *The Collected Writings of John Maynard Keynes* (London: The Macmillan Press, Ltd. for The Royal Economic Society, 1979), 191–193. Clark also met with Keynes at a dinner meeting of the Office of Price Administration and Civilian Supply officials on 10 June 1941. See *ibid.*, 182. On this World War II trip, Keynes arrived in New York on 8 May 1941 and left for London on 28 July 1941.

57.　Keynes to Clark, 26 July 1941; in J.M. Clark Papers. Quoted in Dorfman, "Some Documentary Notes," 13; and vol. 23 of *The Collected Writings of Keynes*, 190–193.

This evidence is inconsistent with the interpretation of Herbert Stein regarding Keynes' view of his "followers" in Washington: "When Keynes visited Washington in June, 1941, on behalf of the British government, he was surprised at the extent to which the Washington economists had absorbed his thinking and the sophistication with which they applied it. At the same time he was critical of some of the procedures used, for reasons which suggested that he was still more classical than his Washington followers. (John M. Keynes to Walter S. Salant, 9 July 1941, 24 July 1941, 27 July 1941 [In Possession of W.S. Salant, Washington, D.C.])." Herbert Stein, *The Fiscal Revolution in America* (Chicago: The University of Chicago Press, 1969), 191, 489.

As will be seen, Clark was concerned not that Keynes was "more classical than his Washington followers" but that the Washington group were becoming epigones of Keynes: rigid and formalistic. In this regard, the opinion that "Despite their criticism, however, both Keynes and Clark recognized the [high] quality of economics being done in Washington" lacks a factual basis. See Byrd L. Jones, "The

Role of Keynesians in Wartime Policy and Postwar Planning, 1940–1946," *The American Economic Review*, 62, No. 2 (May 1972): 127–128.

58. The note is dated 10 December 1950; in the J.M. Clark Papers.
59. Review of Lloyd A. Metzler *et al.*, *Income, Employment and Public Policy* in *The American Economic Review*, 39 (March 1949): 504–507. Samuelson's essay was "The Simple Mathematics of Income Determination," 133–155. Cf. "A Postscript by the Editor [Seymour E. Harris]," *The Review of Economics and Statistics*, 36 (August 1954): esp. 384–386.
60. "The Theoretical Issues," *The American Economic Review*, 32, Supplement 1, Part 2 (March 1942): 8–9. See Dorfman, "Some Documentary Notes," 14–15.
61. "Anti-Inflation Policy Approaches Maturity," (Washington, D.C.: Office of Price Administration, 1943), 1, 3, 10, 9–22.

This evidence is inconsistent with the interpretation that "John M. Clark supported Keynes' view, which was also the classical prescription, that higher taxes were necessary to limit the inflationary threat. Skeptical of the high estimate of potential capacity, Clark urged concurrent use of fiscal and credit controls, rationing, priorities, and direct controls to limit price increases due to bottlenecks and excess demand for consumer goods." Aside from the question of what Keynes' actual views were, this interpretation attempts to portray Clark as a "Keynesian" economist. There is no evidence for this view. See Byrd L. Jones, "The Role of Keynesians in Wartime Policy and Postwar Planning, 1940–1946," 128. As Clark noted in a letter in 1949:

I am just slightly bothered at having Ken Galbraith classify me as an orthodox Keynesian. I don't think Keynes was an orthodox Keynesian, and I did not think I was, except in the sense that pretty much everybody nowadays recognizes that total volume of spending does not take care of itself automatically.

Clark to Frederick C. Mills, 30 March, 1949; Copy in J.M. Clark Papers.

62. *Demobilization of Wartime Economic Controls* (New York: McGraw-Hill, 1944), 166.
63. Washington, D.C.: The Brookings Institution, 1961. This is not to suggest agreement with the assessment of one reviewer than the "volume is essentially a 500–page expansion of that 15–page article." The review, by Richard E. Caves, is in *The Political Science Quarterly*, 77 (December 1962): 632–635. Although Clark wrote in his preface that "The present volume is an elaboration of a line of inquiry dating from . . . 'Toward a Concept of Workable Competition,' . . ." the volume covered a much broader spectrum of theory than that contained in the 1940 article.
64. *The American Economic Review*, Part 1, 30 (June 1940): 241–256. An enlarged and revised version was reprinted in Edgar M. Hoover, Jr.

and Joel Dean (eds.), *Readings in the Social Control of Industry* (Philadelphia: Blakiston, 1942), 452–475.

65.　*Competition as a Dynamic Process*, ix.

66.　See Dorfman, *Economic Mind*, V: 440; and Dorfman, "John Bates and John Maurice Clark on Monopoly and Competition, "Introductory essay to the reprint edition of John Bates Clark and John Maurice Clark, *The Control of Trusts*, rewritten and enlarged edition (New York: Kelley, 1971 [1912]). See also, Benjamin J. Klebaner, "Trusts and Competition: A Note on John Bates Clark and John Maurice Clark," *Social Research*, 29 (Winter 1962): 475, 478–479.

　　As the Clarks stated in the preface to the 1912 edition: "It is a joint production, in that one of its two authors has contributed the earlier work, the other has contributed most of the new material, and both have participated in the revisions demanded by rapid and recent changes in the business world." *The Control of Trusts*, v.

67.　*Ibid.*, 3. This sentence is not in the original edition.

68.　*Ibid.*, 169. This part, from Chapter 7, "Constructive Competition," does not appear in the original edition.

69.　Compare Donald Dewey, *The Theory of Imperfect Competition: A Radical Reconstruction* (New York: Columbia University Press, 1969), 73–74.

70.　See for instance, *Economics of Overhead Costs*, 444–447; *Social Control of Business*, 2d ed., 136.

71.　"Toward a Concept of Workable Competition," in *Readings in the Social Control of Industry*, 453–454.

72.　*Ibid.*, 460. "In fact, it may appear that much of the apparent seriousness of Professor Chamberlin's results derives from what I believe to be the exaggerated steepness of the curves he uses to illustrate them." *Ibid.*

73.　*Ibid.*, 462–463.

74.　*Ibid.*, 460–461.

75.　*Report of the Attorney General's National Committee to Study the Antitrust Laws* (Washington, D.C.: Government Printing Office, 1955), 320.

76.　*Ibid.*, 337,338.

77.　*Alternative to Serfdom*, 70. In a note on the back flyleaf of his copy of George J. Stigler's *The Theory of Competitive Price* (New York: Macmillan, 1942), Clark wrote: "Perfect competition grade B": "i.e., prices fluctuate above & below average cost as demand is less or more than optimum capacity. Price tends to = [equal] marg[inal] cost at least when working below optimum capacity, and total capacity adjusts on av[erage] of fluct[uation], so av[erage] price = [equals] av[erage] (full) cost." J. M. Clark Papers.

78.　Clark to Calkins, 23 December 1961. Copy in J.M. Clark Papers.

79.　*Competition as a Dynamic Process*, ix, 180.

80.　Clark to Simon Kuznets, 11 April 1954. Copy in J.M. Clark Papers. The letter dealt with Clark's subsequent paper, "Competition: Static

Models and Dynamic Aspects," *The American Economic Review*, 45, No. 2 (May 1955): 450–462.

81. Marshall, "Some Aspects of Competition," 1890, quoted in Clark, 179.
82. *Competition as a Dynamic Process*, 212.
83. *Ibid.*, 471.
84. Cf. Donald Dewey, *The Theory of Imperfect Competition*, Chapter 9.
85. *Competition as a Dynamic Process*, 471–472.
86. *Ibid.*, 472, 474.
87. *Ibid.*, 475.
88. *Ibid.*, x.
89. *Ibid.*, 359–360.
90. Clark to Leverett E. Lyon, 30 September 1948. Copy in J.M. Clark Papers. In the same letter, Clark wrote: "As you suggest, the basing-point tangle is a tall order. Arthur R. Burns and I know more about it than most economists, which isn't saying much. I don't think anybody, in the industry, in the Federal Trade Commission, in the Dep't of Justice or among economists knows all about it, few know enough to earn the right to talk very confidently, and those that do have special interests to promote."
91. *Competition as a Dynamic Process*, 301; 338–341; 361–362.
92. Clark to Robert D. Calkins, 19 October 1954. Copy in J.M. Clark Papers.
93. *Competition as a Dynamic Process*, x.
94. J.B. Heath of Manchester University, in the *Economic Journal*, 74 (March 1964): 184–186.
95. "Competition as a Dynamic Process," in *The American Economic Review*, 52 (December 1962): 1970.
96. Review by Ralph F. Fuchs in the *Indiana Law Journal*, 38 (Summer 1963): 731.
97. *The Journal of Political Economy*, 71 (February 1963): 87–89.
98. "Varieties of Economic Law, and Their Limiting Factors," *Proceedings of the American Philosophical Society*, 94, No. 2 (April 1950): 124–126. The reference to "bands or zones" was suggested by Frank W. Taussig's "Is Market Price Determinate?", *Quarterly Journal of Economics*, 35 (May 1921): 394–411. Taussig spoke here of an area of "indeterminateness" and "a penumbra within which market prices fluctuate." See Chapter 2.

6. ECONOMICS AND THE BRIDGE TO ETHICS

1 J.M. Clark Papers. *The Philosophy of Wealth* contains the principal writings by the elder Clark on ethics. In the same note, the younger Clark wrote: "His [John Bates Clark's] ethical attitudes were related in part to those of the German Historical School and in part to the intellectual currents, of a Christian Socialist flavor. . . . " Johnson's sketch appeared in 1958. Cf. Chapter1, above.
Ten years earlier, Clark had noted in a letter: "I was much interested, after writing my W.W. Cook lectures [*Alternative to Serfdom*]

last year, to go back to the "Philosophy of Wealth" and find
how many similarities there were; and that I was nearer to the
general character of that book than to my father's later work."
Clark to Joseph Dorfman, 8 November 1947. Copy in J.M. Clark
Papers.

2. John Neville Keynes, *The Scope and Method of Political Economy*,
4th ed. (1917 [1st ed., 1890], reprint, Augustus M. Kelley, Publishers, 1965), chapter 2, especially 34–35, 60–63.

3. Mary Paley Marshall, *What I Remember* (Cambridge: Cambridge
University Press, 1947), 19. Alfred Marshall, *Principles of Economics*, 9th (variorum) ed. (London: Macmillan, 1961), 2: 685–687.

4. Cf. E.J. Mishan, "A Survey of Welfare Economics, 1939–1959," in
Surveys of Economic Theory: Money Interest, and Welfare, Vol. I
(London: Macmillan, 1965), 4–222. Also, *Readings in Welfare Economics*, Selected by Kenneth J. Arrow and Tibor Scitovsky (Homewood, Ill.: Irwin for The American Economic Association, 1969).

5. "Comment" on Kenneth E. Boulding's "Welfare Economics," in *A
Survey of Contemporary Economics*, vol 2, edited by Bernard F.
Haley (Homewood, Ill.: Irwin for The American Economic Associ-
ation, 1952), 37 (first emphasis added).

6. *An Essay on The Nature and Significance of Economic Science*, 2d
ed. (London: Macmillan and Co., 1952 [1st ed., 1932]), 148–149.

7. *Alternative to Serfdom* (New York: Alfred A. Knopf, 1948; 2d ed.,
Vintage Books, 1960); *Guideposts in Time of Change: Some Essentials for a Sound American Economy* (New York: Harper, 1949);
Economic Institutions and Human Welfare (New York: Knopf,
1957). *Economic Institutions* consists of revised versions of articles
and lectures dating from 1940 to 1955.

8. "Economic Means – To What Ends? A Problem in the Teaching of
Economics," in *Economic Institutions*, 14–15.

9. "The Uses of Diversity: Competitive Bearings of Diversities in Cost
and Demand Functions," *The American Economic Review*, Supplement, 48 (May 1958): 476. See Chapter 3, above.

10. "Economic Means – To What Ends? A Problem in the Teaching of
Economics," in *Economic Institutions and Human Welfare*, 15–16.

11. *Alternative to Serfdom*, 10–11. Cooley's Comprehensive treatment is
in *Social Process*, especially Chapters 26 and 27.

12. Clark to Lionel [Lord] Robbins, 14 March 1951. Copy in J.M. Clark
Papers. Robbins had earlier taken the position that: "In point of
fact I believe that the 'gulf' which divides us is almost entirely
terminological." Robbins to Clark, 31 January 1951, in J.M. Clark
Papers. To this, Clark responded: "I think we could still have a good
argument on the scope of Economics as a science and the relation
between this and value judgments, or between questions of what is
and what ought to be." Clark to Robbins, 14 March 1951.

13. *Guideposts in Time of Change*, 52. This is suggestive of the treatment
of machines in his 1922 essay "The Empire of Machines": what
goals do these devices serve? Cf. Chapter 2, above.

14. *Guideposts in Time of Change*, 52–53.

15. "Economic Means – To What Ends? A Problem in the Teaching of Economics," in *Economic Institutions*, 24–25. The emphasis is in the original.
16. Clark to Lionel Robbins, 14 March 1951. Copy in J.M. Clark Papers. (The emphasis is Clark's.)
17. *Alternative to Serfdom*, 9. References are to the more widely available first edition.
18. In later years, Clark compared the notion of "economic man" to the fable of "Buridan's ass." Jean Buridan, a fourteenth century scholastic philosopher and disciple of William of Occam, wrote a fable depicting an ass who, when placed midway between two similar bundles of hay, was unable to choose and starved to death. See Clark's pencilled notes in his copies of George A. Stigler, *The Theory of Competitive Price* (New York: Macmillan, 1942), and C. Reinhold Noyes, *Economic Man, in Relation to His Natural Environment*, 2 vols. (New York: Columbia University Press, 1948). These volumes are part of the J.M. Clark Papers.
19. See Chapter 2, above.
20. "Economic Means – To What Ends? A Problem in the Teaching of Economics," in *Economic Institutions*, 26.
21. Clark to William S. Maxwell, 2 April 1960. Copy in J.M. Clark Papers.
22. *Alternative to Serfdom*, 11–19, 22.
23. *Ibid.*, 23.
24. *Guideposts in Time of Change*, 67.
25. *Ibid.*, 67–68. In a letter to Lord Robbins, Clark wrote of this passage that he was "calling the attention of economists to the fact that these [ideas] were inconsistent with most of the accepted theoretical positions on utility and kindred matters . . . . Some day perhaps . . . I may try to do that job more formally, in which case people will say 'How interesting! But it is not theory,' and go back to the theoretical orthodoxy; that is, they will unless I succeed in making the point that this is in itself a sounder kind of theory." Clark to Lionel (Lord) Robbins, 21 February 1951. Copy in J.M. Clark Papers.
26. *Alternative to Serfdom*, 25.
27. "Control of Trade Practices by Competitive and Other Forces," in *Proceedings of the Academy of Political Science*, 12, no. 2 (January 1927): 100.
28. See Chapter 2, above, especially.
29. *Economic Institutions*, 71. For an example of Clark's deep sense of urgency concerning these ethical questions, see Appendix A.

7. J. M. CLARK – AN EVALUATION

1. See the original announcement of the award: "Notes," *The American Economic Review*, 37 (June 1947): 519. The announcement further

stressed that the award was to be made "for contributions to the central body of economic thought and knowledge" and was not "to be made for contributions to special branches of economics except in so far as these may contribute vitally to general economic doctrine and knowledge." This award was discontinued by the American Economic Association following introduction of the yearly "The Central Bank of Sweden Prize in Economic Science in Memory of Alfred Nobel." This new Nobel award was introduced to celebrate the 300th anniversary of the Bank of Sweden in 1968 and was to be given for "specific achievements" or specific contributions. See Assar Lindbeck, "The Prize in Economic Science in Memory of Alfred Nobel," *Journal of Economic Literature*, 23 (March 1985): 37–56. Clark had been awarded an honorary doctorate by the University of Paris in 1948.

2.   "The Uses of Diversity: Competitive Bearings of Diversities in Cost and Demand Functions," *The American Economic Review*, Supplement, 48 (May 1958): 476.

3.   "Aims of Economic Life as Seen by Economists," in *Economic Institutions*, 55.

4.   *Overhead Costs*, 482.

5.   "'Administered Prices' in their Relation to Competition and Monopoly," 87.

Appendix A

Clark often used a moral fable to bring out his views. In a note in Clark's papers, his wife, Winifred M. Clark, wrote: "It was characteristic of him that he mulled over a topic, and often much later came up with a sort of allegory or fable. (He was particularly fond of [Robert Louis] Stevenson's 'Fables' and usually carried a copy of the little book about with him in his pocket." (The volume referred to is the 1902 Scribner (New York) edition of Stevenson's *Fables*.)

Illustrative of this characteristic, and of his attitude towards ethical problems, is the "Epilogue" to *Economic Institutions and Human Welfare*:

In that garden where Adam lost his primeval innocence there stood, we have been told, two forbidden trees: the tree of knowledge of good and evil, and the tree of life. Adam ate of the first, and was driven from the garden lest he eat of the second. But between these two stood other trees, of which Adam was not told, and one of which has been found by some of his children.

For Adam taught his children, as he labored to till the soil, that the cure for the ills that come of knowledge is more knowledge. His children did not forget, and in any case they could not have turned back. Some of them came again to the entrance of the garden, where the angel barred the way. Though his flaming sword slew many, some made their way past. But they did not come to the tree of life.

Instead, after many hardships, they came to a great tree which had twin trunks, the branches of which interlaced, and the fruit of the two could not be distinguished. The name of the nearer trunk was the tree of knowledge how worlds are made, and the name of the farther trunk was the tree of knowledge how worlds are destroyed. And Adam's children ate; and they were seized with a great fear, beyond any fear that men had known, which left them no peace nor rest, but drove them on.

The road beyond lies through dark and dangerous chasms; and whether they will win through, it is not given to us to know. If they do, they may come to the tree which bears the knowledge how worlds may be made in which man may safely live. Only then – if their search succeeds thus far – may they be ready to reach out to the tree of life, which stands beyond.

Appendix B: Bibliography of John Maurice Clark

1905 "Ivy Poem," *The Amherst Student* (Commencement Issue), 38, no. 31.

1906 "A Study of the Principles of Railway Rate-Making With a view to ascertaining the possibility of establishing correct rates." Unpublished Master's thesis, Department of Economics, Columbia University.

1909 [Statement concurring with Dean Edward S. Parsons on the need for a college gymnasium.] *The Tiger* [Colorado College], 11, no. 16 (22 January): 8.

1910 *Standards of Reasonableness in Local Freight Discriminations.* New York: Columbia University.[1]

1911 "Rates for Public Utilities," *American Economic Review*, 1 (September): 473–487.

1912 with John Bates Clark, *The Control of Trusts.* Rewritten and enlarged edition. New York: Macmillan.

Review of *Legal Phases of Central Station Rate Making for Electric Supply*, by James U. Oxtoby, *American Economic Review*, 2 (March): 113–114.

1913 "Frontiers of Regulation and What Lies Beyond," *American Economic Review*, 3 (March): 114–125.

"Possible Complications of the Compensated Dollar," *American Economic Review*, 3 (September): 576–588.

Review of *Wealth and Welfare*, by Arthur C. Pigou, *American Economic Review*, 3 (September): 623–625.

1914 "Some Economic Aspects of the New Long and Short Haul Clause," *Quarterly Journal of Economics*, 28 (February): 322–337.

"A Contribution to the Theory of Competitive Price," *Quarterly Journal of Economics*, 28 (August): 747–771.[2]

"Some Neglected Phases of Rate Regulation," *American Economic Review*, 4 (September): 565–574.

"The Panama Canal and the Railroads," *The Commercial and Financial Chronicle*, Section 2 (28 November): 47–50.

Comments on "Recent Trust Decisions and Business," by Willard E. Hotchkiss, *The American Economic Review*, 4, Supplement no. 1, (March): 192–193.

"Davenport's Economics," review of *The Economics of Enterprise*, by Herbert J. Davenport, *Political Science Quarterly*, 29 (June): 315–323.

Review of *Work and Wealth – A Human Valuation*, by John A. Hobson, *Quarterly Journal of Economics*, 29 (November): 177–180.

1915 "The Concept of Value," and "A Rejoinder," *Quarterly Journal of Economics*, 29 (August): 663–673; 709–723.[3]

"A Scholar's Dedication," *The Amherst Monthly*, 30 (December): 211–212.[4]

1916 "The Changing Basis of Economic Responsibility," *Journal of Political Economy*, 24 (March): 209–229.[5]

Review of *A Theory of Interest*, by Clarence G. Hoag, *Political Science Quarterly*, 31 (September): 479–480.

[? 1916] "Is Competition Dead?" Typescript, 21 pp.

1917 "Business Acceleration and the Law of Demand: A Technical Factor in Economic Cycles," *Journal of Political Economy*, 25 (March): 217–235.[6]

"The Basis of War-Time Collectivism," *American Economic Review*, 7 (December): 772–790.

Review of *Transportation Rates and Their Regulation*, by Harry G. Brown, *Journal of Political Economy*, 25 (February): 208–209.

Review of *Second Thoughts of an Economist*, by William Smart, *Journal of Political Economy*, 25 (April): 402–404.

Review of *Prevention and Control of Monopolies*, by W. Jethro Brown, *Political Science Quarterly*, 32 (June): 353–354.

1918 with Walton H. Hamilton and Harold G. Moulton (eds.). *Readings in the Economics of War*. Chicago: The University of Chicago Press.

"Economics and Modern Psychology," *Journal of Political Economy*, 26 (January, February): 1–30; 136–166.[7]

"Concentration of Control in the Railroad Industry," in *Lessons in Community and National Life*. Series A. Prepared under the direction of Charles H. Judd and Leon C. Marshall, Lesson A-26, 219–224. U.S. Bureau of Education, Department of the Interior. Washington, D.C.: Government Printing Office.

"Outline of material for treatise in assumptions of dynamic economics, problems indicated by these assumptions, methodology dictated by the assumptions and the problems, theories in this field already worked out, organization of this material in the central body of economic thought." Handwritten, 2 pp.[8]

Review of *War Time Control of Industry: The Experience of England*, by Howard L. Gray, *Journal of Political Economy*, 26 (November): 918–920.

1919 "Economic theory in an Era of Social Readjustment," and "Rejoinder," *American Economic Review*, 9, Supplement (March): 280–290; 323–324.

"What I Would Like To Do About the High Cost of Living If I Had It To Deal With." Mimeographed, 10 pp.[9]

Review of *Social Process*, by Charles Horton Cooley, *Journal of Political Economy*, 27 (March): 218–221.

Review of *Outlines of Economics*, 3d revised ed., by Richard T. Ely, T.S. Adams, M.O. Lorenz, and A.A. Young, *Journal of Political Economy*, 27 (April): 317–322.

1920 "Coal Production and the Strike Settlement," *Journal of Political Economy*, 28 (January): 80–84.

et al., "The Railway Problem – Discussion," *American Economic Review*, 10, Supplement (March): 186–212.

"Railroad Valuation as a Working Tool," *Journal of Political Economy*, 28 (April): 265–306.

1921 "Soundings in Non-Euclidean Economics," *American Economic Review*, 11, Supplement (March): 132–147.

"An Example of Municipal Research," review of "Report of Commission on Local Transportation of the City of Chicago," *Journal of Political Economy*, 29 (March): 241–249.

Review of *Industry and Trade*, by Alfred Marshall, *Journal of Political Economy*, 29 (October): 684–689.

1922 "The Empire of Machines," *The Yale Review*, New Series, 12 (October): 132–143. Also, "The inspiration of this sketch. . . .", *xxviii*.[10]

"Are We Outgrowing Private Capital?," *The World Tomorrow*, 5 (December): 362–363.

"Appendix B" [report to the Special Board] to "Canal Connecting Lake Erie with the Ohio River," Report of The Special Board of [U.S.] Engineer Officers (appendix not printed, but extracts embodied in the report, 27–28; 30–32; 35), 67th Cong., 2nd sess., House Document no. 188. Washington, D.C.: Government Printing Office. (Report dated 7 May, 1921.)

"The New Leviathan" [outline].[11] Typescript, with many handwritten insertions, 6 pp.

Review of *The American Railroad Problem*, by I. Leo Sharfman, *Journal of Political Economy*, 30 (April): 315–316.

Review of *Modern Economic Tendencies*, by S.A. Reeve, *Literary Review* (6 May): 637.

Review of *A Plan for Railroad Consolidations*, by John E. Oldham, *Amherst Graduates' Quarterly*, no. 43 (May): 194–196.

Review of *Railroad Valuation*, by H.B. Vanderblue, *Journal of Political Economy*, 30 (June): 464–465.

Review of *Prices and Wages*, by Percy Wallis and Albert Wallis, *Journal of Political Economy*, 30 (December): 850–853.

"Jones' Moral Sense." Typescript, 2 pp.

1923 *Studies in the Economics of Overhead Costs.* Chicago: The University of Chicago Press.[12]

"Some Social Aspects of Overhead Costs: An Application of Overhead Costs to Social Accounting, with special reference to the Business Cycle," *American Economic Review*, 13, Supplement (March): 50–59.

Review of *The Threefold Commonwealth*, by Rudolph Steiner, *Journal of Political Economy*, 31 (August): 575–577.

1924 "The Socializing of Theoretical Economics," in *The Trend of Economics*, edited by Rexford Guy Tugwell, 73–105. New York: Knopf.[13]

Review of *The Economic Basis of Public Interest*, by Rexford Guy Tugwell, *Journal of Political Economy*, 32 (February): 133–135.

Review of *Regulation and the Management of Public Utilities*, by Charles S. Morgan, *Journal of Political Economy*, 32 (April): 259–261.

Review of *Absentee Ownership*, by Thorstein Veblen, *American Economic Review*, 14 (June): 289–293.

Review of *Railroads: Rates – Service – Management*, by Homer B. Vanderblue and Kenneth F. Burgess, *Journal of the American Statistical Association*, 19 (June): 259–262.

Review of *A Theory of Social Economy*, by Gustav Cassel, *Political Science Quarterly*, 39 (December): 688–690.

1925 "Problems of Economic Theory – Discussion," *American Economic Review*, 15, Supplement (March): 56–58.

et al., "Report of the Committee on Method of Nomination," *American Economic Review*, 15, Supplement (March): 147.

"Reply to Professor Knight's Remarks [and] Concluding Note," *Journal of Political Economy*, 33 (October): 554–557; 561–562.

"Further Discussion of Three-Dimensional Price Diagrams," *American Economic Review*, 15 (December): 717–719.

Review of *Early Economic Thought*, edited by A.E. Monroe, *Journal of Political Economy*, 33 (April): 256.

et al., "Draft Report on the Pending Local Transportation Ordinance." Submitted by the Local Transportation Committee to the City Club of Chicago, 9 March. 7 pp., mimeographed.

"Memorandum of possible rules for appraisal of public utility property properties [sic] for purposes of purchase by municipalities under the terms of indeterminate permits of franchises." Prepared for the Local Transportation Committee of the City Club of Chicago, May. 5 pp., mimeographed.

[1925?]"Memorandum on Plans for Gradual Extinguishing of Company's Equity in Traction Properties, by 'Amortization' or Otherwise." Submitted to the [Local Transportation] Committee of the City Club of Chicago. 10 pp., mimeographed.

1926 *Social Control of Business.* Chicago: The University of Chicago Press. (2nd ed., New York: McGraw-Hill, 1939.)[14]

"Valuation for the Balance-Sheet and Profit," in *Proceedings*, Second International Congress of Accountants, 369–377. Purmerend, Netherlands: J. Muusses.

"Constitutional Guarantees and Economic Needs." Typescript, 19 pp.[15]

1927 "Adam Smith and the Spirit of '76," in *The Spirit of '76*, by Carl L. Becker, John Maurice Clark, and William E. Dodd, 61–98. Washington, D.C.: Robert Brookings Graduate School of Economics and Government.[16]

"Recent Developments in Economics," in *Recent Developments in the Social Sciences*, edited by Edward C. Hayes, 213–306. Philadelphia: Lippincott.

"The Relation Between Statics and Dynamics," in *Economic Essays, Contributed in Honor of John Bates Clark*, edited by Jacob Harry Hollander, 46–70. New York: Macmillan, on behalf of the American Economic Association.[17]

"Control of Trade Practices by Competitive and Other Forces," *Proceedings of the Academy of Political Science*, 12 (January): 100–107.

"Some Central Problems of Overhead Costs: An Inquiry into Aspects of One of the Most Delicate Problems of Business Policy," *Bulletin of the Taylor Society*, 12 (February): 287–292.

"Economic Conditions and Economic Thinking," "Chap. I". Typescript, 22 pp.[18]

"Adam Smith and the Currents of History," In John Maurice Clark et al., *Adam Smith, 1776–1926*, 53–76. Chicago: The University of Chicago Press.[19]

"Inductive Evidence on Marginal Productivity," *American Economic Review*, 18 (September): 449–467.[20]

Review of *Pollack Prize Essays*, by R.W. Souter, F.L. Olmsted, C.F. Bickerdike, and V.V. Novogilov; and *The Road to Plenty*, by William T. Foster and Waddill Catchings, *Journal of the American Statistical Association*, 23 (June): 220–224.

Review of *Overhead Costs and the Shift to Machinery*, by D.D. Kennedy, *American Economic Review*, 18 (December): 758–759.

"Senator Borah's Plan," letter to *The New York Times*, (11 April), 28.

1929   "Government Control of Industry," *The World Tomorrow*, 12 (February): 74–76.

"Thorstein Bunde Veblen, 1857–1929," *American Economic Review*, 19 (December): 742–745.

1930   "Effects of Public Spending on Capital Formation," in *Capital Formation and Its Elements*, 54–72. New York: National Industrial Conference Board.

Why I do not Believe in Gambling. Chicago: The American Institute of Sacred Literature. (Popular Religion Leaflets, 16 pp.)

1931   *The Costs of the World War to the American People*. New Haven: Yale University Press, for The Carnegie Endowment for International Peace: Division of Economics and History.[21]

"Wesley C. Mitchell's Contribution to the Theory of Business Cycles," in *Methods in Social Science: A Case Book*, edited by Stuart A. Rice, 662–673. Chicago: The University of Chicago Press.[22]

"The Contribution of Economics to Method in Social Science," in W.F.G. Swann et al., *Essays on Research in the Social Sciences*, 67–85. Washington, D.C.: The Brookings Institution.

"The War's Aftermath in America," *Current History*, 34 (May): 169–174.

"Capital Production and Consumer-Taking: a Reply," *Journal of Political Economy*, 39 (December): 814–816.

"By-Products" (III: 129–130), "Diminishing Returns" and "Distribution" (V: 144–146, 167–174), "Government Regulation of Industry" and "Increasing Returns" (VII: 122–129, 639–640), "Monopoly" (X: 623–630), "Overhead Costs" (XI: 511–513), "Adam Smith" and "Statics and Dynamics" (XIV: 112–114, 352–356). *Encyclopaedia of the Social Sciences*. Edited by Edwin R.A. Seligman. 15 Vols. New York: Macmillan, 1930–1934.

"Special Statement," in *Supplementary Economic Brief No. 1*: Quantity Discount, at 22, *United States v. Sugar Institute, Inc, et al.*, 51 F.2d 1066 (S.D.N.Y. 1931), *modified and aff'd*, 297 U.S. 553 (1936).

"The Development of Governmental Characteristics Within Business," in *Business Management as a Human Enterprise*: Business as a

Form of Government, 103–114. Conference 11. New York, N.Y.: Bureau of Personnel Administration (15 January). Mimeographed, 12 pp.

"Sombart's Die Drei Nationalökonomien," [review article] *Quarterly Journal of Economics*, 45 (May): 517–521.

Review of *Corporate Earning Power*, by William L. Crum, *Political Science Quarterly*, 46 (March): 152–153.

Review of *Planning and Control of Public Works*, by Leo Wolman, *Journal of the American Statistical Association*, 26 (March): 101–103.

Review of *Efficiency and Scarcity Profits*, by C.J. Foreman, *Columbia Law Review*, 31 (December): 1390–1391.

1932 (J.M. Clark, chairman; with J. Russell Smith, Edwin S. Smith, and George Soule.) *Long-Range Planning for the Regularization of Industry*: the report of a subcommittee of the Committee on Unemployment and Industrial Stabilization of the National Progressive Conference. *The New Republic*, 69, no. 893, part 2 (13 January). (Also published in Hearings on S. 6215, below, 1932.)[23]

"Business Cycles: The Problem of Diagnosis," *Journal of the American Statistical Association*, 27, Supplement (March): 212–217.

et al., "Institutional Economics [a Round Table Conference]," *American Economic Review*, 22, Supplement (March): 105–116.

"The European Economic Dilemma and the Interests of the United States," *Lloyd's Bank Ltd. Monthly Review*, New Series, 3 (May): 190–209.

"Capital Production and Consumer-Taking: A Further Word," *Journal of Political Economy*, 40 (October): 691–693.

"The Riddle of Business Cycles," *American Federationist*, 39 (October): 1107–1113.

"Production als Organisation von Nutzen und Kosten," [translated by Eva Flügg,] in *Wirtschaftstheorie der Gegenwart*, edited by Hans Mayer *et al*. 4 vols.[24] Wein: Julius Springer, 1927–1932. Vol. 2 (1932), 269–286.

"Characteristics of the American Economic System." Conference on Teaching of Economics to Engineers. Stevens Institute, Hoboken, New Jersey, 6 July. Synopsis, mimeographed.

"Principles of Money and Credit," (notes on second talk at the Stevens Institute of Technology). Handwritten, 2 pp.

[Oral Testimony in] U.S. Congress. Senate. Establishment of National Economic Council: Hearings before a subcommittee of the Committee on Manufactures on S. 6215. 71st Cong., 1st Sess., 22 October – 19 December, 1931, 210–220. (*Long-Range Planning for the Regularization of Industry* published on pp. 737–752.)

Review of *The Masquerade of Monopoly*, by Frank A. Fetter, *The Journal of Business*, 5 (April): 193–195.

Review of *Business Adrift*, by Wallace B. Donham, with an Introduction by Alfred North Whitehead, *The International Journal of Ethics*, 42 (April): 344–346.

"Comments on the Sugar Institute Brief." Typescript, 3 pp.[25]

1933   "The Proposal for a Composite Commodity Currency," in *Economic Essays in Honor of Gustav Cassel*, 75–87. London: Allen & Unwin.
"Convulsion in the Price Structure," *The Yale Review*, New Series, 22 (March): 496–510.
"The General Problem of Cost-Allocation." Paper presented at The Institute of Public Engineering. New York City: The Institute (20 January). Mimeographed.
Review of *Guide Through World Chaos*, by G.D.H. Cole, *Survey Graphic*, 22 (February): 115–116.
Review of *World Social Economic Planning*, edited by M.L. Fleddérus, *Journal of the American Statistical Association*, 28 (September): 360–362.

1934   "Productive Capacity and Effective Demand," in *Economic Reconstruction, Report of the Columbia University Commission*, Robert M. McIver, Chairman, 105–126. New York: Columbia University Press.[26]
Also (joint author), "General Report," 3–76; and "Statement" ("supplementary Statements and Reservations of Individual Members"), 81.
"A Possibility," *The Wharton News of Finance and Commerce*, 7, no. 6 (March): 12–13.
"Economics and the National Recovery Administration," *American Economic Review*, 24 (March): 11–25.
"Factors Making for Instability," *Journal of the American Statistical Association*, 29, Supplement (March): 72–74.
"The State and Economic Life," in *Proceedings of Second Study Conference*, 199, 249–252, 287–289. Paris: International Institute of Intellectual Cooperation.[27]
et al. "Report of Legislative Committee of Westport [Connecticut] Civic League on the Town's Current Borrowing," 20 July. 8 pp., typewritten.
[? 1934] "Alternative Proposal for Sections II & III Recommendations of Legislative Committee of Civic League [of Westport, Connecticut,] on Current Debt." Typescript, 2 pp.
"Report on Financial Plan for the Town of Westport," *Westporter-Herald* (Westport, Connecticut), 24 July, 6.

1935   *Strategic Factors in Business Cycles*. With an introduction by The Committee on Recent Economic Changes. New York: National Bureau of Economic Research in cooperation with The Committee on Recent Economic Changes.
Economics of Planning Public Works. A study made for the National Planning Board of the Federal Emergency Administration of Public Works. Washington, D.C.: U.S. Government Printing Office.
et al., Report of National Recovery Administration on Operation of Basing Point System in Iron and Steel Industry. Washington, D.C. Mimeographed version, 30 November 1934. Revised report, 20 February 1935.
"Cumulative Effects of Changes in Aggregate Spending as Illustrated by Public Works," *American Economic Review*, 25 (March): 14–20.[28]

"The Price of Fire Hose," letter to *The New York Times*, 6 April, 14.

1936 *Preface to Social Economics: Essays on Economic Theory and Social Problems.* Edited with an introduction by Moses Abramovitz and Eli Ginzberg. New York: Farrar & Rinehart.

"Past Accomplishments and Present Prospects of American Economics," *American Economic Review*, 26 (March): 1–11.[29]

"Remarks at Dinner of AEA," *American Economic Review*, 26, Supplement no. 1 (March): 334–336.

Review of *Enquiry on National Public Works* by the League of Nations Organisation for Communications and Transit and *Public Works Policy* by the International Labor Office [Geneva], *Political Science Quarterly*, 51 (June): 294–295.

Review of *Economic Planning*, by G.D.H. Cole, *Political Science Quarterly*, 51 (September): 465–467.

Review of *Lectures on Political Economy*, by Knut Wicksell, *Journal of Political Economy*, 44 (December): 812–814.

1937 "The Possibility of a Scientific Electrical Rate System," *American Economic Review*, 27, Supplement (March): 243–253.

et al., The National Recovery Administration: Report of the President's Committee of Industrial Analysis, 75th Cong., 1st sess., House Doc. no. 158. Washington, D.C.: Government Printing Office.[30]

et al., Studies in Income and Wealth. Vol I. Conference on Research in Income and Wealth, Discussion, 228–229. New York: National Bureau of Economic Research.

Review of *Pioneers of American Economic Thought in the Nineteenth Century*, by E. Teilhac (Translated by E.A.J. Johnson), *American Economic Review*, 27 (March): 123–124.

"The Uprooted Generation; What Can We Tell Our Children?" Typescript, 15 pp.

1938 *et al., John Bates Clark, A Memorial.* New York: privately printed (principal author, A[lden] H. Clark).

"Basing Point Methods of Price Quoting," *The Canadian Journal of Economics and Political Science*, 4 (November): 477–489.

"Industrial Self-Government: A Constitution and a Problem." New York City: Bureau of Personnel Administration, Conference 17, 18 March. Mimeographed, 11 pp.

"Justice to John Treanor," letter to *The New Republic*, 94 (2 March): 103–104.

Review of *The Limits of Economics*, by Oskar Morgenstern, *Journal of Political Economy*, 46 (February): 124–126.

Review of *Market Control in The Aluminum Industry*, by Donald H. Wallace, *American Economic Review*, 28 (March): 144–146.

1939 "Monopolistic Tendencies, Their Character and Consequences," *Proceedings of the Academy of Political Science*, 18, no. 2 (January): 2–9. (Whole vol. 18 [1938–1940], 124–131.)

"An Appraisal of the Workability of Compensatory Devices," *American Economic Review*, 29, Supplement (March): 194–208. Also Published in *Conference Board Bulletin*, 13 (14 April): 80–86.

"One Form of Competition Between Geographically Separated Large Producers," [abstract of paper] *Econometrica*, 7 (April): 174–175.

"What Degree of Cyclical Flexibility in Prices is Socially Desirable? What Degree of Cyclical Flexibility in Prices is Practically Attainable?," in *Revised Summary of Conference on Industrial Price Policies*. Summary prepared by Joel Dean and C.L. Lee of Conference on Price Research, 28 April, 11–14. New York: National Bureau of Economic Research, 11–14. Mimeographed.

Review of *The Causes of Economic Fluctuations, Possibilities of Anticipation and Control*, by W.I. King, *Journal of the American Statistical Association*, 34 (June): 431–432.

1940   "The Attack on the Problem of Full Use," in *The Structure of The American Economy, Part II: Toward Full Use of Resources*. National Resources Planning Board, 20–26. Washington, D.C.: U.S. Government Printing Office.

"Forms of Economic Liberty and What Makes Them Important," in *Freedom: Its Meaning*, by Benedetto Croce, Thomas Mann, Alfred N. Whitehead and others, 305–328. Planned and edited by Ruth Nanda Anshen. New York: Harcourt, Brace.[31]

"Some Speculations on the Requirements of Workable as Distinct from Ideal Competition," *Econometrica*, 8 (April): 187–189.

"Toward a Concept of Workable Competition," *American Economic Review*, 30 (June): 241–256.[32]

"Election Procedure of the American Economic Association," *American Economic Review*, 30 (June): 458–460.

"John A. Hobson: Heretic and Pioneer, 1858–1940," *Journal of Social Philosophy*, 5 (July): 356–359.

Review of *Value and Capital: An Inquiry into some Fundamental Principles of Economic Theory*, by John R. Hicks, *Political Science Quarterly*, 55 (March): 127–129.

Review of *Government and Economic Life: Development and Current Issues of American Economic Policy, vol. I*, by Leverett S. Lyon, Myron W. Watkins, and Victor Abramson, *Columbia Law Review*, 40 (May): 953–955.

"The Baruch Plan for a Defense-Emergency Price-Ceiling." Memo to Leon Henderson, 18 November. 18 pp.

"A Market Society." Talk given before the National League of Women Voters, 30 April. Typescript, 12 pp.

1941   "Investment in Relation to Business Activity and Employment," in W.C. Mitchell *et al.*, *Studies in Economics and Industrial Relations*, 37–51. University of Pennsylvania Bicentennial Conference. Philadelphia: University of Pennsylvania Press.

"Further Remarks on Defense Financing and Inflation," *Review of Economics and Statistics.*, 23 (August): 107–112.

"Instead of Inflation," *Survey Graphic*, 30 (August): 416–420.

"The Relation of Government to the Economy of the Future," *Journal of Political Economy*, 49 (December): 797–816.

"The Defense Program and Economic Policy," in *Price Problems in a Defense Economy*, edited by Edward S. Mason, 1–15. New York: The Conference on Price Research. Mimeographed for Private Circulation.

"J.M. Clark says Profits Tax Would Cause Waste of U.S. Production," *The New Leader*, 26 (11 October): 1.

"Buy Bonds to Help Check Rising Prices," letter to the *Westporter-Herald* [Westport, Connecticut], 25 October.

"The Menace of Inflation." New York: Public Affairs Committee, Inc., November. Mimeographed, 39 pp.[33]

"The Relation of Government to Business." Typescript, 11 pp.[34]

1942 *How to Check Inflation.* (Public Affairs pamphlet no. 64.) New York: Public Affairs Committee.

"How to Meet the Menace of Inflation," with T.O. Yntema and the "Roving Reporter." The University of Chicago Round Table, 11 January. Circulated in pamphlet form.

"Economics and Education for Citizenship [The Role of Economics]," in *Education for Citizen Responsibilities*, edited by Franklin L. Burdette, 31–38. Princeton: Princeton University Press.[35]

[J.M. Clark][36] "Pricing of Joint Products." Price Policy Series, no. 8. Washington, D.C.: Office of Price Administration, Price and Economic Policy Branch, Division of Research, November. 9 pp., mimeographed.

"Wages and Prices in All-Out War," *Survey Graphic*, 31 (February): 85–86.

"Economic Adjustments After Wars: The Theoretical Issues," *American Economic Review*, 32, Supplement (March): 1–12.

"Our Economic Freedom," *Annals of the American Academy of Political and Social Science*, 220 (March): 178–185.

"Problems of Price Control," *Proceedings of the Academy of Political Science*, 20 (May): 11–22, 56.

"Relations of History and Theory," *The Journal of Economic History*, 2, Supplement (December): 132–142.

"Wartime Price Control and the Problem of Inflation," *Law and Contemporary Problems*, 9 (Winter): 6–21.

"Mid-1941 Consumption Level Cannot be Maintained," *The New Leader*, 25 (23 May): 4.

"Income Increase Discussed," letter to *The New York Times*, 25 March, 20.

"Economic Liberties." "Notes for broadcast of Feb. 10, 1942, WABC, New York, 4.15 to 4.30 Eastern Standard Time". Typescript with handwritten insertions, 9 pp.

"Reply to Questionnaire of December 7, 1942" by the Conference on Science, Philosophy and Religion. Mimeographed, 5 pp.

1943 "The Democratic Concept in the Economic Realm," in *Science, Philosophy, and Religion* (Third Symposium, 1942; edited by Lyman Bryson and Louis Finkelstein), 163–182. Also, ["Comment"], 234–235. New York: Conference on Science, Philosophy and Religion in Their Relation to the Democratic Way of Life.

"The Contributions of Price Theory to Price Control," in *A Manual of Price Control*, 4–12. Washington, D.C.: Office of Price Administration.

et al., *Cost Behavior and Price Policy*. (A Study prepared by The Committee on Price Determination for The Conference on Price Research.) New York: National Bureau of Economic Research.

[January 1943][37] "Anti-Inflation Policy Approaches Maturity." [Washington, D.C.: Office of Price Administration.] Mimeographed, 21 pp.; Appendix A, 4 pp; Appendix B, 5 pp.[38]

"Retail Margin Control Program." Memorandum to John K. Galbraith, 21 January. [Washington, D.C.: Office of Price Administration.] Typewritten, 2 pp.

"Curtain-Raiser in Rehabilitation," *Survey Graphic*, 32 (June): 244–249.

"Imperfect Competition Theory and Basing-Point Problems," *American Economic Review*, 33 (June): 283–300.

"Rejoinder," *American Economic Review*, 33 (September): 616–619.

Introduction to *New Firms and Free Enterprise: Pre-War and Post-War Aspects*, by Alfred R. Oxenfeldt, 3–7. Washington, D.C.: American Council on Public Affairs.

Review of *Price Control: The War Against Inflation*, by Erik T.H. Kjellstrom, Gustave H. Gluck, Per Jacobsson, and Evan Wright, *Journal of Political Economy*, 51 (February): 76–77.

"Comments on Outline for Report of League of Nations Depressions Delegation, Part II, Section II." Typescript, 5 pp.

1944 *Demobilization of Wartime Economic Controls*. (Committee for Economic Development Research Study.) New York: McGraw-Hill.

"Educational Functions of Economics After the War," *American Economic Review*, 34, Supplement (March): 58–67.

"Relative Spheres of Business and Government," *American Economic Review*, 34, Supplement (March): 296–297.

"Price Controls in Transition," *Proceedings of the Academy of Political Science*, 21 (May): 89–99.

"How Not to Reconvert," *Political Science Quarterly*, 59 (June): 176–192.

1945 "Economic Controls in Postwar Transition," in *Economic Reconstruction*, edited by Seymour E. Harris, 181–195. New York: McGraw-Hill.

"Financing High-Level Employment," in *Financing American Prosperity: A Symposium of Economists*, edited by Paul T. Homan and Fritz Machlup, 71–125. New York: The Twentieth Century Fund.[39]

"General Aspects of Price Control and Rationing in the Transition Period," *American Economic Review*, 35, no. 2 (May): 152–162.

"Hansen's 'Three Methods of Expansion Through Fiscal Policy'," *American Economic Review*, 35 (December): 926–928.

Letter to Senator Wagner on the Murray Full Employment Bill in *Full Employment Act of 1945*, Hearings, subcommittee of Senate Committee on Banking and Currency, 79th Cong., 1st sess., 1028–1032. Washington, D.C.: Government Printing Office.

"Methods of Determining Objectives in Social Planning: The Economic Approach." Typescript with handwritten insertions, 11 pp.[40]

"Notes for opening lecture in course on Relevant Ec[onomic] Theories." [Economics 109.] Handwritten, 3 pp. (Dated 27 September.)

1946 "Realism and Relevance in the Theory of Demand," *Journal of Political Economy*, 54 (August): 347–353.

et al., "Statement by the Commission," in *Peoples Speaking to Peoples: A Report on International Mass Communication from the Commission on Freedom of the Press*, by Llewellyn White and Robert D. Leigh, *v–vii*. Chicago: The University of Chicago Press.

"Depression or Prosperity?," *The New Leader*, 29 (5 January): 4, 14.

et al., "Price Control Recommended," letter to *The New York Times*, 9 April, 26.

"A World in Revolution." (Alternate title: "The Interdependent World.") Typescript, 4 pp.

"Notes on the Strike Wave and the Wage Issue as a Form of Economic Politics." Typescript, 21 pp.

"Annual Wage." Typescript, 1 p.

1947 "Economic Principles of the New Civilization," in *Our Emergent Civilization*, edited by Ruth N. Anshen, 123–151. New York: Harper.

"The Relation of Wages to Progress," in *The Conditions of Industrial Progress*, 22–39. Philadelphia: The University of Pennsylvania Press.

"Mathematical Economists and Others: A Plea for Communicability," *Econometrica*, 15 (April): 75–78.

"Some Current Cleavages Among Economists," *American Economic Review*, 37, Supplement (May): 1–11.[41]

et al., *A Free and Responsible Press: A General Report on Mass Communications: Newspapers, Radio, Motion Pictures, Magazines, and Books*, by The Commission on Freedom of the Press, with a Foreward by Robert M. Hutchins. Chicago: The University of Chicago Press.

et al., "Summary of Principle: A Statement of The Commission," appendix to *Freedom of The Press: A Framework of Principle*, by William E. Hocking. A Report from the Commission on Freedom of the Press, 209–232. Also signed footnotes, *viii–ix*, 19, 22–23. Chicago: The University of Chicago Press.[42]

et al., "Statement by the Commission," in *The American Radio: A Report on the Broadcasting Industry in the United States from The Commission on Freedom of the Press*, by Llewellyn White, *v–xi*. Chicago: The University of Chicago Press.

et al., "Statement by the Commission," in *Freedom of the Movies: A Report on Self-Regulation from the Commission on Freedom of the Press*, by Ruth A. Inglis, *v–viii*. Chicago: The University of Chicago Press.

et al., "Statement by the Commission," in *Government and Mass Communications: A Report from the Commission on Freedom of the Press*, by Zechariah Chafee, Jr., vol. 1, *vii–x*. 2 vols. Chicago: The University of Chicago Press.

"Note on Income Redistribution and Investment," *American Economic Review*, 37 (December): 931.

"Comments" [on the Hansen-Samuelson Report], in *Guaranteed Wages, Report to the President by the Advisory Board*, 464–466. Office of War Mobilization and Reconversion, Office of Temporary Controls. Washington, D.C.: U.S. Government Printing Office.

Forward to *Private Investment in a Controlled Economy: Germany, 1933–1939*, by Samuel Lurie, *vii–viii*. New York: Columbia University Press.

"Consumer Credit," letter to *The New York Times*, 22 January, 22.

1948   *Alternative to Serfdom.* (vol. 3 of William W. Cook Foundation Lectures.) New York: Knopf.[43] 2nd ed., revised; New York: Vintage Books, 1960.

"Industry and the Worker," *The New Leader*, 31 (17 April): 7.

E.H. Chamberlin; J.M. Clark. "Critics" for "Value and Distribution," by Bernard F. Haley in *A Survey of Contemporary Economics.* Ed. by Howard S. Ellis.[44] Published for The American Economic Association. Philadelphia: The Blakiston Company.

"Preparedness the Answer," letter published as an editorial, *The Amherst Student*, 77, no. 24 (14 April): 2.

"Remarks of J. M. Clark at W. C. Mitchell Memorial Meeting," 4 December. Carbon, 8 pp, with Clark's changes.[45]

1949   *Guideposts in Time of Change: Some Essentials for a Sound American Economy*. (Six lectures delivered at Amherst College in the winter of 1947–1948 on the Merrill Foundation.) New York: Harper.

et al., *National and International Measures for Full Employment.* Lake Success, New York: United Nations, Department of Economic Affairs.

"Free Enterprise and a Planned Economy," in *The Christian Demand for Social Justice*, edited by Bishop William Scarlett, 46–59. New York: New American Library.[46]

"The Law and Economics of Basing Points: Appraisal and Proposals," *American Economic Review*, 39 (March): 430–447.

with Leon H. Keyserling and Jacob Viner, "The President's Economic Program," *Current Business Studies*, no. 3 (June); comments by J.M. Clark, 24–31.

"The Delivered Price Problem (Floor Discussion)," in *Antitrust Law Symposium.* (Section on Antitrust Law of the New York State Bar Association, conference of 26 January), 53–54. New York: Commerce Clearing House.

"Varieties of Economic law, and Their Limiting Factors," *Science*, 110 (25 November): 549. (Abstract of paper presented at Autumn meeting of The American Philosophical Society, full text in 1950 entry.)

"Common and Disparate Elements in National Growth and Decline," in *Problems in the Study of Economic Growth*. New York: Universities-National Bureau of Economic Research Committee. Mimeographed.

("From a Special Correspondent" [J.M. Clark]),[47] "Enforcing Competition," *The Economist*, 157 (24 September): 669–670.

"Machlup on the Basing-Point System," Review article of *The Basing-point System: An Economic Analysis of a Controversial Pricing Practice*, by Fritz Machlup, *Quarterly Journal of Economics*, 63 (August): 315–321.

Review of *Income, Employment and Public Policy: Essays in Honor of Alvin H. Hansen*, by Lloyd A. Metzler *et al.*, *American Economic Review*, 39 (March): 499–507.

Review of *Individualism and Economic Order*, by Friedrich A. Hayek, *Political Science Quarterly*, 64 (March): 108–110.

Review of *Democracy and Progress*, by David McCord Wright, *Journal of Political Economy*, 57 (August): 366–367.

Review of *Maintaining Competition*, by Corwin D. Edwards, *Annals of the American Academy of Political and Social Science*, 265 (September): 203–204.

Review of *Controlling Factors in Economic Development*, by Harold G. Moulton, *The Survey*, 85 (December): 685–686.

"Notes based on off-the-record remarks of J. M. Clark at Group meeting, April 4, 1949. General topic: 'where is this country going, and where should it be going?'" ("Talk to [?Louis] Finkelstein's group".) Typescript, 12 pp.

"The Obligation Assumed by Member Nations Under the United Nation Charter." Typescript, 10 pp.

1950   "Varieties of Economic Law, and their Limiting Factors," *Proceedings of the American Philosophical Society*, 94 (April): 121–126.

"The Orientation of Antitrust Policy," and ["Discussion"], *American Economic Review*, 40, Supplement (May): 93–99, 103–104.

"Employment Policy in a Divided World," *Social Research*, 17 (June):157–167.

"Economic Means – To What Ends? A Problem in the Teaching of Economics," *American Economic Review*, 40, Part 2 (December):34–51.[48]

"Letter on Rufus M. Jones," in *Rufus M[atthew] Jones, In Memoriam*, 27–29. Haverford, [Pennsylvania]. Privately printed.

Review of *The New Society*, by Peter F. Drucker, and *The Social Costs of Private Enterprise*, by K. William Kapp, *The Yale Review*, New Series, 40 (September): 171–174.

1951   *et al.*, "Committee Report," Chapter 9 of *Financing Defense: Federal Tax and Expenditure Policies*, 149–161. New York: The Twentieth Century Fund.

et al., "Policy for the Crisis," Chapter 9 of *Defense Without Inflation*, by Albert G. Hart, 165–186. New York: The Twentieth Century Fund.

"Criteria of Sound Wage Adjustment, with Emphasis on the Question of Inflationary Effects," 1–33; "Comment on Professor Friedman's Position," 361–368; and ["Discussion"], in *The Impact of the Union: Eight Economic Theorists Evaluate the Labor Union Movement*, edited by David McCord Wright. New York: Harcourt, Brace.

"Economics," in *College Teaching and Christian Values*, edited by Paul M. Limbert, 72–95. New York: Association Press.[49]
"Ideas on organization of General Treatise". Dated 8 November. Handwritten, 5 pp.
"J.M.C.'s Views on Business Motives as revealed in his Replies to Questionnaire from Indiana University School of Business, March, 1951." Typescript, 1 p.
"Reports on Discussions of the 'Theory of the Firm' at Three Economic, Econometric, Etc., Sessions." (December.) 1 p, duplicated.[50]

1952 "J.M. Clark on J.B. Clark," in *The Development of Economic Thought: Great Economists in Perspective*, edited by Henry W. Spiegel, 593–612. New York: Wiley.
[Memorial Address on Wesley Clair Mitchell,] in *Wesley Clair Mitchell: The Economic Scientist*, edited by Arthur F. Burns, 139–143. New York: National Bureau of Economic Research.[51]
"Contribution to the Theory of Business Cycles," in *ibid.*, 193–206.[52]
with Eugene L. Grant and Maurice M. Kelso, *Report of Panel of Consultants on Secondary or Indirect Benefits of Water-Use Projects*. Washington, D.C.: U.S. Bureau of Reclamation, 26 June. Mimeographed, 63 pp. (Limited Circulation.)[53]
"Attacking Federal Agencies," letter to *The New York Times*, 16 December, 30.
["Comments" by J. M. Clark on "The O.P.S. Intervention in the Connecticut Public Utilities Commission Hearings,"] *Monthly Economic Report*. Hartford, Connecticut: Office of Price Stabilization, 14 June, 14. Mimeographed.

1953 "Aims of Economic Life as seen by Economists," in *Goals of Economic Life*, edited by Alfred Dudley Ward, 23–51[54]; "memorandum [extracts]," 16–17; 405. New York: Harper.
"Basic Problems and Policies," Chapter 11 of *Economic Controls and Defense*, by Donald H. Wallace, 242–256. New York: The Twentieth Century Fund.
"The Economic Future Looks Good," *The New Leader*, 36 (2 March): 16–18.
Review of *Religion and Economic Responsibility*, by Walter G. Muelder; *The Organizational Revolution*, by Kenneth E. Boulding; and *Social Responsibilities of the Businessman*, by Howard R. Bowen, *The Yale Review*, New Series, 43 (September): 118–121.
Review of *Economics in the Public Service: The Intimate Story of the First Six Years of the Employment Act*, by Edwin G. Nourse, *American Economic Review*, 43 (December): 953–957.
"Comments," *Christian Economics* (New York City), vol. 5, no. 23 (29 December), 1, 3.
"Task of Educators Stressed," letter to *The New York Times*, 4 March, 26.

1954 "Competition and the Objectives of Government Policy," in *Monopoly and Competition and Their Regulation*, edited by Edward H.

Chamberlin, 317–337. (Papers and Proceedings of the 1951 Conference of the International Economic Association.) London: Macmillan.

"America's Changing Capitalism: The Interplay of Politics and Economics," in *Freedom and Control in Modern Society*, edited by Morroe Berger, Theodore Abel, and Charles H. Page, 192–205. New York: D. Van Nostrand.[55]

"McCarthy Methods Queried," letter to *The New York Times*, 9 June, 30.

1955 *The Ethical Basis of Economic Freedom*. Westport, Connecticut: Calvin K. Kazanjian Economic Foundation.[56]

et al., *Report of the Attorney General's National Committee to Study the Antitrust Laws*. Also signed comments, 219–220; 393. Washington, D.C.: Government Printing Office.

"Economic Welfare in a Free Society," in *National Policy for Economic Welfare at Home and Abroad*, edited by Robert Lekachman, 293–334; 349–350. Garden City, New York: Doubleday.[57]

"Legal and Economic Views: With Remarks on Delivered Pricing," in "Crucial Centers of Controversy in the Antitrust Report of the Attorney General's Committee," *Current Business Studies*, no. 22 (April): 14–19.

"Competition: Static Models and Dynamic Aspects," *American Economic Review*, 45, no. 2 (May): 450–462.[58]

1956 "Economic Thought in the East – Discussion," *American Economic Review*, 46, Supplement (May): 416–418.

"Commentary" on "Economic Peace," by Courtney C. Brown, and "Prosperity is no Panacea," by Leo Cherne, *Social Action*, 22 (April): 16–17.

1957 *Economic Institutions and Human Welfare*. New York: Alfred A. Knopf.

"Commentary" on "The Economy of Abundance: An Ethical Problem," by Eduard Heimann, *Social Action*, 23 (January): 16–18.

"Balanced Growth vs. Creeping Inflation," in *Problems of United States Economic Development*. vol. 1, 129–135. New York: Committee for Economic Development.

"The Uses of Diversity: Competitive Bearings of Diversities in Cost and Demand Functions," *American Economic Review*, 48, Supplement (May): 474–482.

"To Save East Front of Capital," letter to *The New York Times*, 12 March, 30.

1958 "Wage Theory in an Age of Organized Labor," in *The Public Stake in Union Power*, edited by Philip D. Bradley, 301–323. Charlottesville, Virginia: The University of Virginia Press.

1959 Review of *Thorstein Veblen: A Critical Reappraisal*, edited by Douglas F. Dowd, *Political Science Quarterly*, 74 (September): 426–429.

1960 *The Wage-Price Problem*. New York: Committee for Economic Growth without Inflation, The American Bankers Association.

1961 *Competition as a Dynamic Process*. Washington, D.C.: The Brookings Institution.

1962   "Statement of John M. Clark on the Relation of Industrial Concentration to the Purposes of the Employment Act," in U.S. Congress, Joint Economic Committee. *State of the Economy and Policies for Full Employment*, 905–908. 87th Congress, 2nd sess., Hearings pursuant to Sec. 5(a) of Public Law 304 (79th Congress), 7–22 August. Washington D.C.: U.S. Government Printing Office.
      Review of *The Corporation in the Emergent American Society*, by W. Lloyd Warner, *Annals of the American Academy of Political and Social Science*, 344 (November): 186–187.

1963   "'Administered Prices' in their Relation to Competition and Monopoly," in *Administered Prices: A Compendium on Public Policy*, 86–96. Subcommittee on Antitrust and Monopoly, Committee on the Judiciary. U.S. Senate, 88th Congress, 1st sess. (pursuant to S. Res. 56). Washington, D.C.: Government Printing Office.
      "Comments" on "The Uses of Price Theory," by Kenneth E. Boulding, in *Models of Markets*, edited by Alfred R. Oxenfeldt, 166–171. New York: Columbia University Press.

1968   "John Bates Clark," in *International Encyclopedia of the Social Sciences*, edited by David L. Sills, vol. 2, 504–508. 17 vols. New York: Macmillan & the Free Press.

Bibliography of
J. M. Clark: Addendum I

As a member of the Commission on Freedom of the Press, Clark contributed the following mimeographed statements and memoranda between 1944 and 1946:[59]

Doc. 16 "Statement on the Importance of the Commission's Work," 26 April 1944, 15–17.

Doc. 37–D: "Clark Memorandum [on 'Question of motivation of press owners; effect of business ownership and management on editorial policy; relation of owner and editor']," 29 March 1945, 10–11.

Doc. 37–J: "Clark Memorandum [on 'The role of professionalization and self regulation in improving the quality of mass communications; proper definition of "profession" in relation to the press']," n.d. [March–April, 1945], 20.

Doc. 91–E: [Letter to J.M. Clark from G.B. Utter; reply by J.M. Clark], 26 March 1946, 3 pp.

Doc. 98C–1: "Comments," 25 June 1946, 2 pp.

Doc. 98–D: "Further Comments on Hocking's Outline of Principles," n.d. [June, 1946], 2 pp.

Doc. 100–A: "Comments on Document no. 100, Outline of Principles (Revised) – W.E. Hocking," 13 June 1946, 3 pp.

Doc. 102–A: "Comments by J.M. Clark on Hocking's Framework of Principle," n.d. [June, 1946], 2 pp.

Doc. 111–D: "Comments on Document no. 111 by J.M. Clark," 4 September 1946, 3 pp.

Doc. 112: "Comments on Hocking's Document 100–F," 27 August 1946, 1 p.

Bibliography of J. M. Clark: Addendum II

MANUSCRIPTS OF UNCERTAIN DATE

n.d. "Kropotkins' 'Mutual Aid as a Factor in Evolution.'" Handwritten, 8 pp. [Book review of *Mutual Aid: A Factor in Evolution*, by Prince Petr A. Kropotkin (New York, 1902).]

[? 1919] "The Behavioristic Man – A Reply." Typescript, 5 pp. Handwritten, 1 p.[60]

[? 1920s] "What is Man? A genetic approach from a biological and psychological standpoint, intended as an introduction to a modern economic treatise." Typescript, 5 pp.

[? 1920s] "What is 'Truth' in Economic Theory?" Typescript, 34 pp.

[early 1920s] "The Present Situation of the Chicago Surface Lines." Typescript, 12 pp.

[early 1920s ?] "Irregular Employment as a Load-factor Problem," Selection 3, pp. 9–10, of Chapter X, "Labor as an Overhead Cost." Readings for Political Economy 5, Department of Political Economy, The University of Chicago.[61] Mimeographed.

[? early 1920s] "Utility and Human Nature." Typescript, 40 pp.

[? 1930] "The Problem of Using Construction Work as a Balance- Wheel of Business Activity." Handwritten, 24 pp.[62]

[?1952] "Economics," 12 pp. "Marketing," 9 pp. "Monopoly and Competition," 21 pp. Typescript.[63]

[1950s] "On Economic Problems of the Next Twenty Years." Typescript, 7 pp.

n.d. "Suggestions Re Problems of Committee on Economics of American Society of American Engineers." Typescript, 3 pp.

[? 1956–1957] "Dilemmas of Abundance." Typescript, 5 pp.[64]

Notes for Appendix B and Biography of J. M. Clark

1. Ph.D. dissertation, Columbia University.
2. Reprinted in *Preface to Social Economics* (1936).
3. Enlarged portions of "A Rejoinder" published as "Toward a Concept of Social Value" in *Preface to Social Economics*, 44–65. "This essay, hitherto unpublished, is the non-controversial portion of a projected enlargement of my rejoinder to B.M. Anderson's criticism of my essay, *The Concept of Value* [1915]." *Preface to Social Economics* (1936), 44.
4. Reprinted with errors, in *Literary Monthly* (University of Chicago), (February 1916): 7.
5. Reprinted in *Preface to Social Economics* (1936).
6. Reprinted, with a note added in 1936, in *Preface to Social Economics*. The 1936 version is reprinted in *Readings in Business Cycle Theory*, edited by Gottfried Haberler et al. (Homewood, Ill.: Irwin, 1951). The 1917 version, without the 1936 note, is reprinted in *Landmarks in Political Economy: Selections from The Journal of Political Economy*, edited by Earl J. Hamilton, Albert Rees, and Harry G. Johnson (Chicago: The University of Chicago Press, 1962).
7. Reprinted in *Preface to Social Economics* (1936).
8. Note in Clark's hand at the bottom of page 2: "Total, 108,000 words, or near 400 pages." Outline dated 11 October 1918.
9. "New York, Aug 17, 1919".
10. Reprinted in *Essays in Contemporary Civilization*, edited by Charles Wright Thomas (New York: The Macmillan Co., 1931), 146–157.
11. The title continued: "Other titles: Our Economic Organism, or Studies in Social Economic Dynamics. Outline done at Mansfield, O[hio], Mar. 1922, revised Jan. 2, 1923 and Mar. 1, 1925."
12. Portions published earlier in 1923: "Overhead Costs in Modern Industry: I. The Scope of the Problem;" "II. The Laws of Return and Economy;" "III. How and Why Large Plants Bring Economy;" *The Journal of Political Economy*, 31 (February, April, October): 47–64; 209–242; 606–636.
   Abridged and translated into Italian: "Stud sull 'Economia dei Costi Constanti," abridged and translated by G. Demaria and A. Piana, *Nuova Collana di Economisti, Straniere e Italiani*, edited by Giuseppe Bottai and Celestino Arena, Vol. 5: *Dinamica Economica* (Torino: Unione Tipografico – Editrice Torinese, 1932), 183–417.
   First twelve chapters reprinted as *The Incidence of Overhead Costs* (Melbourne, Australia: Accountants Publishing Co., 1940).
13. Reprinted in *Preface to Social Economics* (1936).

14. Portions published earlier in 1925: "What is Competition?:" "Law and Economic Life. I;" "Law and Economic Life. II;" *The Journal of Business*, 3 (June, September): 217–240; 350–377; 4 (December): 47–70.
15. Paper read at the 23rd annual meeting of the American Political Science Association, 30 December 1926. Listed as "Constitutional Guarantees and Modern Economic Needs," in *The American Political Science Review*, 21 (February 1927): 152.
16. Revised version in *Adam Smith*, 1776–1926 (1928), reprinted in *Preface to Social Economics* (1936).
17. Reprinted in *Preface to Social Economics* (1936).
18. In longhand an alternative title was inserted with the conjunction "or": "Economic Keynotes, Past and Present." The 1927 date is Clark's.
19. First version appeared in *The Journal of Business*, 6 (October 1926), 348–369. Revised in *The Spirit of '76*. Further revised in this (1928) version and reprinted in *Preface to Social Economics* (1936).
20. Article reviewing "A Theory of Production," by Charles W. Cobb and Paul H. Douglas, *American Economic Review*, 18, Supplement (March 1928): 139–165. Reprinted in *Preface to Social Economics* (1936).
21. Reprinted, with an Introductory essay by Joseph Dorfman, "Some Documentary Notes on the Relations Among J. M. Clark, N. A. L. J. Johansen and J. M. Keynes," (New York: Augustus M. Kelley, Publishers, 1970).
22. Reprinted in *Preface to Social Economics* (1936). Modified version later reprinted in *Wesley Clair Mitchell: The Economic Scientist* (1952).
23. Reprinted in *Preface to Social Economics* (1936).
24. Vol. 1 states: "Friedrich [von] Wieser [1851–1926], In Memoriam."
25. For date, see Clark to E.R.A. Seligman, 1 February, 1932. Copy in J.M. Clark Papers.
26. Reprinted in *Preface to Social Economics* (1936).
27. Reprinted in *Les Nouveau Courants de la Théorie Économique aux États-Unis*, edited by Pirou Gaëtan, (Conférences faites à l'Études en 1934–1935), (Paris: Les Éditions Domat-Monchrestien, F. Loviton, 1935).
28. Reprinted in *Preface to Social Economics* (1936).
29. Reprinted in *Preface to Social Economics* (1936).
30. Also issued as *Report of the President's Committee of Industrial Analysis*. Washington, D.C.: The National Recovery Administration, 17 February. Mimeographed, 240 pp. The other authors were William H. Davis: Pennie, Davis, Marvin and Edmonds; George M. Harrison: President, Brotherhood of Railway and Steamship Clerks; and George H. Mead: President, Mead Corporation. This was their "final review of the effects of the administration of Title I of the National Industrial Recovery Act."
31. Revised version reprinted in *Economic Institutions and Human Welfare* (1957). Not in the British edition; London: George Allen and Unwin, 1942.

32. Enlarged and revised version reprinted in Edgar M. Hoover, Jr. and Joel Dean (eds.), *Readings in the Social Control of Industry* (Philadelphia: Blakiston, 1942), 452–475.
33. On the title page: "This is a first draft, subject to correction and revision. It is not to be quoted in any manner whatsoever." Revised version issued in 1942.
34. Note by Clark: "For [Arthur William] Kornhauser's year-book. Unpublished Jan. 1941 ["]. J.M. Clark Papers.
35. Revised version reprinted in *Economic Institutions and Human Welfare* (1957).
36. Authorship attributed on the basis of a comparison of style and content with previous works by Clark on the subject.
37. Year, and other publication data determined on the basis of internal evidence.
38. "The history of OPA has been a succession of crises, in which the force of inflationary pressures, and of the efforts to resist them, have been progressively increasing." (p. 1.)
39. A condensation by Clark for the Associated Press appeared as: "High-Level Employment Seen Hinging on Balanced Spending," *The Christian Science Monitor*, 26 September, 11.
40. "Final copy" for talk at the New School for Social Research, Conference on Methods in Philosophy and the Sciences, Gail Kennedy, Chair, 25 November.
41. Expanded version of "Mathematical Economists and Others."
42. See Addendum I.
43. Austrian edition: *Sicherheit in Freiheit* (Vienna: Humboldt-Verlag, 1952).
44. Haley's article is on pp 1–48. On p 9, he refers to J.M. Clark's "critique of this chapter."
45. Published in 1952 in *Wesley Clair Mitchell: The Economic Scientist*.
46. Reprinted in *Economic Institutions and Human Welfare* (1957).
47. Authorship attributed on the basis of the following: "I have not written articles for the Times or other papers. I wrote some-thing on the American anti-trust situation which, in sadly-curtailed form, was published in the London Economist, a year or two ago." Clark to Richard E. Shannon, 19 July 1951; in possession of Richard E. Shannon. Copy in possession of Laurence Shute.
48. Revised version reprinted in *Economic Institutions and Human Welfare* (1957).
49. Modified version of "Economic Means – To What End? A Problem in the Teaching of Economics," (1950). Published as a separate pamphlet under original title: *Economic Means – To What Ends? A Problem in the Teaching of Economics* (Haddam, Connecticut: The Hazen Pamphlets [no. 28], 23 pp.).
50. In "quatrain verse-form." Refers to the session, "Issues in Methodology," at the sixty-fourth Annual Meeting of the American Economic Association in Boston, December 26–29, 1951.

    The papers in this session were: "Introductory Remarks," by Fritz Machlup, "Implications for General Economics of More Realistic

Theories of the Firm," by Kenneth E. Boulding, "Institutionalism and Empiricism in Economics," by Frank H. Knight, and "Economic Theory and Mathematics – An Appraisal," by Paul A. Samuelson. Discussion was by Allan G. Gruchy and Fritz Machlup. See: *The American Economic Review*, 42, no. 2 (May 1952).

51.   Earlier version: "Remarks of J.M. Clark at W.C. Mitchell's Memorial Meeting, 4 December 1948." Carbon copy of typescript, with Clark's changes, 8 pp.

52.   Modified version of "Wesley C. Mitchell's Contribution to the Theory of Business Cycles," first published in *Methods in Social Science*, edited by Stuart Rice (1931), and reprinted in *Preface to Social Economics* (1936).

53.   "To Michael W. Straus, Commissioner, Bureau of Reclamation." Grant was Professor of Economics of Engineering and Executive Head of the Department of Civil Engineering, Stanford University. Kelso was Professor of Agricultural Economics and Head, Department of Agricultural Economics and Rural Sociology at Montana State College.

54.   Revised version reprinted in *Economic Institutions and Human Welfare* (1957).

55.   Revised version reprinted in *Economic Institutions and Human Welfare* (1957).

56.   Reprinted in Economic *Institutions and Human Welfare* (1957).

57.   Revised version reprinted in *Economic Institutions and Human Welfare* (1957).

58.   Reprinted in *Readings in Industrial Organization and Public Policy*, selected for The American Economic Association by R.B. Heflebower and G.W. Stocking (Homewood, Illinois: Irwin, 1958), 244–261.

59.   These documents are located in the "Commission on Freedom of the Press – Papers," and the J.M. Clark Papers, Columbia University Libraries.

60.   A reply to "The Behavioristic Man," by Thomas N. Carver, *Quarterly Journal of Economics*, 33 (November 1918): 195–200.

61.   Clark began teaching Political Economy 5 – "Social Control of Business" at Chicago in the Autumn term, 1918, and continued the course until 1925 when he left for Columbia University.

62.   · Apparently in response to reading "Hoover's Fillip to Business," by Leo Wolman, *The Nation*, 129 (11 December 1929): 710–711.

63.   For Collier's Encyclopedia?

64.   (?) *Written for Social Action.*

Selected Bibliography

Library Sources

Amherst College Library: Amherst College Archives.

The University of Chicago Library: Manuscript and Archival Collections

Columbia University Libraries:
The Columbiana Collection
Oral History Collection
Special Collections, Rare Books and Manuscript Division

Yale University Library: The Beinecke Rare Book and Manuscript Library

Books

Abbott, Lawrence. *Quality and Competition: An Essay in Economic Theory.* New York: Columbia University Press, 1955.

Arrow, Kenneth J. *Social Choice and Individual Values.*(Cowles Commission Monograph No. 12.) New York: John Wiley & Sons, 1951.

Ayres, Clarence E. *The Nature of the Relationship Between Ethics and Economics.* Chicago: The University of Chicago Press, 1918.

A Bibliography of the Faculty of Political Science of Columbia University, 1880–1930. New York: Columbia University Press, 1931.

Blaug, Mark. *Great Economists Before Keynes: An Introduction to the Lives & Works of One Hundred Great Economists of the Past.* Cambridge: Cambridge University Press, 1986.

Blaug, Mark. *The Methodology of Economics, or, How Economists Explain.* 2nd ed. Cambridge: Cambridge University Press, 1992.

Blaug, Mark, editor. *Who's Who in Economics: A Biographical Dictionary of Major Economists, 1700–1986.* 2nd ed. Cambridge, Massachusetts: The MIT Press, 1986.

Bonbright, James C. *Principles of Public Utility Rates.* New York: Columbia University Press, 1961.

Boring, Edwin G. *A History of Experimental Psychology.* 2nd ed. New York: Appleton-Century-Crofts, 1950.

Burns, Arthur R. *The Decline of Competition: A Study of The Evolution of American Industry.* New York: McGraw-Hill, 1936.

Butler, Jon. *Awash in a Sea of Faith: Christianizing the American People.* Cambridge, Massachusetts: Harvard University Press, 1990.

Carr, Edward H. *What is History?* London: Macmillan, 1961.

Chamberlin, Edward H. *The Theory of Monopolistic Competition.* Cambridge, Mass.: Harvard University Press, [1933] 1956.

Clark, John Bates. *The Philosophy of Wealth: Economic Principles Newly Formulated.* 1886. Reprint. New York: Augustus M. Kelley Publishers, 1967.

Clark, John Bates. *Social Justice Without Socialism*. (Barbara Weinstock Lectures on the Morals of Trade.) Boston: Houghton Mifflin Company, (April) 1914.

John Bates Clark, A Memorial. Prepared by his children. Privately printed, 1938.

Coats, A.W. Bob. *On the History of Economic Thought. British and American Economic Essays*, Vol. I. London: Routledge, 1992.

Cooley, Charles Horton. *Social Process*. New York: Charles Scribner's Sons, 1918. Reprint. Carbondale Ill: Southern Illinois University Press, 1966.

Copeland, Morris A. *Our Free Enterprise Economy*. New York: Macmillan, 1965.

Critchlow, Donald T. *The Brookings Institution, 1916–1952: Expertise and the Public Interest in a Democratic Society*. Dekalb, Illinois: Northern Illinois University Press, 1985.

Davis, J. Ronnie. *The New Economics and the Old Economists*. Ames, Iowa: Iowa State University Press, 1971.

Deane, Phyllis. *The State and the Economic System*. Oxford: Oxford University Press, 1989.

Dewey, Donald. *The Theory of Imperfect Competition: A Radical Reconstruction*. New York: Columbia University Press, 1969.

Dillard, Dudley. *The Economics of John Maynard Keynes: The Theory of a Monetary Economy*. New York: Prentice-Hall, 1948.

Dorfman, Joseph. *The Economic Mind in American Civilization*. Vols. 3–5: 1865–1933. New York: The Viking Press, 1949–1959.

Duesenberry, James S. *Income, Saving, and the Theory of Consumer Behavior*. Cambridge, Mass.: Harvard University Press, 1967.

Everett, John R. Religion in Economics: A Study of John Bates Clark, Richard T. Ely, Simon N. Patten. New York: King's Crown Press, 1946.

Ferguson, C.E. *A Macroeconomic Theory of Workable Competition*. Durham, N.C.: University of North Carolina Press, 1964.

Flubacher, Joseph F. *The Concept of Ethics in The History of Economics*. New York: Vantage Press, 1950.

Fuchs, Victor R. *The Service Economy*. New York: National Bureau of Economic Research, Inc., 1968.

Fuess, Claude M. *Amherst: The Story of a New England College*. Boston: Little, Brown, and Company, 1935.

Fusfeld, Daniel R. *The Economic Thought of Franklin D. Roosevelt and the Origins of the New Deal*. Columbia Studies in the Social Sciences, edited by The Faculty of Political Science of Columbia University, no. 586. New York: Columbia University Press, 1956.

Galbraith, John K. *A Theory of Price Control*. Cambridge, Mass.: Harvard University Press, 1952.

Ginzberg, Eli. *Human Resources: The Wealth of a Nation*. New York: Simon and Schuster, 1958.

Gordon, Wendell and Adams, John. *Economics as Social Science: An Evolutionary Approach*. Riverdale, Maryland: The Riverdale Company, 1989.

Gruchy, Allan G. *Contemporary Economic Thought: The Contribution of Neo-Institutional Economics*. Clifton, N.J.: Kelley, 1972.

Gruchy, Allan G. *Modern Economic Thought: The American Contribution*. New York: Kelley, [1947] 1967.

Gruchy, Allan G. *The Reconstruction of Economics: An Analysis of the Fundamentals of Institutional Economics*. With a foreward by Donald R. Stabile and Norton T. Dodge. (Contributions in Economics and Economic History No. 71.) New York: Greenwood Press, 1987.

Haberler, Gottfried *et al.*, (eds.). *Readings in Business Cycle Theory*. Homewood, Ill.: Irwin, 1951.

Hadley, Arthur Twining. *Economics: An Account of the Relations Between Private Property and Public Welfare*. New York: G.P. Putnam's Sons, 1896.

Haley, Bernard F. (ed.). *A Survey of Contemporary Economics*. Vol. 2. Homewood, Ill.: Irwin for the American Economic Association, 1952.

Hamilton, Walton H. and Helen R. Wright, with the aid of the council and staff of the Institute of Economics. *The Case of Bituminous Coal*. Brookings Institution, Institute of Economics Investigations in Industry and Labor no. 10. New York: The Macmillan Company, 1925.

Hamilton, Walton H. and Stacy May. *The Control of Wages*. New York, A. M. Kelley, [1927] 1968.

Hamilton, Walton H. *The Pattern of Competition*. New York: Columbia University Press, 1940.

Hamilton, Walton H. *The Politics of Industry*. New York: Knopf, 1957.

Hansen, Alvin H. *Business Cycles and National Income*. Expanded ed. New York: W.W. Norton & Co. Inc., 1964.

Hawkins, David. *The Language of Nature: An Essay in the Philosophy of Science*. San Francisco: Freeman, 1964.

Hodgson, Geoffrey M. *Economics and Institutions: A Manifesto for a Modern Institutional Economics*. Philadelphia: University of Pennsylvania Press, 1988.

Homan, Paul T. *Contemporary Economic Thought*. New York: Harper & Brothers Publisher, 1928.

Jones, Peter d'A. *The Christian Socialist Revival, 1877–1914: Religion, Class, and Social Conscience in Late-Victorian England*. Princeton, N.J.: Princeton Univ. Press, 1968.

Kapp, K. William. *The Social Costs of Private Enterprise*. Paperback edition with new introduction. (1st ed. 1950.) New York: Schocken, 1971.

Keezer, Dexter Merriam and Stacy May. *The Public Control of Business: A Study of Antitrust Law Enforcement, Public Interest Regulation, and Government Participation in Business*. New York: Harper & Brothers, 1930.

Keynes, John Maynard. The Collected Writings of John Maynard Keynes. Edited by Elizabeth Johnson, Donald Moggridge, and others. 29 vols. London: Macmillan, for the Royal Economic Society, 1971–1983.

Keynes, John Maynard. Vol. 13. *The General Theory and After: Part I, Preparation*. Edited by Donald Moggridge. (1973.)

Keynes, John Maymard. Vol. 23. *Activities 1940–1943, External War Finance*. Edited by Donald Moggridge. (1979.)

Keynes, John Neville. *The Scope and Method of Political Economy*. 1890. Reprint of 4th ed., 1917. New York: Augustus M. Kelley, Publishers, 1965.

Knight, Frank H. *The Ethics of Competition and Other Essays*. New York: Harper, 1935.

Knight, Frank H.. *Risk, Uncertainty and Profit*. 1921. Reprint, New York: Augustus M. Kelley, Publishers, 1964.

Langlois, Richard N., ed. *Economics as a Process: Essays in "The New Institutional Economics."* Cambridge: Cambridge University Press, 1986.

Le Duc, Thomas. *Piety and Intellect at Amherst College, 1865–1912*. No. 16 in Columbia Studies in American Culture. New York: Columbia University Press, 1946.

Lewis, W. Arthur. *Overhead Costs*. London: George Allen & Unwin, 1949.

Liebhafsky, H.H. *American Government and Business*. New York: John Wiley & Sons, 1971.

Lutz, Mark A. and Lux, Kenneth. *Humanistic Economics: The New Challenge*. New York: The Bootstrap Press, 1988.

Marshall, Alfred. *Industry and Trade*. London: Macmillan, 1920.

Marshall, Alfred. *Principles of Economics*. 9th (Variorum) ed., 2 vols. with annotations by C.W. Guillebaud. London: Macmillan for the Royal Economic Society, 1961.

Marshall, Mary Paley. *What I Remember*. Cambridge: Cambridge University Press, 1947.

Mendell, Marguerite and Salée, Daniel (eds). *The Legacy of Karl Polanyi: Market, State and Society at the End of the Twentieth Century*. New York: St. Martins Press, 1991.

Myers, Gerald E. *William James: His Life and Thought*. New Haven: Yale University Press, 1986.

Neill, Robin. *A History of Canadian Economic Thought*. Routledge History of Economic Thought Series. London: Routledge, 1991.

Page, Charles H. *Class and American Sociology: From Ward to Ross*. With a New Introduction by the author. New York: Schocken Books, 1969 [1940].

Patinkin, Don, and Leith, J. Clark, eds. *Keynes, Cambridge and **The General Theory**: The process of criticism and discussion connected with the development **of The General Theory***. Proceedings of a conference held at the University of Western Ontario. Toronto: University of Toronto Press, 1978.

Pigou, Arthur C. *The Economics of Welfare*. 1920. Reprint of 4th ed. with eight new appendices. London: Macmillan, 1952.

Pirou, Gaetan. *Les Nouveaux courants de la theorie economique aux États-Unis*. Conferences faites a l'École Pratique des Hautes Études en 1934/1935. Paris: Domat-Montchrestien, F. Loviton, 1935.

Robbins, Lionel. *An Essay on the Nature and Significance of Economic Science*. 2nd ed. London: Macmillan, 1952 (1st ed., 1932).

Robinson, Joan. *The Economics of Imperfect Competition*. London: Macmillan, 1954 (1933).

Ross, Dorothy. *The Origins of American Social Science*. Cambridge: Cambridge University Press, 1991.

Russett, Cynthia E. *The Concept of Equilibrium in American Social Thought*. Yale Historical Publications, Miscellany 84. New Haven: Yale University Press, 1966.

Samuels, Warren J., ed. *Institutional Economics.* 3 vols. No. 5 in *Schools of Thought in Economics.* Series editor, Mark Blaug. Hampshire, England: Edward Elgar Publishing Ltd., [1989].

Scitovsky, Tibor. *Welfare and Competition: The Economics of a Fully Employed Economy.* Chicago, Ill.: Irwin, 1951.

Sievers, Allen M. *Revolution, Evolution, and the Economic Order.* Englewood Cliffs, N.J.: Prentice-Hall, 1962.

Sombart, Werner. *Socialism and the Social Movement in the 19th Century.* With a Chronicle of the Social Movement, 1750–1896. Translated by Anson P. Atterbury with an introduction by John B. Clark. New York: G.P. Putnam's Sons, 1898.

Sowell, Thomas. *Say's Law: An Historical Analysis.* Princeton, N.J.: Princeton University Press, 1972.

Spulber, Nicolas. *Managing the American Economy from Roosevelt to Reagan.* Bloomington: Indiana University Press, 1989.

Stein, Herbert. *The Fiscal Revolution in America.* Chicago: The University of Chicago Press, 1969.

Stigler, George J. *Production and Distribution Theories: The Formative Period.* New York: Macmillan, 1948.

Stigler, George J. *The Theory of Price.* 3rd ed. New York: Macmillan, 1966.

Stocking, George W. *Workable Competition and Antitrust Policy.* Nashville, Tennessee: Vanderbilt University Press, 1961.

Veblen, Thorstein. *Essays, Reviews, and Reports: Previously Uncollected Writings.* Edited and with an Introduction "New Light on Veblen," by Joseph Dorfman. Clifton, New Jersey: Augustus M. Kelley, Publishers, 1973.

Vickrey, William S. *Metastatics and Macroeconomics.* New York: Harcourt, Brace & World, 1964.

Vickrey, William S. *Microstatics.* New York: Harcourt, Brace & World, 1964

Wager, Donald O. *The Church of England and Social Reform Since 1854.* Studies in History, Economics and Public Law, edited by the Faculty of Political Science of Columbia University, No. 325. New York: Columbia University Press, 1930.

Wilson, Harold S. *McClure's Magazine and the Muckrakers.* Princeton, N.J.: Princeton University Press, 1970.

Articles and Periodicals

Ayres, Clarence E. "The Nature and Significance of Institutionalism." *Antioch Review* 26:1 (Spring 1966): 70–90.

[Burns, Arthur R.] "John Maurice Clark." *Political Science Quarterly* 79 (September 1964): whole 641–643.

Chipman, John S. "Charles Frederick Bickerdike." In *The New Palgrave: A Dictionary of Economics,* edited by John Eatwell, Murray Milgate, and Peter Newman, vol. 1, 237–238. London: The Macmillan Press, Ltd., 1987.

Copeland, Morris A.. "Economic Theory and the Natural Science Point of View." *The American Economic Review,* 21 (March 1931): 67–79.

Dalton, George. "Karl Polanyi." In *The New Palgrave: A Dictionary of Economics,* edited by John Eatwell, Murray Milgate, and Peter Newman, vol. 3, 898–899. London: The Macmillan Press, Ltd., 1987.

Dewey, Donald. "Changing Standards of Economic Performance." *The American Economic Review*, Supplement, 50 (May 1960): 1–12.

Dewey, Donald. "John Bates Clark." In *The New Palgrave: A Dictionary of Economics*, edited by John Eatwell, Murray Milgate, and Peter Newman, vol. 1, 428–431. London: The Macmillan Press, Ltd., 1987.

Dillard, Dudley. Review of *The Development of Economic Thought: Great Economists in Perspective*, edited by Henry W. Spiegel. *Political Science Quarterly* 68 (June 1953): 276–278.

Dimand, Robert W. "The New Economics and American Economists in the 1930s Reconsidered." *Atlantic Economic Journal* 18, No. 4 (December 1990): 42–47.

Dorfman, Joseph. "The Department of Economics," in R. Gordon Hoxie, et al., *A History of the Faculty of Political Science, Columbia University*, 161–206. New York: Columbia University Press, 1955.

Dorfman, Joseph. "John Bates and John Maurice Clark on Monopoly and Competition." Introductory essay to reprint of John Bates Clark and John Maurice Clark, *The Control of Trusts*, Rewritten and enlarged edition. New York: Kelley, 1971 [originally published 1912].

Dorfman, Joseph. "Heterodox Economic Thinking and Public Policy." *Journal of Economic Issues*, 4 (March 1970): 1–22.

Dorfman, Joseph. "On A Neglected American Journal in The Social Sciences: *The Yale Review, Old Series*." Introduction to Index of Authors, *The Yale Review*, Old Series – 1892–1911. New York: Kelley, [1969].

Dorfman, Joseph. "Some Documentary Notes on the Relations Among J. M. Clark, N. A. L. J. Johansen and J. M. Keynes." Introductory essay to reprint of John Maurice Clark, *The Costs of the World War to the American People*. New York: Augustus M. Kelley, Publishers, 1970 [1931].

Dorfman, Joseph. "The Role of the German Historical School In American Economic Thought." *The American Economic Review*, Supplement, 45 (May 1955): 17–28.

Dorfman, Joseph. "The Source and Impact of Veblen's Thought." Appendix II, 547–556, to reprint of *Thorstein Veblen and His America* (1934). New York: Kelley, 1961.

Dorfman, Joseph. "Wicksteed's Recantation of the Marginal Productivity Theory." *Economica*, New Series, 31 (August 1964): 294–295.

Eckstein, Otto and Fromm, Gary. "The Price Equation." *The American Economic Review*, 58 (December 1968): 1159–1183.

Ginzberg, Eli. "My Life Philosophy." *The American Economist*, 32, No. 1 (Spring 1988): 3–9.

[Harris, Seymour E.]. "A Postscript by the Editor." *The Review of Economics and Statistics*, 36 (August 1954): 382–386.

Johnson, Alvin. "John Bates Clark." In *Dictionary of American Biography*, Vol. 22, Supplement 2, New York: Scribner's, 1958.

Jones, Byrd L. "The Role of Keynesians in Wartime Policy and Postwar Planning, 1940–1946." *The American Economic Review*, 62, No. 2 (May 1972): 125–133.

Junankar, P.N. "Acceleration Principle." In *The New Palgrave: A Dictionary of Economics*, edited by John Eatwell, Murray Milgate, and

Peter Newman, vol. 1, 10–11. London: The Macmillan Press, Ltd., 1987.

Keyserling, Leon H., Nathan, Robert R., and Lauchlin B. Currie, "Discussion: The Keynesian Revolution and Its Pioneers." *The American Economic Review*, 62, No. 2 (May 1972): 134–141.

Klappholz, Kurt. "Value Judgments and Economics." *The British Journal for the Philosophy of Science*, 15 (August 1964): 97–114.

Klebaner, B.J. "Trusts and Competition: A Note on John Bates Clark and John Maurice Clark." *Social Research*, (January 1963): 475–479.

Knight, Frank H. "'What is Truth' in Economics?" Review article of *The Significance and Basic Postulates of Economic Theory*, by T.W. Hutchinson, in *Journal of Political Economy*, 48 (February 1940): 1–32.

Liebhafsky, H.H.. "Commons and Clark on Law and Economics." *Journal of Economic Issues*, 10, No. 4 (December 1976): 751–764.

Lipsey, Richard G. and Lancaster, Kelvin. "The General Theory of Second Best." *The Review of Economic Studies*, 24(1), No. 63 (October 1956): 11–32.

Markham, Jesse W. "John Maurice Clark." *International Encyclopedia of the Social Sciences*. Edited by David L. Sills. 17 Vols. New York: Macmillan & The Free Press, 1968. Vol. 2, 508–511.

Markham, Jesse W. "J. M. Clark." In *The McGraw-Hill Encyclopedia of World Biography*. 12 Vols. New York: McGraw-Hill Book Co., 1973. Vol. 3, 14.

Meek, Ronald L. "Value Judgments in Economics." *The British Journal for the Philosophy of Science*, 15 (August 1964): 89–96.

Mishan, E.J. "A Survey of Welfare Economics, 1939–59." In *Surveys of Economic Theory: Money, Interest, and Welfare*, London: Macmillan, 1965, 154–222.

Mitchell, Wesley C. "Human Behavior and Economics: A Survey of Recent Literature." *The Quarterly Journal of Economics*, 29 (November 1914): 1–47.

Oi, Walter Y. "Fixed Factors." In *The New Palgrave: A Dictionary of Economics*, edited by John Eatwell, Murray Milgate, and Peter Newman, vol. 2, 384–385. London: The Macmillan Press, Ltd., 1987.

Robinson, Joan. "The Impossibility of Competition." In *Monopoly and Competition and Their Regulation*, edited by Edward H. Chamberlin. London: Macmillan, 1954, 245–254.

Ross, Edward Alsworth. "A Legal Dismissal Wage." In *The American Economic Review*, Supplement, 9 (March 1919): 132–136.

[Samuels, Warren J., editor. Symposium issue "devoted to a semicentennial reconsideration of John R. Common's *Legal Foundations of Capitalism* (1924) and John M. Clark's *Social Control of Business* (1926; 2d ed., 1939.")], *Journal of Economic Issues*, 10, No. 4 (December 1976).

Sharkey, William W. "Natural Monopoly." In *The New Palgrave: A Dictionary of Economics*, edited by John Eatwell, Murray Milgate, and Peter Newman, vol. 3, 603–605. London: The Macmillan Press, Ltd., 1987.

Shepard, William G. "'Contestability' vs. Competition." *The American Economic Review*, 74, No. 4 (September 1984): 572–87.

Shute, Laurence. "John Maurice Clark (1884–1963)," in *The Elgar Companion to Institutional and Evolutionary Economics*, edited by Geoffrey M. Hodgson, Warren J. Samuels, and Marc Tool, 2 vols. Vol 1 (A-K), 50–54. London: Elgar, 1994.

Shute, Laurence. "J.M. Clark on Corporate Concentration and Control." *Journal of Economic Issues*, 19, No. 2 (June 1985), 409–418.

Stigler, George J. "Competition." In *The New Palgrave: A Dictionary of Economics*, edited by John Eatwell, Murray Milgate, and Peter Newman, vol. 1, 531–536. London: The Macmillan Press, Ltd., 1987.

Sweezy, Alan. "The Keynesians and Government Policy, 1933–1939." *The American Economic Review*, 62, No. 2 (May 1972): 116–124.

Taussig, Frank W. "Is Market Price Determinate?" *Quarterly Journal of Economics*, 35 (May 1921), 394–411.

Wiles, R.C. "The Macroeconomics of John Maurice Clark." *Review of Social Economy*, 29, No. 2 (September 1971): 164–179.

Wolfe, A.B. "Neuophysiological Economics." *The Journal of Political Economy*, 58, No. 2 (April 1950): 95–110.

Yamey, Basil S. "Overhead Costs." In *The New Palgrave: A Dictionary of Economics*, edited by John Eatwell, Murray Milgate, and PeterNewman, vol. 3, 764–766. London: The Macmillan Press, Ltd., 1987.

Unpublished Material

Alchon, Guy. "Technocratic Social Science and the Rise of Managed Capitalism, 1910–1933." Ph.D. diss., The University of Iowa, 1982.

Aranoff, Gerald. "Three Economic Essays on Technology and Competition; Applications of John M. Clark's Concepts to the Cement Industry, Transfer Pricing, and Product Pricing." Ph.D. diss., City University of New York, 1991.

Galles, Gary M. "Competition in Imperfect Spatial Markets." Ph.D. diss., University of California, Los Angeles, 1988.

Hirsch, Abraham. "Reconstruction in Economics: The Work of Wesley Clair Mitchell." Unpublished Ph.D. diss., Columbia University, 1958.

Junker, Louis. "The Social and Economic Thought of Clarence E. Ayres." Ph.D. diss., University of Wisconsin (Madison), 1962.

Kennedy, Donald Dwight. "Overhead Costs and the Shift to Machinery." Ph.D. diss., University of Pennsylvania, 1928.

McClintock, Brent. "International Economic Policy and the Welfare State." Ph.D. diss., Colorado State University, 1990.

Powers, Edward J. "The Social Economics of John Maurice Clark." Ph.D. diss., Boston College, 1967.

Raines, James P. "A Theoretical Economic Explanation of the Competition Policy Implemented by the European Economic Community." Ph.D. diss., The University of Alabama, 1983.

Reguero, Miguel A. "The Social Economics of John Maurice Clark." Master's [M.A.] thesis, New York University, 1949.

Rossenfeld, Morris M. "Critical Analysis of the Human Nature Basis in the Economics of John Maurice Clark in an Attempt to Devise a New

Human Nature Basis for Economics." Master's thesis, Department of Economics, Columbia University, 1951.

Shannon, Richard E. "Bibliography of the Works of John Maurice Clark." [1951] 11 pp. Mimeographed.

The Reminiscences of Boris Basil Shishkin. 6 Vols. New York: The Oral History Collection of Columbia University, 1959.

Toyer, Frances A. "The Economic Thought of John Bates Clark." Ph.D. diss., New York University, 1952.

Vukasin, Peter N. "A Study of Davenport's Method: The Employment of the Entrepreneur Point of View." Ph.D. diss., University of California, Berkeley, 1952.

Wyckoff, Viola. "The Psychological theories of J.S. Mill, C.H. Parker, and J.M. Clark." Master's thesis, New York University, 1933.

Index

A leading American economist by mid-century, John Maurice Clark (1884–1963) was recognized by the American Economic Association for 'the most distinguished contribution to economics'. This comprehensive study of his life and work examines his development of a social, dynamic economic theory which he claimed continued the work of his father, John Bates Clark (1847–1938). In addition to the elder Clark, major influences on J. M. Clark were Thorstein Veblen, John A. Hobson, John R. Commons, Charles Horton Cooley, and Wesley Clair Mitchell. His seminal work *Studies in the Economics of Overhead Costs* (1923) argued that cost was an ambiguous expression, reflecting the institutional structure of society. If costs were not precise terms, then prices could not be taken as the final standard to gauge economic activity, and new guidelines of public control were needed in addition to the market. He anticipated much of the work of John Maynard Keynes, brought ethics and social control to the forefront of economics, and spanned virtually the entire range of economic thinking.